Selected Writings of

HANNAH MORE

SELECTED WRITINGS OF

HANNAH
MORE

Edited with Introduction and Notes by

ROBERT HOLE

LONDON

WILLIAM PICKERING

1996

Published by Pickering & Chatto (Publishers) Limited
21 Bloomsbury Way, London WC1A 2TH
Old Post Road, Brookfield, Vermont 05036, USA

British Library Cataloguing in Publication Data
More, Hannah
    Selected Writings of Hannah More. –
    (Pickering Women's Classics)
    I. Title   II. Hole, Robert   III. Series
    828.608

    ISBN 1–85196–266–2

Library of Congress Cataloguing-in-Publication Data
More, Hannah, 1745–1833.
    [Selections, 1995]
    Selected writings of Hannah More / edited with introduction and
notes by Robert Hole.
        p.   cm.
    ISBN 1–85196–266–2
    1. Women—Literary collections.   I. Hole, Robert.   II. Title.
PR3605.M6A6   1995
828'.609—dc20   96–21348
                                                        CIP

Typeset by Waveney Typesetters
Norwich

Printed and bound in Great Britain by
Biddles Ltd
Guildford

CONTENTS

ACKNOWLEDGEMENTS

I am indebted to the staff of the British Library, London, the Bodleian Library, Oxford, Bristol Central Library, Bristol Record Office, the University of Bristol Library, the University of Exeter Library and the University of Plymouth Library, for their unfailing courtesy and helpfulness in the preparation of these texts.

First and foremost, I must thank Mike Edwards for all his help and support, without which this volume would never have been completed. I am also indebted to a number of my friends and colleagues for their expertise and their patience in answering queries concerning the footnotes: Chris Ellis, David Parker, Jeannette Gill, John Highfield, Joseph Staples Smith, Mark Halstead, Nick Smart, Rachel Christofides, Richard Williams and Sara Smart. In addition to this, Nick Smart and Richard Williams have also read drafts of the introduction and Chris Ellis has read both introduction and text. I am most grateful to them all for their criticisms and for their generosity with their time, enthusiasm and encouragement. Lizzie Ash, Dave Thornley and Michael Webb provided invaluable technical assistance in Devon, and Gary Johnston supported me when working in London. I am happy to express my gratitude for financial help to the Research Committee of the Faculty of Arts and Education of the University of Plymouth. I am indebted to the general editor of this series, Janet Todd, for her wise advice on the selection of material for this collection, and to Bridget Frost of Pickering & Chatto for her encouragement and help at all times.

University of Plymouth, 1995   ROBERT HOLE

INTRODUCTION

I

In the late eighteenth century, there were few better exponents of the traditional, orthodox value system and view of the world than Hannah More. She numbered among her friends Samuel Johnson, Joshua Reynolds, David Garrick, Edmund Burke, Horace Walpole and William Wilberforce. She was a poet and a dramatist, a writer of popular propaganda for the poor and didactic religious works for the educated and pious. Her thinking was traditional and conservative. She founded schools for the education of the children of the poor and had a highly developed awareness of the use of religion and education as means of social control.

In her lifetime, More had a huge readership amongst both the educated and the poor. For example, 19,000 copies of her *Strictures on Female Education* were sold to the educated; the work went into seven editions before the end of 1799, and thirteen editions by 1826, in addition to being reprinted in her collected works in 1801, 1818 and 1830. Moreover, by March 1796 over 2,000,000 copies of the tracts in the *Cheap Repository* had been sold or given away to the poor. It is, of course, impossible to say how many of either publication were read, but to some degree or other that is true of all books. Nor do we know how many of the poor agreed with the views with which they were being fed, or what effect the massive propaganda drive had. A few of the educated disliked More and her works but most applauded her; her arguments were the orthodox ones of the governing elite. Although definitive quantitative evidence is lacking, the views she espoused, however unattractive they may be to the late twentieth-century taste, were widely shared two hundred years ago.

The construction of history is, inevitably, the product of an interaction between the evidence of the past and the values of the present. No historian can be entirely value-free in his or her choice of topic or selection of relevant sources. Today, Hannah More appears a less significant figure than her contemporary Mary Wollstonecraft, but the reason for this lies in the values of the late twentieth century. Although many of Wollstonecraft's detailed arguments have been discarded, the general thrust of her principles is one with which men and women at the end of the twentieth century feel comfortable. More, however, takes a stance that most now find unacceptable and it is all too easy to dismiss her simply as a repressed, sterile figure, clinging to traditional ways of thinking in an age of intellectual revolution. However, it would be a mistake to do so.

If the purpose of history is to understand the past, historians must make a conscious effort to construct their history according to the values of the age they are studying. In absolute terms, of course, such an enterprise is impossible. Historians must select, from the myriad of conflicting ideas abounding in any age, those which appear most significant. They frequently find that views that were then in a minority, now have greatest resonance for them. But the temptation to neglect the conventional views of the majority, the established tradition, is one that must be resisted if we are to understand an age aright and so properly to contextualise its radical thinkers.

In the last ten years, our understanding of English society in the age of More and Wollstonecraft has been revolutionised by the work of Jonathan Clark.[1] He argues

> It is often necessary to remind ourselves that the political values of eighteenth-century England were those appropriate to a society Christian, monarchical, aristocratic, rural, traditional and poor; but those of historians of the 1960s and 1970s were drawn from a society indifferent to religion; hostile alike to authority and to social rank; urban; 'plural'; and affluent. This in itself would have posed major problems of sympathetic insight

in an attempt to cross such a divide. But from the 1960s, an increasing number of historians ceased to make such an effort, and chose to believe that fresh historical insights were to be derived, rather, from a celebration of their own values and a reliance on recent experience as a source of analytical categories and analogies.[2]

Clark argues that whilst the old Whig Interpretation of history (as a steady progress to the perfection of the two party democracy of the late nineteenth century) had been discredited, it was being replaced by a *new* Whig Interpretation which

focusses attention on those lines of development in the past which seem to culminate in present arrangements. This allows it, first, to justify present values (concerning those arrangements) by showing their historical rootedness, and, second, to read those values (once allegedly made tenable) back into the past to condemn the forces which are held to have inhibited the earlier emergence of modern practices. By being a theory of the direction of social change, it is enabled also to be a value system.[3]

In arguing so forcibly against the predominant historiography of the 1960s and 1970s, Clark was widely perceived to be taking an adversarial stance that invited response.[4] It is significant that in the opening sentence of his next book, he criticises the fixation of English historical scholarship with the adversary system, 'its desire to see the past as a debate between two 'sides', and to echo this in the rivalry of scholarly interpretations'.[5]

This selection and presentation of some of Hannah More's writings about women is made in the light of Clark's rejection of the new Whig Interpretation of history. If our purpose is to understand English society in the late eighteenth century, a study of More's writings can provide crucial insights into a way of thinking which was then traditional and orthodox but which is to us distant and unfamiliar. However, we must avoid adversarial simplification. We should not think in terms of Burke *versus* Paine, Malthus *versus* Godwin or More *versus* Wollstonecraft.[6] Each writer had his or her own agenda and

More's *Strictures* (1799) no more 'answered' Wollstonecraft's
Vindication (1792), than Paine's *Rights of Man* (1791–2) 'answered'
Burke's *Reflections* (1790). Moreover, instead of taking sides in
such debates, the purpose of historians is rather to understand a
point of view based on premises which very few share today,
and so to resist the temptation to condemn those ideas with
which they disagree.

II

Hannah More was born at Stapleton in Gloucestershire on 2
February 1745 and died on 7 September 1833 at Clifton in
Bristol. Her life stretched from before the Jacobite invasion of
Bonnie Prince Charlie to after the First Reform Act. She was
fifteen years old when George III ascended the throne, thirty-
one when the American Declaration of Independence was
issued, forty-four when the French Revolutionaries stormed the
Bastille, seventy when Napoleon was defeated at Waterloo, and
eighty-eight when the Whigs first provided state money towards education in 1833.

   Hannah More was the fourth of five sisters, the children of a
schoolmaster and a farmer's daughter. A precociously intelligent
child, she was educated first by her father in the home, otherwise a predominantly female environment. When she was twelve her eldest sister opened a boarding school for girls in Bristol
and More learned Italian, Spanish and Latin from the masters at
the school. At the age of twenty-two, she became engaged to be
married to William Turner, a landowner with an estate near
Bristol. Twenty years her senior, Turner kept on delaying the
marriage day. After six years the engagement was called off and
More decided never to marry. Although later referred to, out of
respect, as *Mrs* Hannah More, she never wavered in her decision.
It was the £200 a year which Turner settled on her, by way of
compensation, that allowed More the freedom to become, first,
one of the London literary set and, later, a philanthropist, a
founder of schools, a propagandist and a didactic writer.

In 1774, during a visit to London with two of her sisters, she saw David Garrick play Lear. An admiring letter led to her meeting Garrick and soon she became a close friend of both him and his wife. She met Edmund Burke in Bristol and worked for him in the election campaign of 1774 when he became one of the city's members of parliament. For over twenty years from 1774, she regularly wintered in London for the season and it was there, at the house of Joshua Reynolds, that she first met Samuel Johnson. She met also Elizabeth Montagu, Elizabeth Vesey, Elizabeth Carter, Hester Chapone and Frances Boscawen and became a part of their circle of self-styled 'Blue Stockings'.[7] These eminent hostesses encouraged both men and women to engage in serious conversation at their fashionable assemblies as an alternative to playing cards.

Encouraged in part by this group of intelligent, scholarly women, and in part by the friendship of Garrick, More became a writer, of verse and of plays. She had already, at the age of sixteen, written *A Search after Happiness* for the girls of her sisters' school in Bristol to act, and had published it in 1773. At the same period, she had made a free translation of Metastasio's *Attilio Regolo* and this, as *The Inflexible Captive*, was presented by Garrick at theatres in Bath and Exeter.[8] In 1777 she wrote *Percy*, an historical drama about the twelfth-century Earl of Northumberland, which Garrick presented at Covent Garden. The play was enthusiastically received and More fêted, but it is an unredeemably dreary piece. Her best (and otherwise sympathetic) biographer accurately describes it as '...entirely lacking in dramatic quality. There is no interrelation of character and action, no surprise or suspense in any situation, no variety of tone or pitch, no light or shade, no contrasts of any kind. It begins and ends on the same monotonous tone.'[9]

Garrick died before More finished her next play, *The Fatal Falsehood* in 1779. Without Garrick, the play ran for only three performances at Covent Garden. But his death did more than simply reveal the weakness of More's drama. Whether or not it was the cause, Garrick's death was co-incident with the beginning of More's gradual withdrawal from the fashionable world of London society, what she called the Great and the Gay, and her adoption of a serious life and a high moral and religious tone.

More was a born proselytist and soon she set out to reform the fashionable world of high society. Three of her major works were devoted to this end. Her *Thoughts on the Importance of the Manners of the Great* was published anonymously in 1788. Many attributed it to Wilberforce, but her identity soon became known. *An Estimate of the Religion of the Fashionable World* followed in 1790 and, most importantly, *Strictures on the Modern System of Female Education* in 1799. This campaign drew More into a new circle, that of 'The Saints' – Anglican, Evangelical reformers. This association was inextricably mixed with the campaign for the Abolition of the Slave Trade. More's anti-Slavery credentials are impeccable. In 1788 she published a poem *Slavery*, which roundly and unequivocally denounced the institution:

> Perish th' illiberal thought which would debase
> The native genius of the sable race!
> Perish the proud philosophy, which sought
> To rob them of the pow'rs of equal thought!
> Does then th' immortal principle within
> Change with the casual colour of a skin?[10]

In 1784 More built a cottage, Cowslip Green, in Somerset to enable her to escape from London and write her didactic works. She was, however much visited by her literary, aristocratic and Episcopal friends. With the outbreak of the French Revolution in 1789, Cowslip Green became a centre of counter-revolutionary activity long before the Revolution became unpopular with most Britons. Fears that the French example might spark off a Revolution in Britain were fuelled by the publication of Thomas Paine's *Rights of Man* in two parts in 1791 and 1792. Encouraged by the Bishop of London, Beilby Porteus, and, according to rumours, also by the Prime Minister, William Pitt, More wrote the most famous counter-revolutionary tract of the decade – 'Village Politics' – in November 1792.

Over two years separated the publication of 'Village Politics' and the first of the series of *Cheap Repository Tracts* in 1795. These tracts were published monthly for three years and were widely distributed. Essentially counter-revolutionary in nature, they sought the moral reformation of the poor. By embracing religion and responsibility, the poor would become content with their lot on earth and be reconciled to their place in the divinely ordained hierarchy. Thus political order and social stability would be secured. More read widely in chap-books[11] to catch the demotic style and this major contribution to the popular propaganda of the day is arguably her greatest achievement.

If the tracts were one of More's responses to the French Revolution, the schools were another. When Wilberforce visited Cheddar in August 1789, his horror at the ignorance and irreligion of the place spurred More and her sisters to found a school in the village for the education of the children of the poor. Soon this enterprise was transformed into a larger movement to educate the poor in the Mendips within a radius of about ten miles of Cowslip Green. Cheddar, Shipham and Nailsea were the sites of the three 'great' schools, but there were also a number of 'lesser' schools, which operated only on Sundays and perhaps in the evening, at Sandford, Congressbury, Yatton, Axbridge, Wedmore and Blagdon. The schools were clearly intended to operate as agencies of social control, and More ruled them with an iron rod.

More and her sisters also organised the women of the Mendips into a number of 'Female Friendly Societies'. The women paid in a penny half-penny a week and were promised three shillings and sixpence a week in the event of illness and the considerable sum of seven shillings and sixpence at the time of childbirth. In a letter of 1816, More claimed,

> we have established Female Friendly Societies in several parishes, which, by our constant care, have been very successful. In two places only we have 300 members. In the course of twenty years they have received from the fund near £1,200 in their sickness, and I have just made over £1,200 more to trustees, so that, in the event of my death, things will go on just as they do now. Once a-year we give them a feast at our own

expense; so that their box is never impoverished. They are the mothers of our children, of which we have still near 700.[12]

In 1801 More moved from Cowslip Green a few miles to Barley Wood, a larger house which she shared with her sisters. The ensuing years were dominated by ill-health and writing. In 1805 she published her *Hints towards forming the Character of a Young Princess*. This was dedicated to the Bishop of Exeter who had just been appointed as tutor to Charlotte Augusta, the daughter of George, Prince of Wales, and heir-presumptive to the throne. The work was enthusiastically received. It is, essentially, her anti-Machiavel, her vision of the education proper for a Christian ruler and as such is her most considered work of political theory. In 1808 she produced a novel, *Coelebs in Search of a Wife*. Elsewhere in her writings, notably in *Strictures* and 'Bragwell's Daughters' as is clearly shown in the texts below, she roundly condemned the pernicious effects of modern novels; in *Coelebs*, she sought to write a novel free of these moral dangers. Her ideal young man, Coelebs, seeks and finds a wife who embodies all the Christian virtues. The book seems tedious to the modern reader, as it did to many of her contemporaries. It is devoid of incident and soon becomes a didactic Evangelical tract. Although it sold well, her friends were distressed by it and More never attempted another novel. Her last works were unremittingly religious in character – *Practical Piety* (1811), *Christian Morals* (1812), *The Character and Practical Writings of St Paul* (1815), and *The Spirit of Prayer* (1825).

Her final years were unhappy. At the age of seventy-five she had outlived all her sisters. Chronic ill-health kept her a prisoner in two rooms of Barley Wood for seven years from 1818 to 1825. She was exploited by her eight servants, who neglected her and indulged themselves in the life of pleasure that she had devoted so much of her life to condemning. Rescued by her friends, she left Barley Wood, at the age of eighty-three, to live at Clifton in Bristol, where she died five years later.

If More had died in 1805, or even in 1808, her image might have been a somewhat different one. In 1834, within a year of

her death, William Roberts constructed the first historical representation of More as a pious, narrow old lady. His misleading
memoirs and selected edition of her correspondence concentrated on her later years. Mary Hopkins's suggestion that it is
the earlier years that are the more significant arises, perhaps,
from her desire to portray the 'gay' rather than the 'grave'
Hannah More, and in this way her picture of More is as
incomplete as that of Roberts.[13] The present selection of her
writings covers More's work in the period 1775 to 1805, that
part of her life from thirty to sixty years of age. Within that
period she exhibited the full range and complexity of her
thinking. In it we can see a movement from the society 'blue-
stocking' to the didactic author, but we can see also both the
growth and development of a consistent set of principles and
attitudes which changes in response to current events. By 1805,
More had said everything of interest which she had to say. Her
later writings reveal a decline into old age that it is charitable to
ignore.

III

The writings in this selection generally relate in one way or
another to Hannah More's view of women and their place in
society. Most of her views and attitudes are profoundly political,
and this dimension is extensively explored later in this introduction. But first, one more personal theme needs to be noted. In
her *Strictures on Female Education*, as well as making the predict-
able proposals for educational reform which are similar to those
of many other writers of the period, More also examines the
nature of marriage.

Her Christian orthodoxy and traditionalism demanded that
she support the concept of a perfect, happy marriage as the ideal
state for a woman. But there is enough evidence to suggest that
in many ways she found the idea distasteful. Neither Hannah
More, nor any of her sisters, married. In her twenties, she
avoided the conventional marriage, which would have been her

normal fate, because of the eccentric behaviour of William
Turner. In *Strictures*, she described marriage in very guarded
terms as seldom exquisite though 'often very tolerable'; it took
her nearly twenty years and a dozen editions to change the word
'tolerable' to 'happy'. When she was fifty, she bitterly opposed
Zachary Macaulay's courtship of Selina Mills, the dearest friend
of her sister Patty. Macaulay believed that the sisters dis-
approved of marriage, which Patty considered was hostile to
friendship. M. G. Jones defended More from this charge, but
perhaps the issue is not quite as clear-cut as it appeared to her
to be.[14]

In Chapter Sixteen of *Strictures*, 'On dissipation and the
modern habits of fashionable life', More warns of the dangers of
modern marriage.[15] Ostensibly, this is an attack on the world of
'Fashion' and its indulgence in pleasure. More ridicules the idea
of selecting a marriage partner at a ball, for the qualities
exhibited there are quite contrary to those which she considers
should be looked for in a husband or in a wife. Her profound
distaste for young men who had become accustomed to 'the
voluptuous ease, refined luxuries, soft accommodations, obsequious attendance, and all the unrestrained indulgences' of the
world of fashion seems at least in part to be based on her
awareness, quite evident earlier in the book, that the dual
standard of morality would allow them to indulge in widespread
sexual gratification before marriage.[16] For such a man, marriage
may be 'little more than a selfish stratagem to reconcile health
with pleasure'. His earlier 'excess of gratification' will now make
him 'irritable and exacting', and lead him to affect 'the manners
of a Sybarite'. The London clubs, where young men led their
libertine lives, encouraged luxury and a spirit of play with their
'perfect ease, undress, liberty, and equality of distinction in
rank'. A wife cannot hope, and should not seek, to gratify within
marriage the passions which such men had been used to indulging. The result was that, within a few weeks, the wife would be
left alone at home whilst the man returned to his earlier haunts
of dissipation.

It is possible, of course, to read these passages without

inferring in them a sexual connotation. If they had been written thirty years later, or by the pious, religious recluse whom Roberts constructs in his *Memoirs*, it would be easier to do so. But More lived in the fashionable society of London in the 1770s and 1780s, and was well aware of the realities of the sexual practices of her day. Elsewhere in *Strictures* she discusses openly the dual morality and the dangers of women indulging in the same sexual pleasures as men.[17] When they are read in that context, her expressions of distaste for the sexual dimension of marriage seem to be clear. For her, the pleasures of the family are fundamentally asexual ones.

According to the traditional order which she so strongly defended, men lived their lives in the arena of the world, women in that of the family. Within that arena, women could be intelligent, rational, virtuous, and noble creatures, capable of great intellectual and moral achievements. They had the potential for immense influence on their husbands and sons, on their other relations, their servants and the poor. They also had a greater opportunity than men to devote themselves to religion and, not being involved in public life, were not faced so often with the conflict between the classical and the Christian traditions.[18] It is impossible to know precisely what More's attitude to the position of women in society would have been if that agenda had not been hijacked by the debate on the French Revolution, but there is enough in the *Strictures* to suggest that a degree of moderate, organic change, within the established boundaries, might not totally have appalled her. But More was writing in what she perceived as a time of crisis both for religion and for the social and political order. The views on women which she expressed in the 1790s can be understood only if they are viewed in these political and politico-religious contexts.

IV

Hannah More lived her life during the last phases of the ancien regime in Britain. If the end of that ancien regime is to be identified with the constitutional changes in church and state that took place between 1828 and 1832, with the Repeal of the Test and Corporation Acts and the passing of Catholic Emancipation and the First Reform Act, then her death almost exactly coincides with its passing.[19] The intellectual map of Britain in the period from 1775 to 1805, the thirty years covered by the extracts in this book, is a complex one. In this period, Hannah More's work represents a traditional world view that was doomed soon to disappear, but which had a long heritage and was still the orthodox value system in Britain. The views of Paine, Godwin, Wollstonecraft and other radical thinkers were the views of a minority that can be seen in clear focus only if they are placed in the context of that traditional world view.

One of the most important keys to the understanding of More's thought is the role which religion in general and political theology in particular play in it. Much of the material that has been excluded from the selections presented below relates to religion. For example, the last three chapters of *Strictures on Female Education*, omitted below, are: Chapter 18, 'A worldly spirit incompatible with the spirit of Christianity'; Chapter 19, 'On the leading doctrines of Christianity. – The corruption of human nature. – The doctrine of redemption. – The necessity of a change of heart, and of the divine influences to produce that change. – With a sketch of the Christian character'; and Chapter 20, 'On the duty and efficacy of prayer'. To edit More in this way could appear to be falling into that very trap against which Clark has warned us. However, numerous religious references remain and the reader should be careful not to dismiss them as rhetorical flourishes, obeisances to a dying ideology, as incidental or contingent. Religion played an integral role in More's thinking; it was structural not decorative. Remove it and the spiritual rationale of the ancien regime would collapse. The relationship between the established religion and the political and social structure in Britain, between the Constitution in Church and State, was symbiotic and fundamental.

More was a Trinitarian Christian and a member of the established church. Establishment gave the Church of England great privileges; the political theology of that church provided a sacerdotal sanction of the regime and presented political obligation as a religious duty as well as a civic one. The grounds of political obligation were drawn from Biblical theology. St Paul's statement that 'the powers that be are ordained of God', and St Peter's injunction to 'fear God, honour the king'[20] provided the foundation for a whole range of views. They led some to notions of non-resistance and passive obedience, though others within the Church of England were able to reconcile them with Lockean notions of a right to rebellion. Richard Watson, Bishop of Llandaff from 1782 to 1816, described himself as a 'Christian Whig' and was an acknowledged disciple of John Locke. At the other end of the Anglican spectrum, however, were men like George Horne, vice-chancellor of the University of Oxford from 1776, Dean of Canterbury from 1781, and Bishop of Norwich from 1790 to his death in 1792.[21] Horne looked back not to Locke, but to Filmer and to Hutchinson,[22] and was a patriarchalist in the sense that he justified monarchical authority by tracing it back to the patriarch Adam. In his 1769 Assize sermon 'On the Origin of Civil Government', Horne argued that there was

> an intimate connexion between religion and government; that the latter originally flowed from the same divine source with the former, and was, at the beginning, the ordinance of the most High; that the state of nature was a state of subordination, not one of equality and independence, in which mankind never did, nor ever can exist, and that the civil magistrate is 'the minister of God to us for good'.[23]

Horne's first cousin, William Stevens, the Treasurer of Queen Anne's Bounty, was able to be even more explicit in his patriarchalism. He saw

> the foundation for civil authority in the sentence passed on Eve, *Thy desire shall be to thy husband, and he shall rule over thee.* From that time, at least, the natural equality and independence of individuals was at an end, and Adam became (Oh dreadful sound to republican ears) universal monarch by divine right.[24]

In giving Adam authority over Eve, Stevens argued, God gave him authority over the rest of the human race at that time and this authority was handed down to all subsequent legitimate monarchs, including George III. According to this theory, therefore, the subjection of women to men lay at the very heart of the sacerdotal justification of the authority of government and the obligation of subjects to obey. Horne and Stevens were no more extremists in the Anglican church than was Watson. Locke was relatively neglected in the eighteenth century, although much attention has been paid recently to the minority of radical thinkers who were his disciples; Filmer and Hutchinson remained significant influences on many in the mainstream of orthodox political and social theory.[25] It should not surprise us that George Horne was a close friend of Hannah More; his daughter, Sally, was a boarder at the More sisters' school in Bristol; he encouraged Hannah to write *The Manners of the Great* and visited her in Somerset; she shared his politico-religious beliefs on the divine authority of the established order.[26]

The religious beliefs of high-church Anglicans not only provided them with a Biblical foundation for political obligation, it also sanctified the existing social hierarchy as the work of Divine Providence. Horne preached a sermon on Easter Tuesday 1783, before the Lord Mayor of London, in which he asserted that 'the inequality of mankind is not the effect of chance, but the ordinance of Heaven' and warned that 'politicians should be extremely cautious how they propagate principles tending to render the subordinate ranks in society discontented with their condition, and desirous of aspiring to one for which they were never designed by Providence'.[27] Here, Horne was speaking not from an extreme end of the spectrum but was expressing a view common amongst Anglicans of all persuasions. Edward Tatham, Rector of Lincoln College, Oxford, explained,

> In the subordination and gradation of persons and rights, consists the very life and health of every well constituted state. In this political arrangement, made not by the wisdom or the will

of man, but by the invisible hand of Providence, every man moves in that sphere of life, whether higher or lower, in which that Providence, not his own choice, has placed him at his birth.[28]

Burke, in *An Appeal from the New to the Old Whigs*, assumed that God determined

> our place in the order of existence; and that having disposed and marshalled us by a divine tactic, not according to our will, but according to his, he has, in and by that disposition, virtually subjected us to act the part which belongs to the place assigned us...Men come in that manner into a community with the social state of their parents, endowed with all the benefits, loaded with all the duties, of their situation.[29]

The authority of government, the obligation of subjects, and the existing social hierarchy all rested upon a religious base. The establishment of the Church of England enshrined the union between church and state at the very heart of the constitution. Horne stated the case plainly nine months *before* the Fall of the Bastille:

> We have a church and we have a king; and we must pray for the prosperity of the last, if we wish to retain the first. The levelling principle of the age extends throughout. A republic, the darling idol of many amongst us, would probably, as the taste now inclines, come attended by a religion without bishop, priest, or deacon; without service or sacraments; without a Saviour to justify or a Spirit to sanctify; in short, a classical religion without adoration.[30]

He believed that no rational religion was able to invoke a metaphysical spirituality that could invest kingship and government with sacerdotal powers and with the mystery of state. Jacob More, Hannah's, father was a high-churchman who shared Horne's views. He taught them to his daughter for whom they lasted a lifetime.

V

This traditional, English political theology, which was Hannah More's inheritance, was influenced in her lifetime by two movements: the Evangelical Revival and the French Revolution.

More is often referred to as an Evangelical. While such a description is not inaccurate, it could be misleading if left unqualified. Part of the problem is that Evangelicalism itself is difficult to define accurately. It is often portrayed as a movement within Anglicanism that is somewhat akin to Methodism; as being Low Church, placing the emphasis on the personal relationship between God and the individual rather than on the intercedent role of the Church; as being more Protestant and less Catholic in its theology, with a theological emphasis on 'justification by faith alone' despite its incidental devotion to 'good works'. All of these popular assumptions, although broadly true, are, to some extent, problematic.

More disliked Methodists and Methodism, which she saw as a lower-class movement which weakened the alliance between church and state. If low church was to be identified with latitudinarian, then Evangelicals in general and Hannah More in particular were far removed from it. In political terms, both the high-church patriarchalists, like Horne and Stevens, and the Evangelicals, like Wilberforce and Gisborne, took a conservative stance against the more Whiggish latitudinarians, like Watson or Paley. The concern of Evangelicals for the poor and for slaves should not mislead us. It was informed chiefly by a sense of moral paternalism that they were able easily to reconcile with their belief in an unequal, divinely ordained social hierarchy. This was a hierarchy not only of rank and of wealth, but also of gender.[31]

Leading Evangelicals were forthright in their expression of an hierarchic social theory. John Owen, preaching before the opening of the Cambridge Assizes in the summer of 1794, insisted that 'the whole moral of Christianity...makes for the practice of

Civil Obedience' and that this involved inequality, restraint and subordination. He denounced the idea of rights 'which spurn restraint, and throw off subordination'. Religion should lead people to accept their place in the social hierarchy; by it, 'the passions will be moulded to mildness, and the ebullitions of Discontent effectually subside'; 'a higher and more appropriate use cannot be made of Revealed Religion, than to connect the observance of its Institutes with an exemplary discharge of every Civil and Social Duty.'[32] Wilberforce argued that Christianity taught the rich and powerful to use their wealth and power in a sensitive way:

> Affluence she teaches to be liberal and beneficent; authority, to bear its faculties with meekness, and to consider the various cares and obligations belonging to its elevated station, as being conditions on which that station is conferred. Thus, softening the glare of wealth, and moderating the insolence of power, she renders the inequalities of the social state less galling to the lower orders, whom she also instructs, in their turn, to be diligent, humble, patient; reminding them that their more lowly path has been allotted to them by the hand of God; that it is their part faithfully to discharge its duties, and contentedly to bear its inconveniences; that the present state of things is very short;...if their superiors enjoy more abundant comforts, they are also exposed to many temptations from which the inferior classes are happily exempted;...and finally that all human distinctions will be soon done away, and the true followers of Christ will all, as children of the same father, be alike admitted to the possessions of the same heavenly inheritance. Such are the blessed effects of Christianity on the temporal well-being of political communities.[33]

For the Evangelicals, equality was to be looked for in heaven, not on earth. More's concern for slaves and her paternalistic care of the poor were in the mainstream of Evangelical thinking, but that stream was entirely consistent with the church's traditional teaching of subordination, restraint, inequality, hierarchy and obedience. More's friendship with Wilberforce did not conflict with her relationship with a number of bishops –

Porteus of London, Horne of Norwich, Barrington of Durham – who could certainly not be called evangelical. It does no harm to describe More as an Evangelical, so long as it is remembered that that is only a partial description. She was an Anglican with strong links with the orthodox mainstream of that church – influenced by the evangelical thinking of a wing of the church, but first and foremost a supporter of the Church Establishment.

The second movement that influenced the traditional, English political theology that was More's inheritance, was the French Revolution. This was the most important single event in her life and most of the writings in this selection have to be read in the light of it. More's views of politics and society were rooted in her religious beliefs and the effect of the French Revolution was to accentuate and intensify those views, to make them less flexible and more central to her thinking.

More saw the Revolution as an assault on all that she held sacred. It was an attack on the established order, on constitutional government, on the institution of monarchy, which ran directly counter to the Apostolic injunctions to obedience. It was an attack on the social hierarchy of rank and status, on order, deference and subordination, that showed an irreligious discontent and a desire to anticipate the joys of heaven on earth. It was an attack on Christianity itself that not only confiscated church property and elected bishops, but also, under Robespierre, sought to replace the Christian church with the deist cult of the Supreme Being. This threefold attack, on political authority, social hierarchy and Christian church, was not a coincidence. For More, the three were indivisible. The political and social order could be overthrown only if religion were first destroyed. Voltaire and the *philosophes* in their attack on Christianity had paved the way for the Revolution. Peace and order could return to France, and be preserved in England, only if faith were restored and retained. Like Burke, she believed that a state with no religion would fall either into anarchy or despotism. Without religion to restrain humankind's selfish will there could be no voluntary social order, and government would have to rely on constant coercion. Social and political stability, peace and order rested on a religious foundation and, More believed, it could rest no where else. If Christianity were to be destroyed in England, there could be no order, for only religious restraint made government possible.

This argument depended on a view of human nature that was fundamentally different from that of the French revolutionaries and the English radicals. At its heart was the doctrine of original sin. Trinitarian Christians saw human beings as unregenerate, fallen creatures, whilst many, though not all, Unitarians, Deists and Atheists took an optimistic view of humankind as being capable of progressing towards perfection. The traditional catholic doctrines of original sin and the fall of man were accepted by all Trinitarian Christians but particularly emphasised by Anglican Evangelicals and Methodists. While Mary Wollstonecraft, from a Unitarian perspective, urged her readers of the need to 'get entirely clear of all the notions drawn from the wild traditions of original sin...on which priests have erected their tremendous structures of imposition, to persuade us, that we are naturally inclined to evil', Hannah More insisted that 'the gospel *can* make no part of a scheme...in which poverty and misery are considered as evils arising solely from human governments, and not from the dispensations of God...The gospel can have nothing to do with a system in which sin is reduced to a little human imperfection'.[34] For More, the idea of fundamental human corruption invalidated radical ideas of 'universal benevolence'; humankind was essentially selfish. Just as the greatest of the Christian virtues, humility, arose from a knowledge of fallen man's inherent sinfulness, so the *philosophes*' belief in human perfectibility led to the radicals' greatest vice – inordinate vanity.[35]

VI

Hannah More was a precocious child and an intelligent woman. The political and social theory that her religion prescribed for her placed women in a subordinate position. The established

Constitution in Church and State gave all the significant privileges to adult, male, property-owning Anglicans. Adult, male, property-owning Dissenters, who were excluded from high office, parliament and the universities, managed to support most of the traditional, Christian political and social theory, whilst working for the reform of that part of it that personally disadvantaged them. Theoretically it would have been possible for More to have done the same, but she did not. The reason for this is complex.

More arrived in London when she was in her late twenties. The two major circles in which she mixed, the Garrick-Johnson-Reynolds set and the *Bas Bleu*, were both made up of people considerably older than her. Much of her social success depended upon the fact that in her youth she reinforced the ideas of her seniors. A few of the educated women of the *Bas Bleu* set, like 'the sensible' Mrs Walsingham, felt that she paid too little attention to the place and potential of women in society.[36] She seems at this stage to have thought little about the question. The female characters in her plays do not differ significantly from those in a multitude of bad plays written by men. When she published her *Essays on various subjects, principally designed for young ladies* in 1777, the introduction unthinkingly reproduced traditional stereotyped gender roles:

> Women have generally quicker perceptions; men have juster sentiments. – Women consider how things may be prettily said; men how they may be properly said. – In women, (young ones at least) speaking accompanies, and sometimes precedes reflection; in men, reflection is the antecedent. – Women speak to shine or to please; men, to convince or confute. – Women admire what is brilliant; men what is solid. – Women prefer an extemporaneous sally of wit, or a sparkling effusion of fancy, before the most accurate reasoning, or the most laborious investigation of facts. In literary composition, women are pleased with point, turn, and antithesis; men with observation, and a just deduction of effects from their causes. – Women are fond of incident, men of argument. – Women admire passionately, men approve cautiously. – One sex will think it betrays a

want of feeling to be moderate in their applause, the other will be afraid of expositing a want of judgment by being in raptures with anything. – Men refuse to give way to the emotions they actually feel, while women sometimes affect to be transported beyond what the occasion will justify.[37]

However, by the time she came to write *Strictures on Female Education*, twenty-two years later, More's view was infinitely more subtle and complex. Although the political problematic, which then obsessed her, required More to reinforce the subordinate place of women in the divinely ordained hierarchy,[38] her view of woman's capacity had developed significantly. By 1799 her view of female rationality and intelligence was much more open. The reason women might *appear* to be less rational than men was perhaps simply because they received such a defective education:

> At least, till the female sex are more carefully instructed, this question will always remain as undecided to the degree of difference between the masculine and feminine understanding, as the question between the understandings of blacks and whites; for until men and women, as well as Africans and Europeans, are put more nearly on a par in the cultivation of their minds, the shades of distinction, whatever they be, between their native abilities, can never be fairly ascertained.[39]

When she published her *Works* in 1801, More deliberately excluded the *Essays*, explaining that they were 'a very juvenile production' and that their subject matter had been 'taken up on higher ground' in *Strictures*.[40] In 1810 Sharpe and Hailes of Piccadilly asked her if they could reprint the essays but she explicitly refused and when they proceeded to do so anyway she angrily asked Cadell to issue a disclaimer, which she drafted herself, explaining that the work was 'not only unauthorised by her but against her consent'.[41]

Between the ages of thirty-five and forty-five, More appeared to change significantly. In a letter to Richard Berenger, written from the Garricks' house in the Adelphi shortly after the death

of David Garrick in 1779, the simple joy and fun of past days is
sharply contrasted with her present serious mood:

> When I am in any house but this, I have the secret satisfaction
> to find that my taste for nonsense, is as acute as ever it was; but
> *here*, so far from the comfort of being foolish that I have all the
> difficulty in the world to be cheerful. The table I write upon,
> the too-resembling picture which stares me in the face, the
> speculation in those eyes, and all the hours and unminding
> objects which surround me, make a fool of me indeed but not a
> fool of the *right sort*.[42]

To attribute the new attitude purely to Garrick's death[43] is far
too simplistic, though that event might well have been the
beginning of the process. The triple deaths of Garrick, her father
Jacob More, and of Johnson, in 1779, 1783 and 1784 respectively, no doubt had a cumulative effect, but even this needs to
be set against positive elements. Her meetings with the Middle-
tons and with Wilberforce, her involvement in the Anti Slave
Trade movement and her general attachment to Evangelical
paternalism played as important a part in the process. Nor
should the political perspective be ignored. The impact of the
French Revolution on More was immense and is unquestioned,
but the American Revolution also distressed her sufficiently to
cause a break, albeit temporary, with Burke.

No longer the popular playwright, society 'blue stocking',
light-weight poet and wit of the early days, nor yet the depres-
sive recluse pouring out tedious volume after volume of religious piety unrelieved with political purpose of the last phase,
More experienced the two most productive stages of her life in
the 1780s and 1790s. In one she applied her religious belief to
society and social life; in the other she applied it to politics. In
both, women were her primary target. She was convinced of
their importance and influence. They had a vital role to play in
the preservation of the traditional order of things.

Thoughts on the Importance of the Manners of the Great (1788) and
An Estimate of the Religion of the Fashionable World (1790) are the
major works of that phase of her life in which she applied her

Christianity to social theory. They are earnest and sincere works addressed to women of society, urging them to cast aside the frivolity of their empty and meaningless existence and to live a purposeful Christian life, influencing both their male relations and acquaintances and their female inferiors. Milliners' bills paid on time could save these poor women from a life of prostitution, so practical behaviour as well as moral example was important. In this present collection, however, this phase of her life is represented by her 'Hints towards forming a Bill for the Abolition of the White Female Slave Trade in the Cities of London and Westminster'. Chronologically this is of a later date, appearing in an obscure provincial journal in 1805. It does, however represent her social criticism well. The attitudes and the intellectual position are entirely those of the 1788 and 1790 works, but the touch is perhaps lighter, and the piece is influenced by the fact that the movement for the abolition of the Black Slave Trade, a reform movement to which she was wholly committed, was moving towards a successful conclusion.

It was the outbreak of the French Revolution that turned More's thinking from social to political theory. 'Village Politics' (1792) was written under a male pseudonym and was directed at a male audience. But when, three years later, More began to produce the series of *Cheap Repository Tracts* (1795–7) her thoughts turned increasingly to the moral, social and political influence of women. Three tales and two ballads represent these tracts below. The ballads are of interest for their content not their poetic quality, for however dreadful they may be as verse, they give a clear view of her ideological position and propaganda purpose. The ballad of 'Sinful Sally' is a cautionary tale of a simple country girl, seduced by a member of the local gentry; 'The Sorrows of Yamba' shows that even at the height of her concern with revolution, More still pursued the black slaves' cause; her compassion is heart-felt and her perspective that of a paternalistic Evangelical. Two of the tales relate to poor women, one rural, 'Tawney Rachel', and the other urban, 'Betty Brown'. These, like the other tales, teach acceptance of the divinely ordained social hierarchy, suffering and patience, and advocate

Christianity as the key to this social panacea. More wrote a whole series of tracts that reflected her work among the women of the Mendips. 'The History of Hester Wilmot', 'The Sunday School', 'The Way to Plenty' and 'The Cottage Cook', assume attitudes and values that are profoundly counter-revolutionary. The latter works may read like a pauper's cookery book, but their emphases on suffering, contentment and making-do cheerfully, have a clear political purpose of which More was completely conscious.[44] The tale of 'Mr. Bragwell and his Two Daughters', is directed not at the poor, but at the rising middle class. It is no less political in its purpose. Its emphasis on female sexuality, seduction and ruin, the representation of women in the sentimental novel, the desire to rise out of the social order in which a person had been placed by divine providence, the neglect of religion and the replacement of humility by vanity as the predominant characteristic of the 'revolutionary' world, all mean that it anticipates in its narrative many of the arguments which More was to advance two or three years later in her didactic polemic, *Strictures on Female Education*.

VII

Like Wollstonecraft's *Vindication of the Rights of Woman*, so More's *Strictures on Female Education* was written as part of a controversy concerning the French Revolution. It is informed by a dual fear: a fear of a breakdown of traditional order, control, hierarchy and restraint in the state; and a fear of the power of female sexuality. The two are linked in More's mind, not so much by dint of metaphor, unless she meant her readers to infer a silent and implicit one, but more as the two ends of a causal chain.

The link between religion and order in the state was already well established. In order to overthrow order in the state, it was necessary first to destroy the religion that sustained it. From this position, More moves back a stage; 'religion and morals will stand or fall together'.[45] So, to overthrow religion, first the morality that supports it must be destroyed. Sexual desire was a powerful weapon with which to destroy Christian morality, and women were, to a great extent, the last bastion of that ethic. More was well aware of the double standard of morality that allowed a young man to 'sow his wild oats' and a married man to engage in adultery without undue censure, whilst requiring a woman to remain 'pure'. She dreaded the thought that women 'shall be permitted to indulge in all those gratifications which custom, not religion, has too far overlooked in the male sex!' and is thankful that adultery 'in the female sex at least, is still held in just abhorrence'.[46] Her fear was that if that male indulgence of the sexual passions was to be extended to women, then morality would fall, and that domino would bring down religion, and order in the state, along with it.

More believed that this was the danger of modern literature in general and of the representation of women in novels in particular. She realised that if the popular novels written for women readers made the sexually liberated behaviour of the female characters appear normative, then traditional Christian morality was undermined.[47] French influence, from Rousseau's *La Nouvelle Héloïse* onwards, and German Romantic drama and fiction placed a powerful emphasis on feeling and emotion rather than on reason and principles. The theme of the seduced innocent is a characteristic of the German *Sturm und Drang* movement and the women involved are treated in a highly sympathetic way which disturbed More.[48] But it was an English novel that alarmed her the most. Mary Wollstonecraft's *Maria or the Wrongs of Woman* was published in the year before More's *Strictures* appeared. This asserted, More claimed, 'that adultery is justifiable, and that the restrictions placed on it by the laws of England constitute part of the *wrongs of woman*'.[49] The paragraph which follows this comment in the first edition of *Strictures* is a powerful enough condemnation of such thinking, but by the second edition, published only a few weeks later, More had inserted at this point a remarkable addition, a couple of pages which excoriated Wollstonecraft and her like in the most passionate language as this most destructive class in the whole wide range of modern corruptors, who effect the most desperate work of the passions, without so much as pretending to urge the *violence* of the passions as a plea to extenuate their corruptions. They solicit the indulgence of the grossest appetites with a sort of cold-blooded speculation, and abandon themselves, and debauch the reader, to the most unbounded gratification of the senses, with all the saturnine coolness of a geometrical calculation...It descants on depravity, and details its grossest acts as frigidly as if its object were to *allay* the tumult of the passions, while it is letting them loose on mankind, by "plucking off the muzzle" of the present restraint and future accountableness. The system is a dire infusion compounded of bold impiety, brutish sensuality, and exquisite folly, which creeping fatally around the heart checks the moral circulation, and totally stops the pulse of goodness by the extinction of the vital principle.[50]

More seems convinced that if women were to be persuaded to indulge their sexual passions, they would enjoy the experience and this pleasure would lead them further from the path of Christian virtue. The arts 'become agents of voluptuousness. They excite the imagination; and the imagination thus excited ...becomes the most dangerous stimulant of the passions; promotes a too keen relish for pleasure,...inventing new and pernicious modes of artificial gratification.'[51]

More never moves far from the fundamental *political* point she is making. Female sexual indulgence dissolves morality, which dissolution in turn destroys religion, the removal of which allows the overthrow of order in the state. Radicals and revolutionaries, she believed, understood this process all too well and they encouraged it as part of a conscious conspiracy. Two years before the publication of *Strictures*, two works had appeared in English that argued that the French Revolution was the result of an intellectual conspiracy. The English translation of the Abbé Barruel's *Memoirs of. . . Jacobinism* (1797) and John Robison's *Proofs of a Conspiracy against All the Religions and Governments of Europe* (1797) alleged two connected conspiracies; one that of the French *philosophes*, the other of freemasons and *illuminées*. More extends their argument to the assault on English morality, religion and government. The writings of the French Enlightenment had failed to subvert the English, but now, 'conscious of the influence of women in civil society, conscious of the effect which female infidelity produced in France, they attribute the ill success of their attempts in this country to their having been hitherto chiefly addressed to the male sex.'[52] Women were now the conscious target; destroy their religious principles and church and state could be brought down. To achieve this, 'not only novels and romances have been made the vehicles of vice and infidelity, but the same allurement has been held out to the women of our country, which was employed by the original tempter to our first parent – Knowledge.'[53]

More believed that women were the victims of a dual attack. On the one side were the advocates of sensibility who stressed emotions, sentiment, sympathy and feeling, and sought to re-place moral rectitude with sensual indulgence. On the other were the advocates of female assertiveness, 'the bold and inde-pendent beauty, the intrepid female, the hoyden, the huntress, and the archer; the swinging arms, the confident address, the regimental, and the four-in-hand'. Just as the first led to disaster for society through adultery, so the second led to the 'rights of woman' and the belief of women that 'you need no longer remain in that situation in which Providence has placed you!'[54]

More claimed never to have read Wollstonecraft's *Vindication of the Rights of Woman*. Her opposition to it was twofold. First, like Burke, she rejected the concept of abstract universal rights, for men or women. Rights were concrete privileges won by, or given to, specific groups. Rights were granted by the sovereign; no-one possessed innate rights by virtue of their humanity. Secondly, the divinely ordained social hierarchy, one of the cornerstones of the traditional order More sought to defend, placed women as subordinate to men. St Peter, in the same passage as he instructs his followers to obey the civil magistrate and honour the king, also enjoins, 'servants be subject to your masters with all fear' and 'wives be in subjection to your own husbands'.[55] Again, the position of women was inextricably linked with the safety and security of the traditional order in the state. One of More's major specific objections to Wollstone-craft's *Vindication* was that 'among the innovations of this in-novating period, the imposing term of *rights* has been produced to sanctify the claim of our female pretenders, with a view...to excite in their hearts an impious discontent with the post which God has assigned them in this world'.[56] The basis of the family and the state are the same:

> ...it is pretty clear, in spite of modern theories, that the very frame and being of societies, whether great or small, public or private, is jointed and glued together by dependence. Those attachments, which arise from, and are compacted by, a sense of mutual wants, mutual affection, mutual benefit, and mutual obligation, are the cement which secure the union of the family as well as of the state.[57]

Anyone who wished to support the traditional arguments for the religious sanction of state authority and social order, had no option but to oppose any idea of the rights of woman. Hannah More understood fully all these implications and all these dangers. *Strictures* is, in its way, a sophisticated, counter-revolutionary polemic.

The fall of the ancien regime in England in 1828–32 came when More was in her mid-eighties. The repeal of the Test and Corporation Acts in 1828 gave adult, male, property-owning Dissenters the right to enter parliament and hold office; the passing of Catholic Emancipation in the following year allowed Catholics to become MPs. The Anglican stranglehold on politi-cal power was broken and the established Constitution in the Church breached. Supporters of the traditional order had warned that such a move would lead inevitably to reform of the Constitution in the State, and the First Reform Act duly fol-lowed in 1832. In the event, it was the claims not of women but of male Dissenters to political and civil equality that brought down the old regime. The validity of the state's political author-ity no longer rested on religious sanction, but on the concept of representation; the process of the secularisation of political obligation was effectively complete.

More opposed the reforms strongly. Following the passing of Catholic Emancipation in 1829, Sir Robert Peel, member of parliament for the University of Oxford, who had carried the act in the House of Commons against his constituents' wishes, offered himself for re-election. More encouraged the graduates of Oxford to vote against him, 'the interest of our church and our country is at stake'. When he was defeated she exclaimed in one of the last letters she wrote, 'Joy, joy, joy to you, to me! Joy to the individual victorious Protestant! Joy to the great Protestant cause.'[58] But her joy was misplaced. Peel soon found another seat and the process of reform was unstoppable. Two years later, in October and November 1831, less than a mile from More's sick-bed in Clifton, Bristol was in the throes of Reform Riots; the Bishop's Palace was set on fire and the Chapter House of the Cathedral broken into by the rioters. The old order of church and state was passing. Representation was finally replacing religion as the bed-rock of the social and political order.

More despaired, but things could have appeared worse from her point of view. The claims of 'rights' for women, the denial of the Petrine injunction to subordination, had been thwarted; more important still, the liberation of female sexuality, the destruction of Christian morality, of religion and of the social order had been avoided. However, the political theology which linked these issues so closely for her had been superseded. In its place a new foundation for political society had been established – a foundation that was not only compatible with female suffrage, but eventually perceived to require it.

NOTES

[1] J. C. D. Clark, *English Society 1688–1832: Ideology, social structure and political practice during the ancien regime*, Cambridge University Press, 1985; *Revolution and Rebellion: State and society in England in the seventeenth and eighteenth centuries*, Cambridge University Press, 1986.

[2] Clark, *English Society 1688–1832*, pp. 9–10.

[3] Ibid., pp. 11–12.

[4] An invitation soon taken up by Joanna Innes and others after her. See Innes, 'Jonathan Clark, Social History and England's "Ancien Regime"', *Past and Present*, 115 (May 1987), pp. 165–200.

[5] Clark, *Revolution and Rebellion*, p. 1.

[6] For Malthus as the adversary of Godwin see A. M. C. Waterman, *Revolution, Economics and Religion: Christian Political Economy 1798–1833*, Cambridge University Press, 1991.

[7] See below the Letters from London, pp. 5–19, and the 'Bas Bleu', pp. 25–35 and especially notes 8, 70 and 75 to the main text.

[8] Pietro Metastasio (1698–1782), librettist and lyric poet, wrote the melodrama *Attilio Regolo* in 1732.

[9] Jones, *Hannah More*, p. 35. The appearance of Collingwood's, *Hannah More*, a charming but uncritical biographical sketch, has done nothing to displace Jones's study as the best scholarly biography. For the best literary interpretation of More and her work from a feminist perspective, see Kowaleski-Wallace, *Their fathers' daughters*.

[10] More, *Slavery*, lines 59–64, pp. 4–5.

[11] Popular literature circulated by itinerant dealers or chapmen, consisting chiefly of small pamphlets of popular tales, ballads, tracts, etc.

[12] Letter to Sir W. W. Pepys, March 1816, printed in Martha More, *Mendip Annals*, pp. 245–6.

[13] Roberts, *Memoirs*; Hopkins, *More and Her Circle*.

[14] For marriage as a 'tolerable' state, see *Strictures*, below p. 212. On Selina Mills, see Jones, *Hannah More*, pp. 130–2. Some of More's letters to Macaulay, omitted in Roberts's *Memoirs*, were published by his son Arthur Roberts, *Letters to Zachary Macaulay*, after Macaulay's death. But, as cautious and discrete as his father, he included only three letters before 1806, none of which shed much light on the situation.

[15] See *Strictures*, below, pp. 229–32.

[16] See *Strictures*, below pp. 139, 141.

[17] See below pp. 138–42.

[18] See J. G. A. Pocock, *The Machiavellian Moment: Florentine Political Thought and the Atlantic Republican Tradition*, Princeton, 1975.

[19] For this interpretation of the end of the ancien regime, see Clark, *English Society 1688–1832*, pp. 349–420 and Robert Hole, *Pulpits, Politics and Public Order in England 1760–1832*, Cambridge University Press, 1989, pp. 229–47.

[20] Romans 13: 1–7; 1 Peter 2: 13–18.

[21] See Hole, *Pulpits, Politics and Public Order*, pp. 12–21, 61–3.

[22] Sir Robert Filmer, who died in 1653 and whose *Patriarcha* was published in 1680, and John Hutchinson (1674–1737), who published his *Moses's Principia* in 1724, took contrary views to Locke and Newton respectively.

[23] Horne, 'The Origin of Civil Government', 2 March 1769, *The Works of the Right Reverend George Horne*, 4 vols, London, 1818, II, p. 448.

[24] [Stevens, W.], *Strictures on a Sermon, Entitled The Principles of the Revolution vindicated*, 2nd ed., Cambridge, 1777, pp. 9–10.

[25] See Clark, *English Society 1688–1832*, pp. 74–6, and Hole, *Pulpits, Politics and Public Order*, pp. 61–3.

[26] Hole, *Pulpits, Politics and Public Order*, pp. 16–18, 20–22, 49–50; Hole, 'Sermons and Tracts as a medium of debate', in M. Phelp (ed.), *The French Revolution and British Popular Politics*, Cambridge University Press, 1991; Jones, *Hannah More*, pp. 9, 65–6, 104; & *Strictures*, below, pp. 217–19.

[27] Horne, 'The Duty of Considering the Poor', *Works*, III, pp. 73–88, 76–7.

[28] E. Tatham, *Letters to the Right Honourable Edmund Burke on Politics*, Oxford, 1791, pp. 32, 40.

[29] E. Burke, *The Works of the Right Honourable Edmund Burke*, 6 vols, London, 1877–83, III, pp. 79–80.

[30] Horne, 'The Duty of Praying for Governors', 25 October 1788, *Works*, II, p. 571.

[31] For an interesting feminist reading of More's Evangelicalism see Kowaleski-Wallace, *Their fathers' daughters*, chapter 3, 'Hannah and Her Sister: Women and Evangelicalism', pp. 56–93.

[32] J. Owen, *Subordination considered on the Grounds of Reason and Religion*, Cambridge, 1794, pp. 3, 19, 29, 31.

[33] W. Wilberforce, *A Practical View of the Prevailing Religious System*, London, 1797, pp. 404–6.

[34] M. Wollstonecraft, 'An Historical and Moral View of the French Revolution' (1794), in *Political Writings*, ed. Janet Todd, Pickering & Chatto, 1993, p. 306; More, *Strictures*, below pp. 136–7.

[35] Compare Burke both in the *Reflections on the Revolution in France*, London, 1790, and the *Letters on a Regicide Peace*, London, 1796. More's debt to Burke is obvious and immense. M. G. Jones describes *Village Politics* (1792) as 'Burke for Beginners' and his influence is widespread throughout More's writings. Jones, *Hannah More*, p. 134.

[36] See below p. 10 and note 26 to the main text, and Jones, *Hannah More*, p. 57.

[37] More, *Essays*, pp. 9–10.

[38] See *Strictures*, below p. 181.

[39] See *Strictures*, below p. 183.

[40] More, *Works*, 1801, I, Preface, p. x.

[41] *Essays on Various Subjects principally designed for Young Ladies: A New Edition*, London, Sharpe and Hailes, 1810; Letter to Cadell, 2 July 1810, MS Oxford, Bodleian Library, Autogr. c. 19, f. 83 ᵛ.

[42] MS London, British Library, Add MS 59438, f. 127 ᵛ.

[43] As suggested by Roberts, *Memoirs*, I, p.155. Roberts does not include More's letter to Berenger about her 'taste for nonsense' and playing the fool.

[44] For a fuller analysis of the social control element in these tales, see Robert Hole, 'British Counter-Revolutionary Popular Propaganda in the 1790s' in Colin Jones (ed.), *Britain and Revolutionary France: Conflict, Subversion and Propaganda*, University of Exeter Press, 1983, pp. 53–69, esp. pp. 63–6.

[45] *Strictures*, see below p. 138.

[46] *Strictures*, see below pp. 139, 141.

[47] *Strictures*, see below p. 136.

[48] See, for example, H. L. Wagner , *Die Kindermörden*, 1776, and J. M. R. Lenz, *Die Soldaten*, 1774–5. The depiction of Gretchen in Goethe's *Urfaust*, which was written in this period though not published until 1887, is characteristic.

[49] *Strictures*, see below p. 140.

[50] See below, p. 140, and note 195 to the main text.

[51] *Strictures*, see below p. 151 .

[52] *Strictures*, see below p. 139.

[53] *Strictures*, see below p. 139.

[54] *Strictures*, see below p. 139.

[55] 1 Peter 2: 17–18; 3: 1.

[56] See *Strictures*, below p. 179.

[57] See *Strictures*, below p. 232.

[58] Roberts, *Memoirs*, IV, pp. 334–5.

BIBLIOGRAPHY

Works published by More during her lifetime (in chronological order)

A Search after Happiness: a pastoral drama, Bristol, 1773
The Inflexible Captive: a tragedy, Bristol, 1774
Sir Eldred of the Bower and the Bleeding Rock: two legendary tales, London, 1776
Ode to Dragon, Mr Garrick's house-dog at Hampton, London, 1777
Essays on various subjects, principally designed for Young Ladies, London, 1777
Percy: a tragedy, London, 1778
The Fatal Falsehood: a tragedy, London, 1779
Sacred Dramas, chiefly intended for Young Persons, to which is added Sensibility, A Poem, London, 1782
Florio: a tale, for fine gentlemen and fine ladies: and, The Bas Bleu; or, Conversation: Two Poems, London, 1786.
Slavery, a poem, London, 1788
Thoughts on the importance of the Manners of the Great to general society, London, 1788
Bishop Bonner's Ghost: a poem, Strawberry-hill, 1789
An Estimate of the Religion of the Fashionable World. By one of the Laity, London, 1790
'Village Politics', Canterbury, 1792, (later editions, London).
Remarks on a Speech of M. Dupont, made in the National Convention of France, on the subjects of religion and public education, London, 1793
Cheap Repository Tracts, 1795–7
Strictures on the Modern System of Female Education, London, 1799
Hints towards Forming the Character of a Young Princess, London, 1805

'Hints towards forming a Bill for the Abolition of the White
Female Slave Trade, in the Cities of London and Westmins-
ter', *The Weekly Entertainer; or agreeable and instructive repository*,
Volume 45, Sherborne, Monday 12 August, 1805

*Coelebs in Search of a Wife. Comprehending observations on domestic
habits and manners, religion and morals*, London, 1808

Practical Piety, London, 1811

Christian Morals, London, 1812

An Essay on The Character and Practical Writings of St Paul, London,
1815

Tracts and reprints of the *Cheap Repository Tracts*, 1817–19

Stories for the middle ranks of society and Tales for the Common People,
London, 1818

*Moral Sketches of prevailing opinions and manners, foreign and domestic;
with reflections on prayer*, London, 1819

*The Twelfth of August: or the Feast of Freedom or the Abolition of
Domestic Slavery in Ceylon*, London, 1819

*Bible Rhymes on the names of all the books of the Old and New
Testament, with allusions to some of the principal incidents and
characters*, London, 1821

The Spirit of Prayer, London, 1825

The following collections were also published in her lifetime:

The Works of Miss Hannah More in prose and verse, Cork, 1778
The Works of Hannah More, 8 volumes, London, 1801
Poems, London 1816
The Works of Hannah More, 19 volumes, London, 1818
Poems, London, 1829
The Works of Hannah More, 11 volumes, London, 1830

Works on Hannah More (in alphabetical order)

Anon. [Shaw, W.], *The Life of Hannah More with a critical review of
her writings by the Rev. Sir Archibald MacSarcasm, Bart.*, London,
Hurst, 1802

Balfour, C. L., *A Sketch of Mrs. Hannah More and her sisters*, London, Cash, 1854

Buckland, Anna J., *The Life of Hannah More*, London, Religious Tract Society, not dated [1882]

Collingwood, J. & M. , *Hannah More*, Oxford, Lion, 1990

Cropper, M. B., *Sparks among the Stubble*, London, Longmans, 1955.

Fox, L.P., 'Hannah More, Evangelical Educationalist...', Unpublished thesis, McGill, Montreal, 1949

Harland, Marian, *Hannah More*, New York, Putnam's Sons, 1900

Hopkins, Mary Alden, *Hannah More and Her Circle*, New York, Longmans, 1947

Jones, M. G., *Hannah More*, Cambridge, Cambridge University Press, 1952

Kowaleski-Wallace, E., *Their fathers' daughters, Hannah More, Maria Edgeworth and patriarchal complicity*, New York, OUP, 1991

Meakin, Annette, *Hannah More a biographical study*, London, Smith, Elder & Co., 1911

Miller, P. J., 'Women's Education, "Self-Improvement" and Social Mobility – A Late Eighteenth-Century Debate', *British Journal of Educational Studies*, 20 (1972), pp. 302–14

Myers, Mitzi, 'Hannah More's Tracts for the Times: Social Fiction and Female Ideology', in *Fetter'd or Free?: British Women Novelists 1670–1815*, eds. M.A. Schofield & C. Macheski, Ohio University Press, 1986

Pederson, Susan, 'Hannah More Meets Simple Simon: Tracts, Chapbooks, and Popular Culture in Late Eighteenth-Century England', *Journal of British Studies*, 25 (1986), pp. 84–113

Richardson, William, 'Sentimental Journey of Hannah More: Propaganda and Shaper of Victorian Attitudes', *Revolutionary Worlds*, 11 (1975), pp. 228–39

Roberts, A. (ed.), *Letters of Hannah More to Zachary Macaulay*, London, Nisbet, 1860

Roberts, A. (ed.), *Mendip Annals: or, A Narrative of the Charitable Labours of Hannah and Martha More in their neighbourhood. Being the Journal of Martha More*, 2nd edition, London, Nisbet, 1859

Roberts, W., *Memoirs of the Life and Correspondence of Hannah More*, in four volumes, London, 1834

Silverman J., 'Introduction' to the facsimile reprint, Garland Edition of *Cheap Repository Tracts by Hannah More*, New York, Garland, 1977

Silvester, James, *The Story of Hannah More*, Drummond Tract, not dated, [1928]

Spinney, G. H., 'Cheap Repository Tracts: Hazard and Marshall edition', *The Library*, 4th series, 3 (1939), pp. 295–340

Tabor, M. E., *Pioneer Women*, London, Sheldon Press, 1925–33

Taylor, Thomas, *Memoir of Mrs. Hannah More*, London, 1838

Thompson, Henry, *Life of Hannah More with Notice of her Sisters*, London, Cadell, 1838

Yonge, C. M., *Hannah More*, 1888

HANNAH MORE 1745–1833

AN OUTLINE CHRONOLOGY

Year	Age	
1745		Born at Stapleton, Gloucestershire
1757	12	The More sisters opened a boarding school 6, Trinity Street, Bristol
1767	22	Engaged to be married to William Turner
1767	22	The More sisters' school moved to Park Street, Bristol
1773	28	Engagement to Turner broken off; money settled on her
1773	28	First book published: *A Search after Happiness*, a pastoral drama
1774	29	Helped Burke in his election campaign in Bristol
1774	29	Made the first of her annual visits to London
1775	30	Became a member of the 'Blue Stockings' circle in London
1775	30	Met Frances Reynolds, her brother Sir Joshua, and Samuel Johnson &c.
1775	30	*The Inflexible Captive* produced at Bath Theatre Royal
1776	31	Met the Middletons and was introduced into the Anti-Slave Trade movement
1776	31	Saw David Garrick's farewell performances
1777	32	*Percy* produced at Covent Garden
1779	33	Attended David Garrick's burial in Westminster Abbey

1795	50	Hostile opposition to Zachary Macaulay's courtship of Selina Mills, dearest friend of Patty More
1795–7	50–53	Edited *The Cheap Repository Tracts* and wrote almost half of them herself
1798	54	*The Cheap Repository Tracts* reprinted in volume form
1799	54	Published *Strictures on the Modern System of Female Education* under her own name
1800–03	55–58	The Blagdon Controversy: bitter dispute with the local clergy over the school at Blagdon, Somerset
1801	56	The More sisters left Bath and moved, with Hannah, into Barley Wood a large house in Wrington, Somerset
1805	60	Published *Hints towards forming the Character of a Young Princess*
1808	63	Published her only novel, *Coelebs in Search of a Wife*
1811	66	Published *Practical Piety*
1812	67	Published *Christian Morals*
1815	70	Published *The Character and Practical Writings of St Paul*
1817–19	72–74	Responded to the civil unrest by republishing the *Cheap Repository Tracts* and writing some new ones, including 'The Death of Mr Fantom'
1819	74	Published *Moral Sketches*
1820–28	75–83	Alone, ill and abused by her servants
1821	76	Published *The Feast of Freedom* and *Bible Rhymes*
1825	80	Published *The Spirit of Prayer*
1828	83	Left Barley Wood to live with friends in Bristol
1833	88	Died at Clifton, Bristol

A NOTE ON THE TEXTS

In all cases, the text used in this selection is that of the earliest edition. Often, for publications such as this, it is useful to use a second or third edition in which the author has been able to correct early errors. More however did not just correct, she 'improved'. This usually meant scattering redundant adjectives, adding unnecessary clauses and inserting, at the end of many paragraphs, an additional, tendentious sentence to underline the moral. Any freshness and immediacy in her prose was smothered. So, at the cost of the occasional error, the first edition texts have been preferred.

The 'Sorrows of Yamba', 'Betty Brown', 'Tawney Rachel', 'Sinful Sally' and 'Bragwell's Daughters', first appeared in 1795–7 as unbound tracts and were reprinted several times in this period. They were then collected and reprinted in two bound volumes in 1798, with corrections, 'improvements' and additions. The 1795–7 versions have been preferred, but there is no way of knowing which of these is the earliest. There is, however, no significant difference between any of these pre-1798 versions. What minor variations of punctuation and capitalisation there are, almost certainly owed more to the printer's compositor than to the author.

1. Letters from London 1775–79 are based on the texts in William Roberts, *Memoirs of the Life and Correspondence of Mrs. Hannah More*, 4 vols, London, 1834.

2. 'The Bas Bleu' in *Florio: a tale, for fine gentlemen and fine ladies: and, The Bas Bleu; or, Conversation: Two Poems*, London, Cadell, 1786. The dedication to Horace Walpole is dated 27 January 1786. The poem was written in 1782 and widely circulated in

manuscript before its publication. The work is presented here uncut.

3. 'Hints towards forming a Bill for the Abolition of the White Female Slave Trade, in the Cities of London and Westminster', *The Weekly Entertainer; or agreeable and instructive repository*, Volume 45, Sherborne, Monday 12 August 1805. It is anonymous, signed 'An Enemy to all Slavery'. When More included it in her *Collected Works* in 1818, she gave no indication of the whereabouts of its first appearance and added the title 'The White Slave Trade', making the original title into a sub-title. The work is presented here uncut.

4. 'The Sorrows of Yamba' appeared in November 1795 as one of the *Cheap Repository Tracts*, 1795–7. The work is presented here uncut.

5. 'Betty Brown' appeared in August 1796 as one of the *Cheap Repository Tracts*, 1795–7. The work is presented here uncut.

6. 'Tawney Rachel' appeared in 1797 as one of the *Cheap Repository Tracts*, 1795–7. The work is presented here uncut.

7. 'Sinful Sally' appeared in February 1796 as one of the *Cheap Repository Tracts*, 1795–7. Some have doubted More's authorship of this ballad. Normally the tracts she wrote herself are signed 'Z' and the earliest copies of this one are not. However, when the tract was republished in c. 1805, More clearly acknowledged that it was her work, (see Bodleian, Johnson d. 134). We can speculate on why she concealed the fact earlier, but not on the true attribution. The work is presented here uncut.

8. 'Mr. Bragwell and his two daughters' appeared in seven parts in the *Cheap Repository Tracts*, 1795–7. The parts were published as follows: Part 1 (1795); Parts 3, 4, & 5 (1796); Parts 6 & 7 (1797). The whole of Part 2 has been omitted from this selection. The first part of this story was entitled 'The Two Wealthy Farmers'; by part three it had become 'The History of Mr. Bragwell; or, the Two Wealthy Farmers'; part five was 'The Two Wealthy Farmers with the sad adventures of Miss Bragwell',

and parts six and seven 'The Two Wealthy Farmers or The History of Mr. Bragwell and his two daughters'. This selection concentrates on the story of Bragwell's daughters, so the latter title is chosen.

9. Hannah More, *Strictures on the Modern System of Female Education with a view of the principles and conduct prevalent among women of rank and fortune*, in two volumes, London, Cadell and Davies, 1799. Thirteen editions were published, seven in 1799, and a total of over 19,000 copies were sold. The text as given is that of the first edition, but significant changes and additions in the later editions have been recorded in the endnotes. The notes at the bottom of the page are More's original ones in the first edition. The text is presented here in an edited version.

Throughout the texts the numerical superscript refers to editorial endnotes; the asterisks indicate Hannah More's original footnotes.

Selected Writings of Hannah More

From Miss H. More to Mrs. Gwatkin[1]
[undated, January/February 1775]
Henrietta Street, Covent Garden, London.
My dear Madam

Here have I been a whole week, to my shame be it spoken, without ever having given you the least intimation of my existence, or change of situation; but I doubt not of your having been informed of it by my friend Charlotte. You, who know the hurry, bustle, dissipation, and nonsensical flutter of a town life will, I am sure, excuse me if I have not devoted a few minutes to you before, when I assure you it has not been in my power. Martha and the fair Clarissa are of the party, and we are comfortably situated in Henrietta Street.

We have been to see the new comedy of young Sheridan, 'The Rivals.'[2] It was very unfavourably received the first night, and he had the prudence to prevent a total defeat, by withdrawing it, and making great and various improvements; the event has been successful, for it is now *better* though not *very* much liked. For my own part, I think he ought to be treated with great indulgence: much is to be forgiven in an author of three and twenty, whose genius is likely to be his principal inheritance. I love him for the sake of his amiable and ingenious mother. On the whole I was tolerably entertained. Saturday we were at the 'Maid of the Oaks,' at Drury.[3] The scenery is beautiful – the masquerade scene as good as at the Pantheon.[4] The piece is only intended as a vehicle to the scenery, yet there is some wit and spirit in it, being written by General Burgoyne, and embellished, &c. by Garrick. He is not well enough to play or see company – how mortifying! He has been at Hampton for a week.[5] If he does not get well enough to act soon, I shall break my heart. Monday we dined, drank tea, and supped, at the amiable Sir Joshua Reynolds's;[6] there was a brilliant circle of both sexes; not in general literary, though partly so. We were not suffered to come away till one.

I have not been able to pay my devoirs to my dear Dr. Johnson yet, though Miss Reynolds has offered to accompany me whenever I am at leisure. I wish I could convey his 'Journey to the Hebrides' to you; Cadell tells me he sold 4000 of them the first week.[7] It is an agreeable work, though the subject is sterility itself: he knows how to avail himself of the commonest circumstances, and trifles are no longer trifles when they have passed through his hands. He makes the most entertaining and useful reflections on every occurrence, and when occurrences fail, he has a never-failing fund in his own accomplished and prolific mind. Pray let me hear from you soon. I wish you were with us.

I am so hurried, that I do not know what I write. Adieu, My dear friend,
Your's at all times,
Hannah More.

Miss H. More to one of her sisters.
London, 1775.

Our first visit was to Sir Joshua's, where we were received with all the friendship imaginable. I am going, to-day, to a great dinner; nothing can be conceived so absurd, extravagant, and fantastical, as the present mode of dressing the head. Simplicity and modesty are things so much exploded, that the very names are no longer remembered. I have just escaped from one of the most fashionable disfigurers; and though I charged him to dress me with the greatest simplicity, and to have only a very distant eye upon the fashion, just enough to avoid the pride of singularity, without running into ridiculous excess; yet in spite of all these sage didactics, I absolutely blush at myself, and turn to the glass with as much caution as a vain beauty, just risen from the small-pox; which cannot be a more disfiguring disease than the present mode of dressing. Of the one, the calamity may be greater in its consequences, but of the other it is more corrupt in its cause. We have been reading a treatise on the morality of Shakespeare; it is a happy and easy way of filling a book, that the present race of authors have arrived at – that of criticising the works of some eminent poet; with monstrous extracts, and short remarks. It is a species of cookery I begin to grow tired of; they cut up their authors into chops, and by adding a little crumbled bread of their own, and tossing it up a little, they present it as a fresh dish: you are to dine upon the poet; – the critic supplies the garnish; yet, has the credit, as well as profit, of the whole entertainment.

From the same to the same.
London, 1775.

I had yesterday the pleasure of dining in Hill Street, Berkeley Square, *at a certain Mrs. Montagu's, a name not totally obscure*. The party consisted of herself, Mrs. Carter, Dr. Johnson, Solander, and Matty, Mrs. Boscawen, Miss Reynolds, and Sir Joshua, (the idol of every company;) some other persons of high rank and less wit, and your humble servant, – a party that would not have disgraced the table of Lælius, or of Atticus.[8] I felt myself a worm, the more a worm for the consequence which was given me, by mixing me with such a society; but, as I told Mrs. Boscawen, and with great truth, I had an opportunity of making an experiment of my heart, by which I learnt that I was not envious, for I certainly did not repine at being the meanest person in company.

Mrs. Montagu received me with the most encouraging kindness; she is not only the finest genius, but the finest lady I ever saw: she lives in the highest style of magnificence; her apartments and table are in the most splendid taste; but what baubles are these when speaking of a Montagu! her form (for she has no *body*) is delicate even to fragility; her countenance the most animated in the world; the sprightly vivacity of fifteen, with the judgment and experience of a Nestor. But I fear she is hastening to decay very fast; her spirits are so active, that they must soon wear out the little frail receptacle that holds them. Mrs. Carter has in her person a great deal of what the gentlemen mean when they say such a one is a 'poetical lady;' however, independently of her great talents and learning, I like her much; she has affability, kindness, and goodness; and I honour her heart even more than her talents; but I do not like one of them better than Mrs. Boscawen; she is at once polite, learned, judicious, and humble, and Mrs. Palk tells me, her letters are not thought inferior to Mrs. Montagu's. She regretted (so did I) that so many suns could not possibly shine at one time; but we are to have a smaller party, where, from fewer luminaries, there may emanate a clearer, steadier, and more beneficial light. Dr. Johnson asked me how I liked the new tragedy of Braganza.[9] I was afraid to speak before them all, as I knew a diversity of opinion prevailed among the company: however, as I thought it a less evil to dissent from the opinion of a fellow-creature, than to tell a falsity, I ventured to give my sentiments; and was satisfied with Johnson's answering, 'You are right, Madam.'

From the same to the same.
Sunday night, 9 o'clock.

Perhaps you will say I ought to have thought of it again to-day, when I tell you I have dined abroad; but it is a day I reflect on without those uneasy sensations one has when one is conscious it has been spent in trifling company. I have been at Mrs. Boscawen's. Mrs. Montagu, Mrs. Carter, Mrs. Chapone, and myself only were admitted.[10] We spent the time, not as wits, but as reasonable creatures; better characters, I trow. The conversation was sprightly but serious. I have not enjoyed an afternoon so much since I have been in town. There was much sterling sense, and they are all ladies of high character for piety; of which, however, I do not think their visiting on Sundays any proof: for though their conversation is edifying, the example is bad.[11] You do not, I presume, expect I should send you a transcript of the conversation: I have told you the interlocutors, but you are not to expect the dialogue. Patty says if she had such rich subjects, she could make a better hand of them: I believe her: my outlines are perhaps more just, but she beats me all to nothing in the colouring.[12] She is but a young painter, and is fond of drapery and ornament: for my own part the more I see of the 'honoured, famed, and great,' the more I see of the littleness, the unsatisfactoriness of all created good; and that no earthly pleasure can fill up the wants of the immortal principle within. One need go no farther than the company I have just left, to be convinced that 'pain is for man,' and that fortune, talents, and science are no exemption from the universal lot. Mrs. Montagu, eminently distinguished for wit and virtue, 'the wisest where all are wise,' is hastening to insensible decay by a slow, but sure hectic. Mrs. Chapone has experienced the severest reverses of fortune; and Mrs. Boscawen's life has been a continued series of afflictions that may almost bear a parallel with those of the righteous man of Uz.[13] Tell me, then, what is it to be wise? This you will say is exhibiting the unfavourable side of the picture of humanity, but it is the right side, the side that shows the likeness.

Miss H. More to one of her sisters.
London, 1776.

Just returned from spending one of the most agreeable days of my life, with the female Mæcenas of Hill Street; she engaged me five or six days ago to dine with her, and had assembled half the wits of the age.[14] The only fault that charming woman has, is, that she is fond of collecting too many of them together at one time. There were nineteen persons assembled at dinner, but after the repast, she has a method of dividing her guests, or rather letting them assort themselves into little groups of five or six each. I spent my time in going from one to the other of these little societies, as I happened more or less to like the subjects they were discussing. Mrs. Scott, Mrs. Montagu's sister, a very good writer, Mrs. Carter, Mrs. Barbauld,[15] and a man of letters, whose name I have forgotten, made up one of these little parties. When we had canvassed two or three subjects, I stole off and joined in with the next group, which was composed of Mrs. Montagu, Dr. Johnson, the Provost of Dublin, and two other ingenious men. In this party there was a diversity of opinions, which produced a great deal of good argument and reasoning. There were several other groups less interesting to me, as they were more composed of rank than talent, and it was amusing to see how the people of sentiment singled out each other, and how the fine ladies and pretty gentlemen naturally slid into each other's society.

I had the happiness to carry Dr. Johnson home from Hill Street, though Mrs. Montagu publicly declared she did not think it prudent to trust us together, with such a declared affection on both sides. She said she was afraid of a Scotch elopement. He has invited himself to drink tea with us to-morrow, that we may read Sir Eldred together.[16] I shall not tell you what he said of it, but to me the best part of his flattery was, that he repeats all the best stanzas by heart, with the energy, though not with the grace of a Garrick.

London, 1776.

Let the Muses shed tears, for Garrick has this day sold the patent of Drury Lane Theatre, and will never act after this winter.[17] *Sic transit gloria mundi!* He retires with all his blushing honours thick about him, his laurels as green as in their early spring. Who shall supply his loss to the stage? Who shall now hold the master-key of the human heart? Who direct the passions with more than magic power? Who purify the stage; and who, in short, shall direct and nurse my dramatic muse?

Yesterday was another of the few sunshiny days with which human life is so scantily furnished. We spent it at Garrick's, he was in high good humour, and inexpressibly agreeable. Here was likely to have been another jostling and intersecting of our pleasures; but as they knew Johnson would be with us at seven, Mrs. Garrick was so good as to dine a little after three, and all things fell out in comfortable succession. We were at the reading of a new tragedy, and insolently and unfeelingly pronounced against it. We got home in time: I hardly ever spent an evening more pleasantly or profitably. Johnson, full of wisdom and piety, was very communicative. To enjoy Dr. Johnson perfectly, one must have him to oneself, as he seldom cares to speak in mixed parties. Our tea was not over till nine, we then fell upon Sir Eldred: he read both poems through, suggested some little alterations in the first, and did me the honour to write one whole stanza; but in the Rock, he has not altered a word.[18] Though only a tea visit, he staid with us till twelve. I was quite at my ease, and never once asked him to eat (drink he never does any thing but tea); while you, I dare say, would have been fidgeted to death, and would have sent half over the town for chickens, and oysters, and asparagus, and Madeira. You see how frugal it is to be well-bred, and not to think of such vulgar renovation as eating and drinking.

London, 1776.

Again I am annoyed by the foolish absurdity of the present mode of dress. Some ladies carry on their heads a large quantity of fruit, and yet they would despise a poor useful member of society, who carried it there for the purpose of selling it for bread. Some, at the back of their perpendicular caps, hang four or five ostrich feathers, of different colours, &c. Spirit of Addison! thou pure and gentle shade, arise! thou who, with such fine humour, and such polished sarcasm, didst lash the cherry-coloured hood, and the party patches; and cut down, with a trenchant sickle, a whole harvest of follies and absurdities! awake! for the follies thou didst lash were but the beginning of follies; and the absurdities thou didst censure, were but the seeds of absurdities![19] Oh, that thy master-spirit, speaking and chiding in thy graceful page, could recal the blushes, and collect the scattered and mutilated remnants of female modesty.

Adelphi, 1776.[20]

Did I tell you we had a very agreeable day at Mrs. Boscawen's? I like Mr. Berenger prodigiously.[21] I met the Bunbury family at Sir Joshua's. Mr. Boswell (Corsican Boswell)[22] was here last night; he is a very agreeable good-natured man; he perfectly adores Johnson; they have this day set out together for Oxford, Lichfield, &c. that the Doctor may take leave of all his old friends and acquaintances, previous to his great expedition across the Alps. I lament his undertaking such a journey at his time of life, with beginning infirmities; I hope he will not leave his bones on classic ground. I have here most spacious apartments, three rooms to myself. David Hume is at the point of death in a jaundice.[23] Cadell told me today he had circulated six thousand of Price's book, and was rejoiced to hear that the Dean of Gloucester intended to answer it.[24]

Adelphi, 1776.

We have had a great evening in the Adelphi...Did I excel in the descriptive, here would be a fine field for me to expatiate on the graces of the host and hostess, whose behaviour was all cheerfulness and good breeding: but lords delight not me, no, nor ladies neither, unless they are very chosen ones.

A relation of the Duchess of Chandos died at the Duchess's a few days ago, at the card-table; she was dressed most sumptuously; – they stripped off her diamonds, stuck her upright in a coach, put in two gentlemen with her, and sent her home two hours after she was dead; at least so the story goes.

Baron Burland died as suddenly; after having been at the house of lords he dined heartily, and was standing by the fire, talking politics to a gentleman. So you see, even London has its warnings if it would but listen to them. These are two signal ones in one week; but the infatuation of the people is beyond anything that can be conceived.

A most magnificent hotel in St. James's Street was opened last night for the first time, by the name of the 'Savoir Vivre;' none but people of the very first rank were there, so you may conclude the diversion was cards; and in one night, the very first time the rooms were ever used, the enormous sum of sixty thousand pounds was lost! Heaven reform us!

We had the other night a conversazione at Mrs. Boscawen's. What a comfort for me that none of my friends play at cards. Soame Jenyns and the learned and ingenious Mr. Cambridge were of the party.[25] We had a few sensible ladies, and a very agreeable day, till the world broke in upon us, and made us too large for conversation. The sensible Mrs. Walsingham was there, as was Mrs. Newton, who gave me many invitations to St. Paul's.[26] Mr. Jenyns was very polite to me, and as he, his lady, and I were the first visitants, he introduced me himself to everybody that came afterwards, who were strangers to me. There is a fine simplicity about him, and a meek innocent kind of wit, in Addison's manner, which is very pleasant. The kind Mrs. Boscawen had made another party for me at her house, with Mr. Berenger, who is everybody's favourite, (even Dr. Johnson's) but I am unluckily engaged.

Cumberland's odes are come out.[27] I tried to prevail on Mr. Cambridge to read them, but could not; he has a natural aversion to an ode, as some people have to a cat; one of them is pretty, but another contains a literal description of administering a dose of James's powders! Why will a man who has real talents, attempt a species of writing for which he is so little qualified? But so little do we poor mortals know ourselves, that I should not be surprised, if he were to prefer these odes to his comedies, which have real merit.

London, 1776.

I dined yesterday with Captain and Mrs. Middleton. Tell Dr. Stonehouse that I recommended the translation of Saurin's Sermons to Captain Middleton and Mrs. Bouverie; and Captain M. intends writing to the doctor about them.[28] How nobly eloquent they are! One little peculiarity I remark, – his more frequent use of the word *vice* than generally occurs in religious writings. I think sin is a theological, vice a moral, and crime a judicial term. There are so few people I meet with in this good town to whom one can venture to recommend sermons, that the opportunity is not to be lost; though the misfortune is, that those who are most willing to read them, happen to be the very people who least want them. Mrs. Boscawen, Mrs. Carter, and some other of my friends, were there.

Mrs. Boscawen came to see me the other day with the duchess, in her gilt chariot, with four footmen (as I hear), for I happened not to be at home. It is not possible for anything on earth to be more agreeable to my taste than my present manner of living. I am so much at my ease; have a great many hours at my own disposal, to read my own books and see my own friends; and, whenever I please, may join the most polished and delightful society in the world! Our breakfasts are little literary societies; there is generally company at meals, as they think it saves time, by avoiding the necessity of seeing people at other seasons. Mr. Garrick sets the highest value upon his time of anybody I ever knew. From dinner to tea we laugh, chat, and talk nonsense; the rest of his time is generally devoted to study. I detest and avoid public places more than ever, and should make a miserably bad fine lady! What most people come to London *for*, would keep me *from* it...

Adelphi, 1776.

I wish it were possible for me to give you the slightest idea of the scene I was present at yesterday. Garrick would make me take his ticket to go to the trial of the Duchess of Kingston;[29] a sight which, for beauty and magnificence, exceeded anything which those who were never present at a coronation or a trial by peers, can have the least notion of. Mrs. Garrick and I were in full dress by seven. At eight we went to the Duke of Newcastle's,[30] whose house adjoins Westminster Hall, in which he has a large gallery, communicating with the apartments in his house. You will imagine the bustle of five thousand people getting into one hall! yet in all this hurry, we walked in tranquilly. When they were all seated, and the king-at-arms had commanded silence on pain of imprisonment, (which however, was very ill observed,) the gentleman of the black rod was commanded to bring in his prisoner. Elizabeth, calling herself Duchess Dowager of Kingston, walked in, led by black rod and Mr. la Roche, courtesying profoundly to her judges: when she bent, the lord steward called out, 'Madam, you may rise;' which, I think, was literally taking her up before she was down. The peers made her a slight bow. The prisoner was dressed in deep mourning, a black hood on her head, her hair modestly dressed and powdered, a black silk sacque,[31] with crape trimmings; black gauze, deep ruffles, and black gloves. The counsel spoke

about an hour and a quarter each. Dunning's manner is insuffer-
ably bad, coughing and spitting at every three words; but his
sense and his expression, pointed to the last degree; he made her
grace shed bitter tears.[32] I had the pleasure of hearing several of
the lords speak, though nothing more than proposals on common things. Among these were Lyttleton, Talbot, Townsend,
and Camden. The fair victim had four virgins in white behind
the bar. She imitated her great predecessor, Mrs. Rudd,[33] and
affected to write very often, though I plainly perceived she only
wrote as they do their love epistles on the stage, without
forming a letter. I must not omit one of the best things: we had
only to open a door, to get at a very fine cold collation of all
sorts of meats and wines, with tea, &c. a privilege confined to
those who belonged to the Duke of Newcastle. I fancy the
peeresses would have been glad of our places at the trial, for I
saw Lady Derby and the Duchess of Devonshire with their work-
bags full of good things. Their rank and dignity did not exempt
them from the 'villainous appetites' of eating and drinking.

Foote says that the Empress of Russia, the Duchess of
Kingston, and Mrs. Rudd, are the three most extraordinary
women in Europe;[34] but the duchess disdainfully, and I think
unjustly, excludes Mrs. Rudd from the honour of deserving to
make one in the triple alliance. The duchess has but small
remains of that beauty of which kings and princes were once so
enamoured; she looked very much like Mrs. Pritchard;[35] she is
large and ill shaped; there was nothing white but her face, and
had it not been for that, she would have looked like a bale of
bombazeen. There was a great deal of ceremony, a great deal of
splendour, and a great deal of nonsense: they adjourned upon
the most foolish pretences imaginable, and did *nothing* with such
an air of business as was truly ridiculous. I forgot to tell you the
duchess was taken ill, but performed it badly.

Adelphi, 1776.

We did not come to town till yesterday, and even then left
Hampton with regret, as it is there we spend the pleasantest
part of our time, uninterrupted by the idle, the gossiping, and

the impertinent. On Tuesday Lord and Lady Pembroke dined with us.[36] The Countess is a pretty woman, and my Lord a good-humoured, lively, chatty man; but Roscius[37] was, as usual, the life and soul of the company, and always says so many home things, pointed at the vices and follies of those with whom he converses, but in so indirect, well-bred, and good-humoured a manner, that every body must love him, and none but fools are ever offended, or will expose themselves so much as to own they are. Politicians say that there is a great prospect of an accommodation with America. Heaven grant it, before more human blood is spilt! But even this topic has, I think, a little given place to the trial. For my part, I cannot see why there should be so much ceremony used, to know whether an infamous woman has one or two husbands. I think a *lieutenant de police* would be a better judge for her than the peers, and I do not see why she should not be tried by Sir John Fielding, as a profligate of less note would have been.[38]

Adelphi, 1776.

I have the great satisfaction of telling you that Elizabeth, calling herself duchess-dowager of Kingston, was this very afternoon *undignified* and *unduchessed*, and very narrowly escaped being burned in the hand. If you have been half as much interested against this unprincipled, artful, licentious woman as I have, you will be rejoiced at it as I am. All the peers, but two or three (who chose to withdraw), exclaimed with great emphasis, 'Guilty, upon my honour!' except the Duke of N – ,[39] who said, 'Guilty erroneously, but not intentionally.' Great nonsense, by the bye, but peers are privileged.

On Wednesday we had a very large party to dinner, consisting chiefly of French persons of distinction and talents, who are come over to take a last look at the beams of the great dramatic sun, before he sets.[40] We had beaux esprits, femmes sçavantes, academicians, &c. and no English person except Mr. Gibbon, the Garricks, and myself; we had not one English sentence the whole day. Last night we were at our friends the Wilmots', in Bloomsbury Square. There was a great deal of good company –

the Bishop of Worcester, his lady, Sir Ralph Paine and lady,
Mrs. Boscawen, and half a score others.

This morning Lord Camden breakfasted with us.[41] He was
very entertaining. He is very angry that the Duchess of Kingston
was not burned in the hand. He says, as he was once a professed
lover of her's, he thought it would have looked ill-natured and
ungallant for him to propose it; but that he should have acceded
to it most heartily, though he believes he should have recommended a cold iron.

This evening I am engaged to spend with a foreigner. He is a
Dane, unjustly deprived of his father's fortune by his mother's
marrying a second time. I have never yet seen him, but I hear
that all the world is to be there, which I think is a little
unfeeling, as he is low-spirited at times, even to madness. For
my part, from what I have heard, I do not think the poor young
man will live out the night.

Gerrard Street, 1777.

It is impossible to tell you of all the kindness and friendship
of the Garricks; he thinks of nothing, talks of nothing, writes of
nothing but Percy.[42] He is too sanguine; it will have a fall, and
so I tell him. When Garrick had finished his prologue and
epilogue, (which are excellent) he desired I would pay him.
Dryden, he said, used to have five guineas a piece, but as he was
a richer man he would be content if I would treat him with a
handsome supper and a bottle of claret. We haggled sadly about
the price, I insisting that I could only afford to give him a beef
steak and a pot of porter; and at about twelve we sat down to
some toast and honey, with which the temperate bard contented himself. Several very great ones made interest to hear
Garrick read the play, which he peremptorily refused. I supped
on Wednesday night at Sir Joshua's; spent yesterday morning at
the Chancellor's, and the evening at Mrs. Boscawen's, Lady
Bathurst being of the party.

What dreadful news from America! we are a disgraced,
undone nation.[43] What a sad time to bring out a play in! when,
if the country had the least spark of virtue remaining, not a

creature would think of going to it. But the levity of the times will, on this occasion, be of some service to me.

Mr. Garrick's study, Adelphi, ten at night.

He himself puts the pen into my hand, and bids me say that all is just as it should be. Nothing was ever more warmly received. I went with Mr. and Mrs. Garrick; sat in Mr. Harris's box,[44] in a snug dark corner, and behaved very well, that is, very quietly. The prologue and epilogue were received with bursts of applause; so indeed was the whole; as much beyond my expectation as my deserts! Mr. Garrick's kindness has been unceasing.

H. More to her sister
Gerrard Street, 1777.

I may now venture to tell you, (as you exhorted a promise from me to conceal nothing) what I would not hazard last night, – that the reception of Percy exceeded my most sanguine wishes. I am just returned from the second night, and it was, if possible, received more favourably than on the first. One tear is worth a thousand hands, and I had the satisfaction to see even the men shed them in abundance.

The critics, (as is usual) met at the Bedford last night, to fix the character of the play. If I were a heroine of romance, and was writing to my confidante, I should tell you all the fine things that were said, but as I am a real living Christian woman, I do not think it would be so modest: I will only say, as Garrick does, that I have had so much flattery, that I might, if I would, choke myself in my own pap.

Gerrard Street, 1777.

Yesterday morning Dr. Percy[45] was announced to me. When he came in he told me he was sent by the Duke of Northumberland and Earl Percy to congratulate me on my great success; to inform me of the general approbation, and to thank me in their names for the honour I had done them.[46] That the duke and my lord were under much concern at not being able to attend the play; both father and son having the gout. They sent, however, each for a ticket, for which they paid as became the blood of the Percys; and in so genteel and respectful a manner, that it was impossible for the nicest pride to take umbrage at it.

I am more flattered with the honour this noble family have done me, because I did not solicit their attention, nor would I even renew my acquaintance with Dr. Percy on coming to town, lest it should look like courting the notice of his patrons. *Je suis un peu fiere*.[47]

They are playing Percy at this moment for the seventh time: I never think of going. It is very odd, but it does not amuse me. I had a very brilliant house last night. It is strange, but I hear Lord Lyttleton has been every night since the play came out.[48] I do not deserve it, for I always abuse him. I have the great good fortune to have the whole town warm in my favour, and the writers too...The Duke of Northumberland has sent to thank me for a copy of the play. My Lord bid Dr. Percy tell me it was impossible to express how exactly I had pleased him in the manner of wording the inscription.

Last night was the ninth night of Percy. It was a very brilliant house; and *I* was there. Lady North[49] did me the honour to take a stage-box. I trembled when the speech against the wickedness of going to war was spoken, as I was afraid my lord was in the house, and that speech, though not written with any particular design, is so bold, and always so warmly received, that it frightens me; and I really feel uneasy till it is well over.[50] Mrs. Montagu had a box again; which, as she is so consummate a critic, and is hardly ever seen at a public place, is a great credit to the play. Lady B.[51] was there of course; and I am told she has not made an engagement this fortnight, but on condition she should be at liberty to break it for Percy. I was asked to dine at the chancellor's two or three days ago, but happened to be engaged to Mrs. Montagu, with whom I have been a good deal lately. We also spent an agreeable evening together at Dr. Cadogan's,[52] where she and I, being the only two monsters in the creation who never touch a card, (and laughed at enough for it we are) had the fireside to ourselves; and a more elegant and instructive conversation I have seldom enjoyed. I met Mrs.

Chapone one day at Mrs. Montagu's; she is one of Percy's warmest admirers; and as she does not go to plays, but has formed her judgement in the closet, it is the more flattering. I have been out very little except to particular friends. I believe it was a false delicacy, but I could not go to any body's house, for fear they should think I came to be praised or to hear the play talked of.

1778.

Yesterday I dined at Sir Joshua's. Just as they were beginning to offer their nightly sacrifice to their idol Loo, I took it into my head to go and see Mrs. Barry[53] in the mad-scene in the last act of Percy, in which she is so very fine, that though it is my own nonsense, I always see that scene with pleasure. I called on a lady, not choosing to go alone, and we got into the front boxes. On opening the door I was a little hurt to see a very indifferent house. I looked on the stage, and saw the scene was the inside of a prison, and that the heroine, who was then speaking, had on a linen gown. I was quite stunned, and really thought I had lost my senses, when a smart man, in regimentals, began to sing, 'How happy could I be with either.' I stared and rubbed my eyes, thinking I was in a dream; for all this while I was such a dunce, that I never discovered that they were acting the 'Beggar's Opera.'[54] At length, upon inquiry, I found that Lewis[55] had been taken extremely ill, and that hand-bills had been distributed to announce another play. Many sober personages shook their heads at me, as much as to say – How finely we are caught. Among these...was Dr. Percy, who, I vainly thought, looked rather glum. But the best of all was Sir William Ashurst, who sat in a side box, and was perhaps one of the first judges who ever figured away at the 'Beggar's Opera,' that strong and bitter satire against the professions, and particularly his.[56]

Monday night, 1778.

At the latter part of this evening Mr. Home came in;[57] I was quite hurt to see him. He is a worthy gentlemanlike man. He congratulated me on my success, and said Alfred had not hurt me much. There was no replying to this: so I said nothing: condolence would have been insult. Tuesday I dined at Mr. Wilmot's, with an agreeable party. When I came home I found an invitation to dine the following day at Sir Joshua's, and in the Adelphi. I could accept of neither, being pre-engaged to dine with Mrs. Delany.[58] Our party, like our dinner, was small, excellent, and well chosen. It consisted only of Mrs. Delany, Mrs. Boscawen, Mrs. Chapone, and one very agreeable man. The Duchess of Portland, and all Mrs. Delany's chosen friends were appointed for the evening. I dined yesterday at Garrick's, with the sour crout party.[59] Lady Bathurst came to see me yesterday before I was up: 'tis well I was ill, or I should have had a fine trimming, for she makes breakfast for the chancellor every day before nine, during the whole winter. She is very angry that I go to see her so seldom. I am not sorry that if I do affront my friends, it is generally in this way; but I always think people will like me the less the more they see of me.

Mrs. Garrick came to me this morning, and wished me to go to the Adelphi, which I declined, being so ill. She would have gone herself to fetch me a physician, and insisted upon sending me my dinner, which I refused: but at six this evening, when Garrick came to the Turk's head to dine, there accompanied him, in the coach, a minced chicken in the stew-pan, hot, a canister of her fine tea, and a pot of cream. Were there ever such people! Tell it not in Epic, or in Lyric, that the great Roscius rode with a stew-pan of minced meat with him in the coach for my dinner. Percy is acted again this evening: do any of you choose to go? I can write you an order; for my own part, I shall enjoy a much superior pleasure – that of sitting by the fire, in a great chair, and being denied to all company; What is Percy to this?

Well, if you do not desire I should write you an order, I will write something that will give some pleasure to your sisterly vanity. A friend has just sent me a letter she received from Mrs. Clive,[60] from which here follows an extract. 'I suppose you have heard of the uncommon success Miss More's play has met with, indeed, very deservedly. I have not seen it, but have read it: it is delightful, natural, and affecting, and by much the best modern tragedy that has been acted in my time, which you know is a pretty while ago. As you are acquainted with her family, I know you will be pleased with her success. Mr. Garrick had the conducting it, and you know whatever he touches turns to gold.'

My friends have been so excessively kind to me in my little illness, that it was worth suffering some pain, (though perhaps not quite so much) to try them. The Garricks have been to see me every morning. The other day he told me he was in a violent hurry – that he had been to order his own and Mrs. Garrick's mourning – had just settled every thing with the undertaker, and called for a moment to take a few hints for my epitaph. I told him he was too late, as I had disposed of the employment, a few days before, to Dr. Johnson: but as I thought *he* (Garrick) would praise me most, I should be glad to change; as to hints, I told him I had only one to give; which was to romance as much as he could, and make the character as fine as possible.

Adelphi, Jan. 1779.

From Dr. Cadogan's, I intended to have gone to the Adelphi, but found that Mrs. Garrick was that moment quitting her house, while preparations were making for the last sad cere-mony; she very wisely fixed on a private friend's house for this purpose, where she could be at her ease.[61] I got there just before her; she was prepared for meeting me; she ran into my arms, and we both remained silent for some minutes; at last she whispered, 'I have this moment embraced his coffin, and you come next.' She soon recovered herself, and said with great composure, 'The goodness of God to me is inexpressible; I desired to die, but it is his will that I should live, and he has convinced me he will not let my life be quite miserable, for he gives astonishing strength to my body and *grace* to my heart; neither do I deserve, but I am thankful for both.' She thanked me a thousand times for such a real act of friendship, and bade me be comforted, for it was God's will. She told me they had just returned from Althorp, Lord Spencer's, where he had been reluctantly dragged, for he had felt unwell for some time; but during his visit he was often in such fine spirits that they could not believe he was ill. On his return home he appointed Dr. Cadogan to meet him, who ordered him an emetic, the warm bath, and the usual remedies, but with very little effect. On the Sunday he was in good spirits and free from pain; but as the suppression still continued, Dr. Cadogan became extremely alarmed, and sent for Pott, Heberden, and Schomberg, who gave him up the moment they saw him. Poor Garrick stared to see his room full of doctors, not being conscious of his real state. No change happened till the Tuesday evening, when the surgeon who was sent for to blister and bleed him, made light of his illness, assuring Mrs. Garrick that he would be well in a day or two, and insisted on her going to lie down. Towards morning she desired to be called if there was the least change. Every time that she administered the draughts to him in the night, he always squeezed her hand in a particular manner, and spoke to her with the greatest tenderness and affection. Immediately after he had taken his last medicine, he softly said, 'Oh! dear,' and yielded up his spirit without a groan, and in his perfect senses. His behaviour during the night was all gentleness and patience, and he frequently made apologies to those about him, for the trouble he gave them.

On opening him, a stone was found that measured five inches and a half round one way, and four and a half the other, yet this was not the immediate cause of his death; his kidneys were quite gone. I paid a melancholy visit to his coffin yesterday, where I found room for meditation, till the mind 'burst with thinking.' His new house is not so pleasant as Hampton, nor so splendid as the Adelphi, but it is commodious enough for all the wants of its inhabitant; and besides, it is so quiet, that he never will be disturbed till the eternal morning, and never till then will a sweeter voice than his own be heard. May he then find mercy! They are preparing to hang the house with black, for he is to lie in state till Monday. I dislike this pageantry, and cannot help thinking that the disembodied spirit must look with contempt upon the farce that is played over its miserable relics. But a

splendid funeral could not be avoided, as he is to be laid in the
Abbey with such illustrious dust, and so many are desirous of
testifying their respect by attending.

I can never cease to remember with affection and gratitude,
so warm, steady, and disinterested a friend; and I can most truly
bear this testimony to his memory, that I never witnessed, in
any family, more decorum, propriety, and regularity than in his:
where I never saw a card, or even met, (except in one instance)
a person of his own profession at his table: of which Mrs.
Garrick, by her elegance of taste, her correctness of manners,
and very original turn of humour, was the brightest ornament.
All his pursuits and tastes were so decidedly intellectual, that it
made the society, and the conversation which was always to be
found in his circle, interesting and delightful.

From H. More to her sister.
Adelphi, Feb. 2, 1779.

We (Miss Cadogan and myself,) went to Charing Cross to see
the melancholy procession.[62] Just as we got there we received a
ticket from the Bishop of Rochester,[63] to admit us into the
Abbey. No admittance could be obtained but under his hand.
We hurried away in a hackney coach, dreading to be too late.
The bell of St. Martin's and the Abbey gave a sound that smote
upon my very soul. When we got to the cloisters, we found
multitudes striving for admittance. We gave our ticket, and
were let in, but unluckily we ought to have kept it. We followed
the man who unlocked a door of iron, and directly closed it
upon us, and two or three others, and we found ourselves in a
tower, with a dark winding staircase, consisting of half a hundred stone steps. When we got to the top there was no way out;
we ran down again, called, and beat the door till the whole pile
resounded with our cries. Here we staid half an hour in perfect
agony; we were sure it would be all over: nay, we might never
be let out; we might starve; we might perish. At length our
clamours brought an honest man, – a guardian angel I then
thought him. We implored him to take care of us, and get us
into a part of the abbey whence we might see the grave. He

asked for the Bishop's ticket; we had given it away to the wrong person; and he was not obliged to believe we ever had one; yet he saw so much truth in our grief, that though we were most shabby, and a hundred fine people were soliciting the same favour, he took us under each arm – carried us safely through the crowd, and put us in a little gallery directly over the grave, where we could see and hear everything as distinctly as if the Abbey had been a parlour. Little things sometimes affect the mind strongly! We were no sooner recovered from the fresh burst of grief than I cast my eyes, the first thing, on Handel's monument and read the scroll in his hand, "I know that my Redeemer liveth." Just at three the great doors burst open with a noise that shook the roof: the organ struck up, and the whole choir in strains only less solemn than the "archangel's trump," began Handel's fine anthem. The whole choir advanced to the grave, in hoods and surplices, singing all the way: then Sheridan, as chief mourner; then the body, (alas! whose body!) with ten noblemen and gentlemen, pall-bearers; then the rest of the friends and mourners; hardly a dry eye, – the very players, bred to the trade of counterfeiting, shed genuine tears.

As soon as the body was let down, the bishop began the service, which he read in a low, but solemn and devout manner. Such an awful stillness reigned, that every word was audible. How I felt it! Judge if my heart did not assent to the wish, that the soul of our dear brother now departed was in peace. And this is all of Garrick! Yet a very little while, and he shall "say to the worm, Thou art my brother; and to corruption, thou art my mother and my sister." So passes away the fashion of this world. And the very night he was buried, the playhouses were as full, and the Pantheon was as crowded, as if no such thing had happened: nay, the very mourners of the day partook of the revelries of the night, – the same night too!

As soon as the crowd was dispersed, our friend came to us with an invitation from the bishop's lady,[64] to whom he had related our disaster, to come into the deanery. We were carried into her dressing room, but being incapable of speech, she very kindly said she would not interrupt such sorrow, and left us; but sent up wine, cakes, and all manner of good things, which was really well-timed. I caught no cold, notwithstanding all I went through.

On Wednesday night we came to the Adelphi, – to this house! She bore it with great tranquillity; but what was my surprise to see her go alone into the chamber and bed, in which he had died that day fortnight. She had a delight in it beyond expression. I asked her the next day how she went through it? She told me very well; that she first prayed with great composure, then went and kissed the dear bed, and got into it with a sad pleasure.

THE BAS BLEU:
or,
CONVERSATION.
Addressed to Mrs. Vesey.[65]
ADVERTISEMENT

The following Trifle owes its birth and name to the mistake of a Foreigner of Distinction, who gave the literal appellation of the *Bas-bleu* to a small party of friends, who had been sometimes called, by way of pleasantry the Blue Stockings. The slight performance, occasioned by this little circumstance, was never intended to appear in print: Its is, in general, too local, and too personal for publication; and was only written with a wish to amuse the amiable Lady to whom it is addressed, and a few partial friends. But copies having been multiplied, far beyond the intention of the Author, she has been advised to publish it, lest it should steal into the world in a state of still greater imperfection; though she is almost ashamed to take refuge in so hackneyed an apology, however true.

Vesey! of Verse the judge and friend!
Awhile my idle strain attend:
Not with the days of early Greece,
I mean to ope' my slender piece;
The rare Symposium to proclaim,
Which crown'd th' Athenians' social name;
Or how ASPASIA's[66] parties shone,
The first *Bas-bleu* at Athens known;
Nor need I stop my tale, to shew,
At least to Readers such as you,
How all that Rome esteem'd polite,
Supp'd with LUCULLUS[67] every night;

10

LUCULLUS, who, from Pontus come,
Brought conquests, and brought cherries home:
Name but the suppers in th' Apollo,
What classic images will follow!
How wit flew round, while each might take
Conchylia from the Lucrine lake;
And Attic Salt, and Garum Sauce,
And Lettuce from the Isle of Cos;   20
The first and last from Greece transplanted,
Us'd here − because the rhyme I wanted:
How Pheasants' heads, with cost collected,
And Phenicopters' stood neglected,[68]
To laugh at SCIPIO's lucky hit,
POMPEY's bon-mot, or CÆSAR's wit!
Intemperance, list'ning to the tale,
Forgot the Mullet growing* stale;
And Admiration, balanc'd, hung
'Twixt PEACOCKS' brains, and TULLY's tongue.   30
I shall not stop to dwell on these,
But be as epic as I please,
And plunge at once in medias res.
To prove the privilege I plead,
I'll quote some Greek I cannot read;
Stunn'd by Authority, you yield,
And I, not Reason, keep the field.
    Long was Society o'er-run
By Whist, that desolating Hun;
Long did Quadrille despotic sit,   40
That Vandal of colloquial wit;
And Conversation's setting light
Lay half-obscur'd in Gothic night;
Till LEO's triple crown, to you,
BOSCAWEN[70] sage, bright MONTAGU,[71]
Divided, fell; − your cares in haste

---

* Seneca says, that in his time the Romans were arrived at such a pitch of
luxury, that the mullet was considered stale that did not die in the hands of
the guest.[69]

Rescued the ravag'd realms of Taste;
And LYTTELTON's accomplish'd name,
And witty PULTENEY[72] shar'd the fame;
The Men, not bound by pedant rules,   50
Nor Ladies' *precieuses ridicules*:[73]
For polish'd WALPOLE[74] shew'd the way,
How Wits may be both learn'd and gay;
And CARTER taught the female train,
The deeply wise are never vain;
And she, who SHAKSPEARE's wrongs redrest,
Prov'd that the brightest are the best.[75]

   O! how unlike the wit that fell,
Rambouillet!* at thy quaint Hotel;
Where point, and turn, and equivoque,   60
Distorted every word they spoke!
All so intolerably bright,
Plain Common Sense was put to flight;
Each speaker, so ingenious ever,
'Twas tiresome to be quite so clever;
There twisted Wit forgot to please,
And Mood and Figure banish'd ease:
Poor exil'd Nature houseless stray'd,
'Till SEVIGNÉ[77] receiv'd the maid.

   Tho' here she comes to bless our isle,   70
Not universal is her smile.
Muse! snatch the lyre which CAMBRIDGE[78] strung,
When he the *empty ball-room* sung;
'Tis tun'd above thy pitch, I doubt,
And thou no music wou'dst draw out;
Yet, in a lower note, presume
To sing the full, dull Drawing-room.

   Where the dire *Circle* keeps its station,
Each common phrase is an oration;
And cracking fans, and whisp'ring Misses,   80

---

* The society at the Hotel de RAMBOUILLET, though composed of polite
and ingenious persons, was much tainted with affectation and false taste. See
VOITURE, MENAGE, &c.[76]

Compose their Conversation blisses.
The Matron marks the goodly shew,
While the tall daughter eyes the Beau –
The frigid Beau! – Ah! luckless fair,
'Tis not for you that studied air;
Ah! not for you that sidelong glance,
And all that charming nonchalance;
Ah! not for you the three long hours
He worship'd the "Cosmetic powers;"
That finish'd head which breathes perfume,   90
And kills the nerves of half the room;
And all the murders meant to lie
In that large, languishing, grey eye;
Desist; – less wild th' attempt would be,
To warm the snows of Rhodope:
Too cold to feel, too proud to feign,
For him you're wise and fair in vain.
Chill shade of that affected Peer,[79]
Who dreaded Mirth! come safely here;
For here no vulgar joy effaces   100
Thy rage for polish, ton,[80] and graces.
Cold Ceremony's leaden hand,
Waves o'er the room her poppy wand;
Arrives the stranger; every guest
Conspires to torture the distrest;
At once they rise – so have I seen –
You guess the simile I mean,
Take what comparison you please,
The crowded streets, the swarming bees,
The pebbles on the shores that lie,   110
The stars, which form the galaxy;
This serve t' embellish what is said,
And shews, besides, that one has read; –
At once they rise – th' astonish'd guest
Back in a corner slinks, distrest;
Scar'd at the many bowing round,
And shock'd at her own voice's sound,

Forgot the thing she meant to say,
Her words, half utter'd, die away;
In sweet oblivion down she sinks,   120
And of her ten appointments thinks:
While her loud neighbour on the right,
Boasts what she has to do to-night;
So very much, you'd swear her pride is
To match the labours of ALCIDES;
'Tis true, in hyperbolic measure,
She nobly calls her labours PLEASURE;
In this, unlike ALCMENA's son,
She never means they shou'd be done;
Her fancy of no *limits* dreams,   130
No! *ne plus ultra* bounds her schemes;
Fir'd at th' idea, out she flounces,
And a new Martyr JOHN announces.
We pass the pleasures vast and various
Of Routs, not social, but gregarious;
And, pleas'd, to gentler scenes retreat,
Where Conversation holds her seat.
    Small were that art which would ensure
The Circle's boasted quadrature!
See VESEY's[81] plastic genius make   140
A Circle every figure take;
Nay, shapes and forms which wou'd defy
All science of Geometry;
Isosceles, and Parallel,
Names hard to speak, and hard to spell!
Th' enchantress wav'd her wand, and spoke!
Her potent wand the Circle broke;
The social Spirits hover round,
And bless the liberated ground.
Ask you what charms this gift dispense?   150
'Tis the strong spell of Common Sense.
Away fell ceremony flew,
And with her bore Detraction too.
    Nor only Geometric Art

Does this presiding power impart;
But Chymists too, who want the essence,
Which makes or mars all coalescence,
Of her the secret rare might get,
How different kinds amalgamate:
And he, who wilder studies chose,   160
Find here a new metempsychose;
How forms can other forms assume,
Within her Pythagoric room;
Or be, and stranger is th' event,
The very things which Nature meant;
Nor strive, by art and affectation,
To cross their genuine destination.
Here sober Duchesses are seen,
Chaste Wits, and Critics void of spleen;
Physicians, fraught with real science,   170
And Whigs and Tories in alliance;
Poets, fulfilling Christian duties,
Just Lawyers, reasonable Beauties;
Bishops who preach, and Peers who pay,
And Countesses who seldom play;
Learn'd Antiquaries, who, from college,
Reject the rust, and bring the knowledge;
And, hear it, age, believe it, youth,
Polemics, really seeking truth;
And Travellers of that rare tribe,   180
Who've *seen* the countries they describe;
Ladies who point, nor think me partial,
An Epigram as well as MARTIAL;
Yet in all female worth succeed,
As well as those who cannot read.
     Right pleasant were the task, I ween,
To name the groups which fill the scene;
But Rhyme's of such fastidious nature,
She proudly scorns all Nomenclature,
Nor grace our Northern names her lips,   190
Like HOMER's Catalogue of Ships.

Once – faithful Memory! heave a sigh,
Here Roscius gladden'd every eye.
Why comes not Maro?[82] Far from town,
He rears the Urn to Taste, and Brown;[83]
His English garden breathes perfume,
And promises perennial bloom.
Here, rigid Cato,[84] awful Sage!
Bold Censor of a thoughtless age,
Once dealt his pointed moral round,   200
And, not unheeded, fell the sound;
The Muse his honour'd memory weeps,
For Cato now with Roscius sleeps!
Here once Hortensius[85] lov'd to sit,
Apostate now from social Wit:
Ah! why in wrangling senates waste
The noblest parts, the happiest taste?
Why Democratic Thunders wield,
And quit the Muses' calmer field?
Taste thou the gentler joys they give   210
With Horace and with Lelius live.

Hail! Conversation, soothing Power,
Sweet Goddess of the social hour!
Not with more heart-felt warmth, at least,
Does Lelius bend,[86] thy true High Priest;
Than I, the lowest of thy train,
These field-flow'rs bring to deck thy fane?
Who to thy shrine like him can haste,
With warmer zeal, or purer taste?
O may thy worship long prevail,   220
And thy true votaries never fail!
Long may thy polish'd altars blaze
With wax-lights' undiminish'd rays!
Still be thy nightly offerings paid,
Libations large of Limonade!
On silver Vases, loaded, rise
The biscuits' ample sacrifice!
Nor be the milk-white streams forgot

Of thirst-assuaging, cool orgeat;[87]
Rise, incense pure from fragrant Tea,   230
Delicious incense, worthy Thee!
    Hail, Conversation, heavenly fair,
Thou bliss of life, and balm of care!
Calls forth the long-forgotten knowledge
Of school, of travel, and of college!
For thee, best solace of his toil!
The sage consumes his midnight oil;
And keeps late vigils, to produce
Materials for thy future use.
If none behold, ah! wherefore fair?   240
Ah! wherefore wise, if none must hear?
Our intellectual ore must shine,
Not slumber, idly, in the mine.
Let Education's moral mint
The noblest images imprint;
Let taste her curious touchstone hold,
To try if standard be the gold;
But 'tis thy commerce, Conversation,
Must give it use by circulation;
That noblest commerce of mankind,   250
Whose precious merchandise is MIND!
    What stoic Traveller wou'd try
A sterile soul and parching sky,[88]
Or dare th' intemperate Northern zone,
If what he saw must ne'er be known?
For this he bids his home farewell,
The joy of seeing is to tell.
Trust me, he never wou'd have stirr'd,
Were he forbid to speak a word;
And Curiosity wou'd sleep,   260
If her own secrets she must keep:
The bliss of telling what is past,
Becomes her rich reward at last.
Yet not from low desire to shine
Does Genius toil in Learning's Mine;

Not to indulge in idle vision,
But strike new light by strong collision.
   O'er books, the mind inactive lies,
Books, the mind's food, not exercise
Her vigorous wing she scarcely feels,   270
'Till use the latent strength reveals;
Her slumbering energies call'd forth,
She rises, conscious of her worth;
And, at her new-found powers elated,
Thinks them not rous'd, but new created.
Enlighten'd spirits! you, who know
What charms from polish'd converse flow,
Speak, for you can, the pure delight
When kindling sympathies unite;
When correspondent tastes impart   280
Communion sweet from heart to heart;
You ne'er the cold gradations need
Which vulgar souls to union lead;
No dry discussion to unfold
The meaning, caught as soon as told:
But sparks electric only strike
On souls electrical alike;
The flash of Intellect expires,
Unless it meet congenial fires.
The language to th' Elect alone   290
Is, like the Mason's mystery, known;[89]
In vain th' unerring sign is made
To him who is not of the *Trade*.
What lively pleasure to divine,
The thought implied, the hinted line,
To feel Allusion's artful force,
And trace the Image to its source!
Quick Memory blends her scatter'd rays,
'Till Fancy kindles at the blaze;
The works of ages start to view,   300
And ancient Wit elicits new.
   But wit and parts if thus we praise,

What nobler altars shou'd we raise,
Those sacrifices cou'd we see
Which Wit, O Virtue! makes to Thee.
At once the rising thought to dash,
To quench at once the bursting flash!
The shining Mischief to subdue,
And lose the praise, and pleasure too!
This is high Principle's controul!   310
This is true continence of soul!

   Blush, heroes, at your cheap renown,
A vanquish'd realm, a plunder'd town!
Your conquests were to gain a name,
This conquest triumphs over Fame;
So pure its essence, 'twere destroy'd
If known, and if commended, void.
Amidst the fairest deeds believ'd,
Amidst the brightest truths achiev'd,
Shall stand recorded and admir'd,   320
That Virtue sunk what Wit inspir'd.

   But let the letter'd, and the fair,
And, chiefly, let the Wit beware;
You, whose warm spirits never fail,
Forgive the hint which ends my tale.
Tho' Science nurs'd you in her bow'rs,
Tho' Fancy crown your brow with flowers,
Each thought, though bright Invention fill,
Tho' Attic bees each word distil;
Yet, if one gracious power refuse   330
Her gentle influence to infuse,
In vain shall listening crowds approve,
They'll praise you, but they will not love.
What is this power, you're loth to mention,
This charm, this witchcraft? 'tis ATTENTION:
Mute angel, yes; thy looks dispense
The silence of intelligence;
Thy graceful form I well discern,
In act to listen and to learn;

'Tis Thou for talents shalt obtain   340
That pardon Wit wou'd hope in vain;
Thy wond'rous power, thy secret charm,
Shall Envy of her sting disarm;
Thy silent flattery soothes our spirit,
And we forgive eclipsing merit;
The sweet atonement screens the fault,
And love and praise are cheaply bought.
   With mild complacency to hear,
Tho' somewhat long the tale appear, –
'Tis more than Wit, 'tis moral Beauty,   350
'Tis Pleasure rising out of Duty.

THE WHITE SLAVE TRADE

Hints towards forming a Bill for the Abolition of the White Female Slave Trade, in the Cities of London and Westminster

Whereas many members of both houses of parliament have long been indefatigably labouring to bring in a bill for the amelioration of the condition of slaves in our foreign plantations, as well as for the abolition of the trade itself; by which trade multitudes of fresh slaves are annually made: and whereas it is presumed that the profound attention of these grave legislators to this great foreign evil prevents their attending to domestic grievances of the same nature; it is, therefore, humbly proposed, that whilst these benevolent senators are thus meritoriously labouring for the deliverance of our black brethren, the printer will, as in duty bound, insert these loose hints of a bill for the abolition of slavery at home; a slavery which, in some few instances, as it is to be feared, may be found to involve the wives, daughters, aunts, nieces, cousins, and grandmothers even of these very zealous African abolitionists themselves.

In our West India plantations the lot of slaves is of all descriptions; here, it is uniform. There, there are diversities of masters; if some are cruel, others are kind; and the worst are mortal: here, there is one, arbitrary, universal tyrant, and like the lama of Thibet he never dies. FASHION is his name. Here, indeed, the original subjection is voluntary, but, once engaged, the subsequent servility of the slaves keeps pace with the tyranny of the despot. They hug their chains, and because they are gilt and shining, this prevents them, not from feeling, but from acknowledging that they are heavy. With astonishing fortitude they carry them about, not only without repining, but as their glory and distinction. A few females are every where to be found who have manfully resisted the tyrant, but *they are people whom nobody knows*; as the free people are the minority, and as, in this one instance, the minority are peaceable persons, no one envies them an exemption from chains, and their freedom is considered only as a proof of their insignificance.

I propose to take up the question on the two notorious grounds of *inhumanity* and *impolicy*;[90] and first of the first, as our good old divines say. Here are great multitudes of beautiful white creatures, forced away, like their prototypes in Africa, from all the endearing connections of domestic life, separated from their husbands, dragged from their children, 'till these last are old enough to be also engaged as slaves in the same labour: nay, in some respects, their condition is worse than that of their African brethren; for, if they are less restricted in the article of food, they are more abridged in that of rest. It is well known that in some of our foreign plantations, under mild masters, the slaves have, in one instance, more indulgence than the English despot here allows them. Some of them have at least the Sunday to themselves, in which they may either serve God, or attend to their own families. Here, the tyrant allows of no such alleviation. So far from it, his rigour peculiarly assigns the sabbath for acts of superior fatigue and exertion, such as long journeys, crowded markets, &c. And whereas, in our foreign plantations, slaves too frequently do the work of horses in the system of domestic slavery, horses partake of the labour of the slave without diminishing his sufferings; many hundreds being regularly condemned, after the labours of the day are closed, to transport the slaves to the scene of their nightly labours, which scene shifts so often, that there is scarcely an interval of rest; so that the poor animals are exposed the greater part of the night to all the rigors of a northern winter.

Again – if the African slaves go nearly naked, their burning clime prevents the want of covering from being one of their greatest hardships: whereas, though the female slaves of London and Westminster were aforetime comfortably cloathed, and were allowed by the despot to accommodate their dress to the season, wearing the lightest raiment in the hottest weather, and thick silks trimmed with skins of beasts in cold and frost; now nakedness is of all seasons, and many of the most delicate females are allowed so little clothing as to give pain to the humane beholder. In the most rigorous seasons, they are so exposed as to endanger their own health, and shock the feelings of others.

The younger slaves are condemned to violent bodily labour, from midnight to sunrise. For this public service they are many years preparing by a severe drill under a great variety and succession of posture-masters.[91] More compassion, indeed, seems to be shown to the more aged slaves, who are nightly allowed to sit, and do their work at a multitude of tables provided for that purpose. Some of these employments are quiet enough, well suited to weakness and imbecility, and just serve to keep the slaves out of harm's way; but at other tables, the labour of the slave is most severe; and though you cannot perceive their fetters, yet they must undoubtedly be firmly chained to the spot, as appears by their inability to quit it; for by their long continuance in the same attitude one can hardly suppose them to be at liberty.

But if their bodies labour less than those of the more active slaves, they seem to suffer the severest agitations of mind; their colour often changes, their lips tremble, and their voice faulters; and no wonder, for sometimes all they have in the world is at stake, and depends on the next slight motion of the hand. In one respect the comparison between the African, and this part of the London slave trade fails: the former, though incompatible with the *spirit* of our laws, yet is not, alas! carried on in direct opposition to the *letter* of them; whereas these tables, at which some of the English slaves are so cruelly exercised, have the cannon of an act of parliament planted directly in their face; and the oddity of the thing is, that the act is not, as in most other cases, made by one set of people and broken by another, but in many instances the law-maker is the law-breaker.[92]

Many of these elderly female slaves excuse their constant attendance in the public markets, (for it is thought that, at a certain age, they might be emancipated if they wished it,) by asserting the necessity of their attendance, 'till their daughters are disposed of. They are often heard to lament the hardship of this slavery, and to anticipate the final period of their labours; but it is observable, that not only when their daughters, but even their grand-daughters, are taken off their hands, they still continue, from the mere force of habit, and when they are past their labour, to hover about the markets.

A multitude of fine fresh young slaves are annually imported at the age of seventeen or eighteen; or, according to the phrase of the despot, *they come out.*[93] This despot so completely takes them in as to make these lovely young creatures believe that the assigned period at which they lose the gaiety and independence of their former free life is, in fact, the day of their emancipation.

I come now to the question of *impolicy*. This white slavery, like the black, is evidently an injury to fair and lawful commerce, for the time spent in training and overworking these fair slaves might be better employed in promoting the more profitable articles of health, beauty, simplicity, modesty, and industry; articles which many think would fetch a higher price, and by which traffic, both the slave and the slave-owner would be mutually benefitted.

Those who take up this question on this ground maintain also that it does not answer to the slave holders; for that the markets are so glutted that there is less chance of a good bargain, in the best sense of the word, where there are so many competitors, and where there is so little opportunity of discriminating, than if the young slaves were disposed of by private contract; in which the respective value of each individual could be more exactly ascertained.

In the article of policy also, the slaves themselves are not only great losers; youth and beauty, by this promiscuous huddling of slaves together, failing to attract attention; but moreover youth and beauty are so soon impaired by hard labour, foul air, and late hours, that those who are not early disposed of, on the novelty of a first appearance, soon become withered, and are apt to lie a good while upon hands.

One strong argument brought to prove the impolicy of the

African slave trade is, that it is a most improvident waste of the human species. What devastation is made in the human frame among our white slaves, by working over hours, by loss of sleep, want of clothing, fetid atmospheres, being crammed in the holds of smaller ships without their proper proportion of inches – what havoc, I say, is made by all those, and many other causes, let all the various baths and watering places, to which these poor exhausted slaves are sent every summer to recruit, after the working season is over, declare.

Some candid members have hoped for a *gradual* abolition, concluding that if no interference took place, the evil was become so great, it must needs be cured by its very excess; the event, however, has proved so far otherwise, that the grievance is actually grown worse and worse.

And whereas, aforetime, the slaves were comfortably covered, and were not obliged to labour through the *whole* night, nor to labour *every* night, nor to labour at several places in the *same* night; and whereas, aforetime, the hold in which they were confined was not obliged to receive more slaves than it could contain; it is now a notorious fact, that their cloathing is stripped off in the severest weather; that their labours are protected 'till the morning; and that since the late great increase of trade, three hundred panting slaves are often crammed into an area which cannot conveniently accommodate more than fourscore, to the great damage of the healths and lives of his majesty's fair and faithful subjects.

From all the above causes it is evident, that the white slave trade has increased, is increasing, and ought to be diminished.[94]

'Till, therefore, there be some hope that a complete abolition may be effected, the following regulations are humbly proposed.

Regulation 1st. That no slave be allowed to spend more than three hours in preparing her chains, beads, and other implements for the nightly labour.

2d. That no slave be allowed to paint her person of more than two colours for any market.

3d. That each slave be at least allowed sufficient covering for the purposes of decency, if not for those of health and comfort.

4th. That no slave be put under more than four posture masters, in order to teach her such attitudes and exercises as shall enable her to fetch more money in the markets.

5th. That no slave be carried to more than three markets on the same night.

6th. That no trader be allowed to press more slaves into one hold than three times as many as it will contain.

7th. That the same regard to comfort, which has led the black factor to allow the African slaves a ton to a man, be extended to the white slaves, not allowing them less than one chair to five slaves.

8th. That no white negro driver or horses be allowed to stand in the street more than five hours in a dry night, or four in a rainy one.

9th. That every elderly female slave, as soon as her youngest grandchild is fairly disposed of, be permitted to retire from her more public labours, without any fine or loss of character, or any other punishment from the despot.

To conclude: – the black slave trade has been taken up by its opposers, not only on the ground of *inhumanity* and *impolicy*, but on that of *religion* also. On the first two points alone have I ventured to examine the question of the white slave trade. It would be a folly to enquire into it on this last principle; it can admit no such discussion, as in this view it could not stand its ground for a single moment; for if that principle were allowed to operate, mitigations, nearly approaching to abolition, must inevitably and immediately take place.

AN ENEMY TO ALL SLAVERY

THE SORROWS OF YAMBA

or the Negro Woman's Lamentation
To the tune of *Hosiers Ghost*

In St Lucie's distant isle,[95]
   Still with Afric's love I burn;
Parted many a thousand mile,
   Never, never to return.

Come, kind death! and give me rest;
   Yamba has no friend but thee;
Thou can'st ease my throbbing breast;
   Thou can'st set the Prisoner free.

Down my cheeks the tears are dripping,
   Broken is my heart with grief;
Mangled my poor flesh with whipping,
   Come, kind death! and bring relief.

Born on Afric's Golden Coast,
   Once I was as blest as you;
Parents tender I could boast,
   Husband dear, and children too.

Whity man he came from far,
   Sailing o'er the briny flood;
Who, with help of British Tar,
   Buys up human flesh and blood.

With the Baby at my breast
   (Other two were sleeping by)

10

20

In my Hut I sat at rest,
    With no thought of danger nigh.

From the Bush at even tide,
    Rush'd the fierce man-stealing Crew;
Seiz'd the children by my side,
    Seiz'd the wretched Yamba too.

Then for love of filthy Gold,
    Strait they bore me to the Sea,   30
Cramm'd me down a Slave Ship's hold,
    Where were hundreds stow'd like me.

Naked on the Platform lying,
    Now we cross the tumbling wave;
Shrieking, sickening, fainting, dying,
    Deed of shame for Britons brave.

At the savage Captain's beck;
    Now like Brutes they make us prance;
Smack the Cat about the Deck,[96]
    And in scorn they bid us dance.   40

Nauseous horse-beans they bring nigh,
    Sick and sad we cannot eat;
Cat must cure the Sulks, they cry,
    Down their throats we'll force the meat.

I in groaning pass'd the night,
    And did roll my aching head;
At the break of morning light,
    My poor Child was cold and dead.

Happy, happy, there she lies,
    Thou shalt feel the lash no more,   50
Thus full many a Negro dies
    Ere we reach the destin'd shore.

Thee, sweet infant, none shall sell,
  Thou has't gained a wat'ry Grave;
Clean escap'd the Tyrants fell,
  While thy mother lives a Slave.

Driven like Cattle to a fair,
  See they sell us young and old;
Child from Mother too they tear,
  All for love of filthy Gold.   60

I was sold to Massa hard,
  Some have Massas kind and good:
And again my back was scarr'd,
  Bad and stinted was my food.

Poor and wounded, faint and sick,
  All expos'd to burning sky;
Massa bids me grass to pick,
  And I now am near to die.

What and if to death he send me,
  Savage murder tho' it be,   70
British Law shall ne'er befriend me,
  They protect not Slaves like me.

Mourning thus my wretched state,
  (Ne'er may I forget the day)
Once in dusk of evening late
  Far from home I dar'd to stray;

Dar'd, alas! with impious haste
  Tow'rds the roaring Sea to fly;
Death itself I long'd to taste,
  Long'd to cast me in and Die.   80

There I met upon the Strand
  English Missionary Good,

He had Bible book in hand,
  Which poor me no understood.

Led by pity from afar
  He had left his native ground;
Thus if some inflict a scar,
  Others fly to cure the wound.

Strait he pull'd me from the shore,
  Bid me no self-murder do; 90
Talk'd of state when life is o'er,
  All from Bible good and true.

Then he led me to his Cot,
  Sooth'd and pity'd all my woe;
Told me 'twas the Christian's lot
  Much to suffer here below.

Told me then of God's dear Son,
  (Strange and wond'rous is the story)
What sad wrong to him was done,
  Tho' he was the Lord of Glory. 100

Told me too, like one who knew him,
  (Can such love as this be true ?)
How he died for them that slew him,
  Died for wretched Yamba too.

Freely he his mercy proffer'd,
  And to Sinners he was sent;
E'en to Massa pardon's offer'd:
  O, if Massa would repent!

Wicked deed full many a time
  Sinful Yamba too hath done 110
But she wails to God her crime,
  But she trusts his only Son.

O ye slaves whom Massas beat,
   Ye are stain'd with guilt within;
As ye hope for Mercy sweet,
   So forgive your Massas' sin.

And with grief when sinking low,
   Mark the Road that Yamba trod;
Think how all her pain and woe
   Brought the Captive home to God.   120

Now let Yamba too adore
   Gracious Heaven's mysterious Plan;
Now I'll count my mercies o'er,
   Flowing thro' the guilt of man.

Now I'll bless my cruel capture,
   (Hence I've known a Saviour's name)
Till my grief is turn'd to Rapture,
   And I half forget the blame.

But tho' here a Convert rare,
   Thanks her God for Grace divine;   130
Let not man the glory share,
   Sinner, still the guilt is thine.

Here an injur'd Slave forgives,
   There a Host for vengeance cry;
Here a single Yamba lives,
   There a thousand droop and die.

Duly now baptiz'd am I,
   By good Missionary Man:
Lord, my nature purify
   As no outward water can!   140

All my former thoughts abhorr'd,
   Teach me now to pray and praise;

Joy and Glory in my Lord,
   Trust and serve him all my days.

Worn indeed with Grief and Pain,
   Death I now will welcome in:
O, the Heavenly Prize to gain!
   O, to 'scape the power of Sin!

True of heart, and meek, and lowly,
   Pure and blameless let me grow!   150
Holy may I be, for Holy
   Is the place to which I go.

But tho' death this hour may find me,
   Still with Afric's love I burn,
(There I've left a spouse behind me)
   Still to native land I turn.

And when Yamba sinks in death,
   This my latest prayer shall be,
While I yield my parting breath,
   O, that Afric might be free.   *160*

Cease, ye British Sons of murder!
   Cease from forging's Afric's chain
Mock your Saviour's name no further,
   Cease your savage lust of gain.

Ye that boast *"Ye rule the waves,"*
   Bid no Slave Ship soil the sea,
Ye, that *"never will be slaves,"*[97]
   Bid poor Afric's land be free.

Where ye gave to war it's birth,
   Where your traders fix'd their den,   170
There go publish *"Peace on Earth,"*
   Go proclaim *"good-will to men."*

Where ye once have carried slaughter,
   Vice, and Slavery, and Sin;
Seiz'd on Husband, Wife, and Daughter,
   Let the Gospel enter in.

Thus, where Yamba's native home,
   Humble Hut of Rushes stood,
Oh if there should chance to roam
   Some dear Missionary good;   180

Thou in Afric's distant land,
   Still shalt see the man I love;
Join him to the Christian band,
   Guide his Soul to Realms above.

There no Fiend again shall sever
   Those whom God hath join'd and blest;
There they dwell with Him for ever,
   There "*the weary are at rest.*"

BETTY BROWN

THE ST. GILES'S ORANGE GIRL
WITH SOME ACCOUNT OF MRS. SPONGE, THE MONEY LENDER

Betty Brown, the Orange Girl, was born nobody knows where, and bred nobody knows how. No girl in all the streets of London could drive a barrow more nimbly, avoid pushing against passengers more dexterously, or cry her "Fine China Oranges" in a shriller voice. But then she could neither sew, nor spin, nor knit, nor wash, nor iron, nor read, nor spell. Betty had not been always in so good a situation as that in which we now describe her. She came into the world before so many good gentlemen and ladies began to concern themselves so kindly that the poor might have a little learning. There was no charitable Society[98] then, as there is now, to pick up poor friendless children in the streets, and put them into a good house, and give them meat, and drink, and lodging, and learning, and teach them to get their bread in an honest way into the bargain. Whereas, this now is often the case in London, blessed be God for all his mercies.

The longest thing that Betty can remember is, that she used to crawl up out of a night cellar, stroll about the streets, and pick cinders from the scavengers' carts. Among the ashes she sometimes found some ragged gauze and dirty ribbons; with these she used to dizen herself out, and join the merry bands on the first of May. This was not, however, quite fair, as she did not lawfully belong either to the female dancers who foot it gaily round the garland, or to the sooty tribe,[99] who, on this happy holiday, forget their whole year's toil; she often, however, got a few scraps by appearing to belong to both parties.

Betty was not an idle girl; she always put herself in the way of doing something. She would run of errands for the footmen, or sweep the door for the maid of any house where she was known; she would run and fetch some porter, and never was once known either to sip a drop by the way or steal the pot. Her quickness and fidelity in doing little jobs, got her into favour with a lazy cook-maid, who was too apt to give away her master's cold meat and beer, not to those who were most in want, but to those who waited upon her, and did the little things for her which she ought to have done herself.

The cook, who found Betty a dexterous girl, soon employed her to sell ends of candles, pieces of meat and cheese, and lumps of butter, or any thing else she could crib from the house. These were all carried to her friend, Mrs. Sponge, who kept a little shop and a kind of eating-house for poor working people, not far from the Seven Dials.[100] She also bought as well as sold many kinds of second hand things, and was not scrupulous to know whether what she bought was honestly come by, provided she could get it for a sixth part of what it was worth. But if the owner presumed to ask for its real value, she had sudden qualms of conscience, suspected the things were stolen, and gave herself airs of honesty, which often took in poor silly people, and gave her a sort of half reputation among the needy and the ignorant, whose friend she pretended to be.

To this artful woman Betty carried the cook's pilferings, and as Mrs. Sponge would give no great price for these in money, the cook was willing to receive payment for her eatables in Mrs. Sponge's drinkables; for she dealt in all kinds of spirits. I shall only just remark here, that one receiver, like Mrs. Sponge, makes many pilferers, who are tempted to these petty thieveries, by knowing how easy it is to dispose of them at such iniquitous houses.

Betty was faithful to both her employers, which is extraordinary, considering the greatness of the temptation, and her utter ignorance of good and evil. One day, she ventured to ask Mrs. Sponge if she could not assist her to get into a more settled way of life. She told her, that when she rose in the morning, she never knew where she should lie at night, nor was she ever sure of a meal before hand. Mrs. Sponge asked her what she thought herself fit for. Betty, with fear and trembling, said, there was one trade for which she thought herself qualified, but she had not the ambition to look so high. It was far above her humble views. This was, to have a barrow, and sell fruit, as several other of Mrs. Sponge's customers did, whom she had often looked at with envy.

Mrs. Sponge was an artful woman. Bad as she was, she was always aiming at something of a character; this was a great help to her trade. While she watched keenly to make every thing turn to her own profit, she had a false fawning way of seeming to do all she did out of pity and kindness to the distressed; and she seldom committed an extortion, but she tried to make the persons she cheated believe themselves highly obliged to her kindness. By thus pretending to be their friend she gained their confidence, and she grew rich herself while they thought she was only shewing favour to them. Various were the arts she had of getting rich. The money she got by grinding the poor, she spent in the most luxurious living; while she would haggle with her hungry customers for a farthing, she would spend pounds on the most costly delicacies for herself.

Mrs. Sponge, laying aside that haughty look and voice, well known to such as had the misfortune to be in her debt, put on the hypocritical smile and soft tone, which she always assumed when she meant to *take in* her dependants. "Betty," said she, "I am resolved to stand your friend. These are sad times to be sure. Money is money now. Yet I am resolved to put you into a handsome way of living. You shall have a barrow, and well furnished too." Betty could not have felt more joy or gratitude, if she had been told that she should have a coach. "O, Madam," said Betty, "it is impossible. I have not a penny in the world towards helping me to set up." "I will take care of that," said Mrs. Sponge; "only you must do as I bid you. You must pay me interest for my money. And you will of course be glad also to pay so much every night for a nice hot supper which I get ready, quite out of kindness, for a number of poor working people. This will be a great comfort for such a friendless girl as you, for my victuals and drink are the best; and my company the merriest of any house in all St. Giles's." Betty thought all this only so many more favours, and courtesying to the ground, said, "to be sure, Ma'am, and thank you a thousand times into the bargain."

Mrs. Sponge knew what she was about. Betty was a lively girl, who had a knack at learning any thing; and so well looking through all her dirt and rags, that there was little doubt she would get custom. A barrow was soon provided, and five shillings put into Betty's hands. Mrs. Sponge kindly conde-scended to go to shew her how to buy the fruit, for it was a rule with this prudent gentlewoman, and one from which she never departed, that no one should cheat but herself.[101]

Betty had never possessed such a sum before. She grudged to lay it out all at once, and was ready to fancy she could live upon the capital. The crown, however, was laid out to the best advantage. Betty was carefully taught in what manner to cry her Oranges; and received many useful lessons how to get off the bad with the good, and the stale with the fresh. Mrs. Sponge also lent her a few bad sixpences, for which she ordered her to bring home good ones at night. – Betty stared. Mrs. Sponge said, "Betty, those who would get money must not be too nice about trifles. Keep one of these sixpences in your hand, and if an ignorant young customer gives you a good sixpence do you immediately slip it into your other hand, and give him the bad one, declaring, that it is the very one you have just received, and that you have not another sixpence in the world. You must also learn how to treat different sorts of customers. To some you may put off with safety goods which would be quite unsaleable to others. Never offer bad fruit, Betty, to those who know better; never waste the good on those who may be put off with worse; put good Oranges at top and the mouldy ones under."

Poor Betty had not a nice conscience, for she had never learnt that grand but simple rule of all moral obligation, "Never do that to another which you would not have another do to you." She set off with her barrow as proud and as happy as if she had been set up in the finest shop in Covent Garden. Betty had a sort of natural good-nature, which made her unwilling to impose, but she had no principle which told her it was a sin. She had such good success, that when night came she had not an Orange left. With a light heart, she drove her empty barrow to Mrs. Sponge's door. She went in with a merry face, and threw down on the counter every farthing she had taken. "Betty," said Mrs. Sponge, "I have a right to it all, as it was got by my money. But I am too generous to take it. I will therefore only take sixpence for this day's use of my five shillings. This is a most reasonable interest, and I will lend you the same sum to trade with to-morrow, and so on; you only paying me sixpence for the use of it every night, which will be a great bargain to you. You must also pay me my price every night for your supper, and you shall have an excellent lodging above stairs; so you see every thing will now be provided for you in a genteel manner, through my generosity."

Poor Betty's gratitude blinded her so completely that she forgot to calculate the vast proportion which this generous benefactress was to receive out of her little gains. She thought herself a happy creature, and went in to supper with a number of others of her own class. For this supper, and for more porter and gin than she ought to have drank, Betty was forced to pay so high, that it ate up all the profits of the day, which, added to the daily interest, made Mrs. Sponge a rich return for her five shillings.

Betty was reminded again of the gentility of her new situation, as she crept up to bed in one of Mrs. Sponge's garrets five stories high. This loft, to be sure, was small, and had no window, but what it wanted in light was made up in company, as it had three beds, and thrice as many lodgers. Those gentry had one night, in a drunken frolic, broke down the door, which happily had never been replaced; for, since that time, the lodgers had died much seldomer of infectious distempers. For this lodging Betty paid twice as much to her good friend as she would have done to a stranger. Thus she continued, with great industry and a thriving trade, as poor as on the first day, and not a bit nearer to saving money enough to buy her even a pair of shoes, though her feet were nearly on the ground.

One day, as Betty was driving her barrow through a street near Holborn, a lady from a window called out to her that she wanted some Oranges. While the servants went to fetch a plate, the lady entered into some talk with Betty, having been struck with her honest countenance and civil manner. She questioned her as to her way of life, and the profits of her trade – and Betty, who had never been so kindly treated before by so genteel a person, was very communicative. She told her little history as far as she knew it, and dwelt much on the generosity of Mrs. Sponge, in keeping her in her house, and trusting her with so large a capital as five shillings. At first it sounded like a very good-natured thing; but the lady, whose husband was one of the Justices of the new Police,[102] happened to know more of Mrs. Sponge than was good, which led her to enquire still further. Betty owned, that to be sure, it was not all clear profit, for that besides that the high price of the supper and bed ran away with all she got, she paid sixpence a day for the use of the five shillings. "And how long have you done this" said the lady?. "About a year, Madam."

The lady's eyes were at once opened. "My poor girl," said she, "do you know that you have already paid for that single five shillings the enormous sum of 7l. 10s.?[103] I believe it is the most profitable five shillings Mrs. Sponge ever laid out." "O, no, madam," said the girl; "that good gentlewoman does the same kindness to ten or twelve other poor friendless creatures like me." "Does she so?" said the lady; "then I never heard of a better trade than this woman carries on, under the mask of charity, at the expence of her poor deluded fellow-creatures."

"But, madam," said Betty, who did not comprehend this lady's arithmetic, "what can I do? I now contrive to pick up a morsel of bread without begging or stealing. Mrs. Sponge has been very good to me, and I don't see how I can help myself."

"I will tell you," said the lady. "If you will follow my advice, you may not only maintain yourself honestly but independently. Only oblige yourself to live hard for a little time, till you have saved five shillings out of your own earnings. Give up that expensive supper at night, drink only one pint of porter, and no gin at all. As soon as you have scraped together the five shillings, carry it back to your false friend, and if you are industrious, you will at the end of the year, have saved seven pounds ten shillings. If you can make a shift to live now, when you have this heavy interest to pay, judge how things will mend when your capital becomes your own. You will put some cloaths on your back, and by leaving the use of spirits, and the company in which you drink them, your health, your morals, and your condition, will mend."

The lady did not talk thus to save her money. She would gladly have given the girl the five shillings; but she thought it was beginning at the wrong end. She wanted to try her. Besides, she knew there was more pleasure as well as honour in possessing five shillings of one's own saving, than of another's giving. Betty promised to obey. She owned she had got no good by the company or the liquor at Mrs. Sponge's. She promised that very night to begin saving the expence of the supper, and that she would not taste a drop of gin till she had the five shillings beforehand. The lady, who knew the power of good habits, was contented with this, thinking, that if the girl could abstain for a certain time, it would become easy to her. She therefore, at present, said little about the *sin* of drinking.

In a very few weeks, Betty had saved up the five shillings. She went to carry back this money with great gratitude to Mrs. Sponge. This kind friend began to abuse her most unmercifully. She called her many hard names, not fit to repeat, for having forsaken the supper, by which she swore she herself got nothing at all; but as she had the charity to dress it for such beggarly wretches, she insisted they should pay for it whether they ate it or not. She also brought in a heavy score for lodging, though Betty had paid for it every night, and given notice of her intending to quit her. By all these false pretences, she got from her not only her own five shillings but all the little capital with which Betty was going to set up for herself. As all was not sufficient to answer her demands, she declared she would send her to prison, but while she went to call a Constable, Betty contrived to make off.

With a light pocket and a heavy heart she went back to the lady, and with many tears told her sad story. The lady's husband, the Justice, condescended to listen to Betty's tale. He said Mrs. Sponge had long been upon his books as a receiver of stolen goods. Betty's evidence strengthened his bad opinion of her. "This petty system of usury," said the gentleman, "may be thought trifling, but it will no longer appear so, if you reflect, that if one of these female sharpers possesses a capital of seventy shillings, or 3l. 10s. with fourteen steady regular customers, she can realize a fixed income of 100 guineas a year. Add to this the influence such a loan gives her over these friendless creatures, by compelling them to eat at her house; or lodge, or buy liquors, or by taking their pawns, and you will see the extent of the evil. I pity these poor victims: You, Betty, shall point out some of them to me. I will endeavour to open their eyes on their own bad management. It is one of the greatest acts of kindness, to the poor to mend their œconomy, and to give them right views of laying out their little money to advantage. These poor blinded creatures look no further than to be able to pay this heavy interest every night, and to obtain the same loan on the same hard terms the next day. Thus are they kept in poverty and bondage all their lives; but I hope as many as hear of this will get on a better plan, and I shall be ready to help any who are willing to help themselves." This worthy Magistrate went directly to Mrs. Sponge's with proper officers, and he soon got to the bottom of many iniquities. He not only made her refund poor Betty's money, but committed her to prison for receiving stolen goods, and various other offences, which may, perhaps, make the subject of another history.

Betty was now set up in trade to her heart's content. She had found the benefit of leaving off spirits, and she resolved to drink them no more. The first fruits of this resolution was that in a fortnight she bought her a new pair of shoes, and as there was now no deduction for interest or for gin, her earnings became considerable. The lady made her a present of a gown and a hat, on the easy condition that she should go to church. She accepted the terms, at first rather as an act of obedience to the

lady than from a sense of higher duty. But she soon began to
go from a better motive. This constant attendance at church,
joined to the instructions of the lady, opened a new world to
Betty. She now heard for the first time that she was a sinner;
that God had given a law which was holy, just, and good, that
she had broken this law, had been a swearer, a sabbath-
breaker, and had lived without God in the world. All this was
sad news to Betty; she knew, indeed, that there were sinners,
but she thought they were only to be found in the prisons, or at
Botany Bay, or in those mournful carts which she had sometimes followed with her barrow, with the unthinking crowd to
Tyburn.[104] – She was deeply struck with the great truths
revealed in the Scripture, which were quite new to her. She was
desirous of improvement, and said, she would give up all the
profits of her barrow, and go into the hardest service, rather
than live in sin and ignorance.

"Betty," said the lady, "I am glad to see you so well disposed,
and will do what I can for you. Your present way of life, to be
sure, exposes you to much danger; but the trade is not unlawful
in itself, and we may please God in any calling, provided it be
not a dishonest one. In this great town there must be barrow
women to sell fruit. Do you, then, instead of forsaking your
business, set a good example to those in it, and shew them, that
though a dangerous trade, it need not be a bad one. Till
Providence points out some safer way of getting your bread, let
your companions see, that it is possible to be good even in this.
Your trade being carried on in the open street, and your fruit
bought in an open shop, you are not so much obliged to keep
sinful company as may be thought. Take a garret in an honest
house, to which you may go home in safety at night. I will give
you a bed and a few necessaries to furnish your room; and I will
also give you a constant Sunday's dinner. A barrow woman,
blessed be God and our good laws, is as much her own mistress
on Sundays as a Duchess; and the Church and the Bible are as
much open to her. You may soon learn all that such as you are
expected to know. A barrow woman may pray as heartily
morning and night, and serve God as acceptably all day, while

she is carrying on her little trade, as if she had her whole time
to spare.

To do this well, you must mind the following

RULES FOR RETAIL DEALERS

Resist every temptation to cheat.

Never impose bad goods on false pretences.

Never put off bad money for good.

Never use profane or uncivil language.

Never swear your goods cost so much, when you know it is
false. By so doing you are guilty of two sins in one breath, a lie
and an oath.

To break these rules, will be your chief temptation. God will
mark how you behave under them, and will reward or punish
you accordingly. These temptations will be as great to you as
higher trials are to higher people; but you have the same God to
look to for strength to resist them as they have. You must pray
to him to give you this strength. You shall attend a Sunday
School, where you will be taught these good things, and I will
promote you as you shall be found to deserve.[105]

Poor Betty here burst into tears of joy and gratitude, crying
out, "What, shall such a poor friendless creature as I be treated
so kindly and learn to read the word of God too? Oh, Madam,
what a lucky chance brought me to your door." "Betty," said
the lady, "what you have just said shews the need you have of
being better taught; there is no such thing as chance, and we
offend God when we call that luck or chance which is brought
about by his will and pleasure. None of the events of your life
have happened by chance – but all have been under the
direction of a good and kind Providence. He has permitted you
to experience want and distress, that you might acknowledge
his hand in your present comfort and prosperity. Above all, you
must bless his goodness in sending you to me, not only because
I have been of use to you in your worldly affairs, but because he
has enabled me to shew you the danger of your state from sin

and ignorance, and to put you in a way to know his will and to keep his commandments.

How Betty, by industry and piety, rose in the world, till at length she came to keep a handsome Sausage-shop near the Seven Dials, and was married to an honest Hackney Coachman, may be told at some future time, in a Second Part.[106]

TAWNEY RACHEL

or THE FORTUNE-TELLER

WITH SOME ACCOUNT OF DREAMS, OMENS AND CONJURORS

Tawney Rachel was the wife of poaching Giles.[107] There seemed
to be a conspiracy in Giles's whole family to maintain themselves by tricks and pilfering. Regular labour and honest industry did not suit their idle habits. They had a sort of genius at
finding out every unlawful means to support a vagabond life.
Rachel travelled the country with a basket on her arm. She
pretended to get her bread by selling laces, cabbage-nets,[108]
ballads and history books, and to buy old rags and rabbit-skins.
Many honest people trade in these things, and I am sure I don't
mean to say a word against honest people, let them trade in
what they will. But Rachel only made this traffic a pretence for
getting admittance into farmers' kitchens, in order to tell fortunes. She was continually practising on the credulity of silly
girls; and took advantage of their ignorance to cheat and deceive
them. Many an innocent servant has she caused to be suspected
of a robbery, while she herself, perhaps, was in league with the
thief. Many a harmless maid has she brought to ruin by first
contriving plots and events, and then pretending to foretell
them. She had not, to be sure, the power of really foretelling
things, because she had no power of seeing into futurity; but she
had the art sometimes to bring them about according as she had
foretold them. So she got that credit for her wisdom which
really belonged to her wickedness.

Rachel was also a famous interpreter of dreams, and could
distinguish exactly between the fate of any two persons who
happened to have a mole on the right or the left cheek. She had
a cunning way of getting herself off when any of her prophecies

failed. When she explained a dream according to the natural appearance of things, and it did not come to pass; then she would get out of that scrape by saying, that "this sort of dreams went by contraries." Now of two very opposite things the chance always is that one of them may turn out to be true; so in either case she kept up the cheat.

Rachel in one of her rambles stopped at the house of Farmer Jenkins. She contrived to call when she knew the master of the house was from home, which indeed was her usual way. She knocked at the door; the maids being out hay-making, Mrs. Jenkins went to open it herself. Rachel asked her if she would please to let her light her pipe? This was a common pretence, when she could find no other way of getting into a house. While she was filling her pipe, she looked at Mrs. Jenkins and said, she could tell her some good fortune. The farmer's wife, who was a very inoffensive, but a weak and superstitious woman, was curious to know what she meant. Rachel then looked about very carefully, and shutting the door with a mysterious air, asked her if she was sure nobody would hear them. This appearance of mystery was at once delightful and terrifying to Mrs. Jenkins, who bid the cunning woman[109] speak out. "Then," said Rachel in a solemn whisper, "there is to my certain knowledge a pot of money hid under one of the stones in your cellar." "Indeed," said Mrs. Jenkins, "it is impossible, for now I think of it, I dreamt last night I was in prison for debt." "Did you indeed?" said Rachel, "that is quite surprising. Did you dream before twelve o'clock or after?" "O it was this morning, just before I awoke." "Then I am sure it is true, for morning dreams always go by contraries," cried Rachel. "How lucky it was you dreamt it so late." Mrs. Jenkins could hardly contain her joy, and asked how the money was to be come at.[110] "There is but one way," said Rachel, "I must go into the cellar. I know by my art under which stone it lies, but I must not tell." Then they both went down into the cellar, but Rachel refused to point at the stone unless Mrs. Jenkins would put five pieces of gold into a bason and do as she directed. The simple woman instead of turning her out of doors for a cheat, did as she was bid. She put the guineas into a bason which she gave into Rachel's hand. Rachel strewed some white powder over the gold, muttered some barbarous words, and pretended to perform the black art. She then told Mrs. Jenkins to put the bason quietly down within the cellar; telling her that if she offered to look into it, or even to speak a word the charm would be broken. She also directed her to lock the cellar door, and on no pretence to open it in less than forty eight hours. "If," added she, "you closely follow these directions, then, by the power of my art, you will find the bason conveyed to the very stone under which the money lies hid, and a fine treasure it will be." Mrs. Jenkins, who believed every word the woman said, did exactly as she was told, and Rachel took her leave with a handsome reward.

When farmer Jenkins came home he desired his wife to draw him a cup of cider; this she put off doing so long that he began to be displeased. At last she begged he would be so good as drink a little beer instead. He insisted on knowing the reason, and when at last he grew angry she told him all that had past; and owned that as the pot of gold happened to be in the cider cellar, she did not dare open the door, as she was sure it would break the charm. "And it would be a pity you know," said she, "to lose a good fortune for the sake of a draught of cider." The farmer, who was not so easily imposed upon, suspected a trick. He demanded the key, and went and opened the cellar door. He found the bason, and in it five round pieces of tin covered with powder. Mrs. Jenkins burst out a-crying; but the farmer thought of nothing but of getting a warrant to apprehend the cunning woman. Indeed she well proved her claim to that name, when she insisted that the cellar door might be kept locked till she had time to get out of the reach of all pursuit.

Poor Sally Evans! I am sure she rued the day that ever she listened to a fortune teller! Sally was as harmless a girl as ever churned a pound of butter; but Sally was ignorant, and superstitious. She delighted in dream-books,[111] and had consulted all the cunning women in the country to tell her whether the two moles on her cheek denoted that she was to have two husbands, or only two children. If she picked up an old horse-shoe going to church she was sure that would be a lucky week. She never made a black-pudding without borrowing one of the Parson's old wigs to hang in the chimney, firmly believing there were no other means to preserve them from bursting. She would never go to-bed on Midsummer eve without sticking up in her room the well known plant called Midsummer-man,[112] as the bending of the leaves to the right or to the left, would not fail to tell her whether Jacob, of whom we shall speak presently, was true or false. She would rather go five miles about than pass near a church-yard at night. Every seventh year she would not eat beans because they grew downward in the pod, instead of upward; and she would rather have gone with her gown open than have taken a pin of an old woman, for fear of being bewitched. Poor Sally had so many unlucky days in her calendar, that a large portion of her time became of little use, because on these days she did not dare set about any new work. And she would have refused the best offer if made to her on a Friday, which she thought so unlucky a day that she often said what a pity it was that there were any Friday in the week. Sally had twenty pounds left her by her grandmother. She had long been courted by Jacob a sober lad with whom she lived fellow servant at a creditable farmer's. Honest Jacob, like his namesake of old,[113] thought it little to wait seven years to get this damsel to wife, because of the love he bore her, for Sally had promised to marry him when he could match her twenty pounds with another.

Now there was one Robert, a rambling, idle young gardener, who instead of sitting down steadily in one place, used to roam about the country, and do odd jobs where he could get them. No one understood any thing about him, except that he was a down-looking fellow, who got his bread nobody knew how, and never had a penny in his pocket. Robert, who was now in the neighbourhood, happened to hear of Sally Evans and her twenty pounds. He conceived a longing desire for the latter. So he went to his old friend Rachel, told her all he had heard of Sally, and promised if she could bring about a marriage between them, she should go shares in the money.

Rachel undertook the business. She set off to the farm house and fell to singing one of her most enticing songs just under the dairy window. Sally was so struck with the pretty tune, which was unhappily used to set off some very loose words, that she jumped up, dropped the skimming dish into the cream and ran out to buy the song. While she stooped down to rummage the basket for these songs which had the most tragical pictures, for Sally had a tender heart and delighted in whatever was mournful, Rachel looked steadfastly in her face, and told her she knew by her art that she was born to good fortune, but advised her not to throw herself away. "These two moles on your cheek," added she, "shew you are in some danger." "Do they denote husbands or children," cried Sally? starting up, and letting fall the song of the children in the wood;[114] "Husbands," muttered Rachel, "Alas! poor Jacob!" said Sally mournfully, "then he will die first won't he?" "Mum for that," quoth the fortune-teller, "I will say no more." Sally was impatient; but the more curiosity she discovered, the more mystery Rachel affected. At last she said, "If you will cross my hand with a piece of silver I will tell your fortune. By the power of my art I can do this three ways; first, by cards, by the lines of your hand, or by turning a cup of tea-grounds: which will you have?" "O, all! all!" cried Sally, looking up with reverence to this sun-burnt oracle of wisdom, who knew no less than three different ways of diving into the secrets of futurity. Alas! persons of better sense than Sally have been so taken in; the more is the pity! The poor girl said she would run up stairs to her little box where she kept her money tied up in a bit of an old glove, and would bring down a bright queen Ann's six-pence, very crooked. "I am sure," added she, "it is a lucky one, for it cured me of a very bad ague last spring, by only laying it nine nights under my pillow without speaking a word. But then you must know what gave the virtue to this sixpence was, that it had belonged to three young men of the name of John; I am sure I had work enough to get it. But true it is, it certainly cured me. It must be the six-pence you know, for I am sure I did nothing else for my ague, except indeed taking some bitter stuff every three hours which the doctor called bark. Indeed I lost my ague soon after I took it, but I am certain it was owing to the crooked six-pence, and not to the bark. And so, good woman, you may come in if you will, for there is not a soul in the house but me." This was the very thing Rachel wanted to know.

While Sally was above stairs untying her glove, Rachel slipped into the parlour, took a small silver cup from the beaufet,[115] and clapped it into her pocket. Sally ran down lamenting she had lost her six-pence, which she verily believed was owing to her having put it into a left glove, instead of a right one. Rachel comforted her by saying, that if she gave her two plain ones instead, the charm would work just as well. Simple Sally thought herself happy to be let off so easily, never calculating that a smooth shilling was worth two crooked six-pences. But this skill was a part of the black art in which Rachel excelled. She took the money and began to examine the lines of Sally's left hand. She bit her withered lip, shook her head, and bade her poor dupe beware of a young man, who had black hair. "No, indeed," cried Sally all in a fright, "you mean black eyes, for our Jacob has got brown hair, 'tis his eyes that are black." "That is the very thing I was going to say," muttered Rachel, "I meant eyes though I said hair, for I know his hair is as brown as a chestnut, and his eyes as black as a sloe." "So they are sure enough," cried Sally, "how in the world could you know that?" forgetting that she herself had just told her so. And it is thus that these hags pick out the credulous all which they afterwards pretend to reveal to them. "O, I know a pretty deal more than that," said Rachel, "but you must be aware of this man."[116] "Why so?" cried Sally with great quickness, "Because," answered Rachel, "you are *fated* to marry a man worth a hundred of him who has blue eyes, light hair, and a stoop in the shoulders." "No, indeed, but I can't," said Sally, "I have promised Jacob, and Jacob I will marry." "You cannot child," returned Rachel, in a solemn tone, " it is out of your power; you are fated to marry the grey eyes and light hair." "Nay, indeed," said Sally, sighing deeply, "if I am fated, I must; I know there is no resisting one's fate." This is a common cant with poor deluded girls, who are not aware that they themselves make their fate by their folly, and then complain there is no resisting it. – "What can I do?" said Sally. "I will tell you that too," said Rachel. "You must take a walk next Sunday afternoon to the church-yard, and the first man you meet in a blue coat, with a large posy of pinks and sutherwood[117] in his bosom, sitting on the church-yard wall, about seven o'clock, he will be the man." "Provided," said Sally, much disturbed, "that he has grey eyes, and stoops." "O, to be sure," said Rachel, "otherwise it is not the right man." "But if I should mistake," said Sally, "for two men may happen to have a coat and eyes of the same colour?" "To prevent that," replied Rachel, "if it is the right man, the two first letters of his name will be R.P. This man has got money beyond sea." "O, I do not value his money," said Sally, with tears in her eyes, "for I love Jacob better than house or land; but if I am fated to marry another, I can't help it. You know there is no struggling against my fate."

Poor Sally thought of nothing, and dreamt of nothing all the week but the blue coat and the grey eyes. She made a hundred blunders at her works. She put her rennet into the butter-pan, instead of the cheese-tub. She gave the curd to the hogs, and put the whey into the vats. She put her little knife out of her pocket for fear it should cut love, and would not stay in the kitchen, if there was not an even number of people, lest it should break the charm. She grew cold and mysterious in her behaviour to faithful Jacob, whom she truly loved. But the more she thought of the fortune-teller, the more she was convinced that brown hair and black eyes were not what she was fated to marry, and therefore though she trembled to think it, Jacob could not be the man.

On Sunday she was too uneasy to go to church; for poor Sally had never been taught that her being uneasy was only a fresh reason why she ought to go thither. She spent the whole afternoon in her little garret, dressing in all her best. First she put on her red ribbon, which she had bought at last Lammas fair:[118] then she recollected that red was an unlucky colour, and changed it for a blue ribbon, tied in a true lover's knot; but suddenly calling to mind that poor Jacob had bought this knot for her of a pedlar at the door, and that she had promised to wear it for his sake, her heart smote her, and she laid it by, sighing to think she was not fated to marry the man who had given it to her. When she had looked at herself twenty times in the glass, for one vain action always brings on another, she set off, trembling and quaking every step she went. She walked eagerly towards the church-yard, not daring to look to the right or left, for fear she should spy Jacob, who would have offered to walk with her. As soon as she came within sight of the wall, she spied a man sitting upon it. Her heart beat violently. She looked again; but, alas! the stranger not only had on a black coat, but neither hair nor eyes answered the description. She happened to cast her eyes on the church-clock, and found she was two hours before her time. This was some comfort. She walked away and got rid of the two hours as well as she could, paying great attention as she went not to walk over any straws which lay across. While the clock was striking seven, she returned to the church-yard, and, O! the wonderful power of fortune-tellers! there she saw him! there sat the very man! his hair as light as flax, his eyes as blue as butter-milk, and his shoulders as round as a tub. Every tittle agreed, to the very nosegay in his waistcoat button-hole. At first indeed she thought it had been sweetbriar, and, glad to catch at a straw, whispered to herself, it is not he, and I shall marry Jacob still; but on looking again, she saw it was southernwood plain enough, and that all was over. The man accosted her with some very nonsensical, but too acceptable compliments. Sally was naturally a modest girl, and but for Rachel's wicked arts, would not have talked with a strange man; but how could she resist her fate, you know? After a little discourse, she asked him, with a trembling heart, what might be his name? "Robert Price, at your service," was the answer. "Robert Price! that is R. P. as sure as I am alive, and the fortune-teller was a witch! It is all out! it is all out! O the wonderful art of fortune-tellers!"

The little sleep she had that night was disturbed with dreams of graves, and ghosts, and funerals; but as they were morning dreams, she knew those always went by contraries, and that a funeral denoted a wedding. Still a sigh would now and then heave, to think that in that wedding Jacob could have no part. Such of my readers as know the power which superstition has over the weak and credulous mind, scarcely need be told, that poor Sally's unhappiness was soon compleated. She forgot all her vows to Jacob; she at once forsook an honest man whom she loved, and consented to marry one of whom she knew nothing, from a ridiculous notion that she was compelled to do so by a decree which she had it not in her power to resist. She married this Richard Price,[119] the strange gardener, whom she soon found to be very worthless, and very much in debt. He had no such thing as "money beyond sea," as the fortune-teller had told her; but he had another wife there. He got immediate possession of Sally's 20*l*[120] Rachel put in for her share, but he refused to give her a farthing, and bid her get away, or he would have her taken up on the vagrant act. He soon ran away from Sally, leaving her to bewail her own weakness; for it was that indeed, and not any irresistible fate, which had been the cause of her ruin. To compleat her misery, she herself was suspected of having stolen the silver cup which Rachel had pocketed. Her master, however, would not prosecute her, as she was falling into a deep decline, and she died in a few months of a broken heart.

Rachel, whenever she got near home, used to drop her trade of fortune-teller, and only dealt in the wares of her basket. Mr. Wilson, the clergyman, found her one day dealing out some very wicked ballads to some children. He went up with a view to give her a reprimand; but had no sooner begun his exhortation than up came a constable, followed by several people. "There she is, that is she, that is the old witch who tricked my wife out of the five guineas," said one of them. "Do your office constable, seize that old hag.[121] She may tell fortunes and find pots of gold in Taunton gaol, for there she will have nothing else to do?" This was that very farmer Jenkins, whose wife had been cheated by Rachel of the five guineas. He had taken pains to trace her to her own parish: he did not so much value the loss

of the money, but he thought it was a duty he owed the public
to clear the country of such vermin. Mr. Wilson immediately
committed her.[122] She took her trial at the next assizes, when
she was sentenced to a year's imprisonment. In the mean time
the pawnbroker to whom she had sold the cup, which she had
stolen from poor Sally's master, impeached; and as the robbery
was fully proved upon Rachel, she was sentenced for this crime
to Botany Bay; and a happy day it was for the county of
Somerset, when such a nuisance was sent out of it. She was
transported much about the same time that her husband Giles
lost his life in stealing the net from the garden wall.[123]

I have thought it my duty to print this little history as a kind
warning to all you young men and maidens not to have any
thing to say to CHEATS,[124] IMPOSTERS, CUNNING-WOMEN,
FORTUNE-TELLERS, CONJURERS, and INTERPRETERS OF DREAMS. –
Listen to me, your true friend, when I assure you that God
never reveals to weak and wicked women those secret designs
of his Providence, which no human wisdom is able to foresee.
To consult these false oracles is not only foolish, but sinful. It is
foolish, because they are themselves as ignorant as those whom
they pretend to teach, and it is sinful, because it is prying into
that futurity which God, as kindly as wisely, hides from men.
God indeed *orders* all things; but when you have a mind to do a
foolish thing, do not fancy you are *fated* to do it. This is tempting
Providence, and not trusting him. It is indeed, "charging God
with folly". Prudence is his gift, and you obey him better when
you make use of prudence under the direction of prayer, than
when you madly run into ruin, and think you are only submit-
ting to your fate. Never fancy that you are compelled to undo
yourself. Never believe that God conceals his will from a sober
Christian who obey his laws, and reveals it to a vagabond Gipsy,
who runs up and down breaking the laws, both of God and man.
King Saul never consulted the witch till he had left off serving
God.[125] The Bible will direct us what to do better than any
conjurer, and no days are unlucky but those which we make so
by our own vanity, folly, and sin.

THE STORY OF SINFUL SALLY
told by herself, shewing

How from being SALLY of the GREEN she was first led to become
SINFUL SALLY, and afterwards DRUNKEN SAL, and how at last she
came to a most melancholy and almost hopeless End; being therein
a Warning to all young Women both in Town and Country.

Come each maiden lend an ear,
    Country Lass and London Belle!
Come and drop a mournful tear
    O'er the tale that I shall tell!

I that ask your tender pity,
    Ruin'd now and all forlorn,
Once, like you, was young and pretty,
    And as cheerful as the morn.

In yon distant cottage sitting,
    Far away from London town,   10
Once you might have seen me knitting
    In my simple Kersey Gown.[126]

Where the little lambkins leap,
    Where the meadows look so gay,
Where the drooping willows weep,
    Simple Sally used to stray.

Then I tasted many a Blessing,
    Then I had an honest fame;
Father Mother me caressing,
    Smil'd, and thought me free from blame.   20

Then, amid my friends so dear,
 Life it speeded fast away;
O, it moves a tender tear,
 To bethink me of the day!

From the villages surrounding,
 Ere I well had reach'd Eighteen,
Came the modest youths abounding,
 All to Sally of the Green.

Courting days were thus beginning,
 And I soon had prov'd a wife;   30
O! if I had kept from sinning,
 Now how blest had been my life.

Come each maiden lend an ear,
 Country Lass and London Belle!
Come ye now and deign to hear
 How poor sinful Sally fell.

Where the hill begins inclining,
 Half a furlong from the Road,
O'er the village white and shining
 Stands Sir William's great abode.   40

Near his meadow I was tripping,
 Vainly wishing to be seen,
When Sir William met me skipping,
 And he spoke me on the Green.

Bid me quit my cloak of scarlet,
 Blam'd my simple Kersey Gown;
Ey'd me then, so like a Varlet,
 Such as live in London town.

With his presents I was loaded,
 And bedeck'd in ribbons gay;   50

Thus my ruin was foreboded,
   O, how crafty was his way!

Vanish'd now from Cottage lowly,
   My poor parents' hearts I break;
Enter on a state unholy,
   Turn a Mistress to a Rake.

Now no more by morning light
   Up to God my voice I raise;
Now no shadows of the night
   Call my thoughts to prayer and praise.   60

Hark! a well-known sound I hear!
   'Tis the Church's Sunday Bell;
No; I dread to venture near:
   No; I'm now the Child of Hell.

Now I lay my Bible by,
   Chuse that impious book so new,
Love the bold blaspheming lie,
   And that filthy novel too.

Next to London town I pass
   (Sinful Sally is my name)   70
There to gain a front of brass,
   And to glory in my Shame.

Powder'd well, and puff'd, and painted,
   Rivals all I there out-shine;
With skin so white and heart so tainted,
   Rolling in my chariot fine.

In the Park I glitter daily,
   Then I dress me for the play,
Then to masquerade so gaily,
   See me, see me tear away.   80

When I meet some meaner Lass
   Then I toss with proud disdain;
Laugh and giggle as I pass,
   Seeming not to know a pain.

Still at every hour of leisure
   Something whispers me within,
O! I hate this life of pleasure,
   For it is a Life of Sin.

Thus amidst my peals of laughter
   Horror seizes oft my frame: 90
Pleasure now – Damnation after,
   And a never-dying flame.

Save me, Save me, Lord, I cry,
   Save my soul from Satan's chain!
Now I see Salvation nigh,
   Now I turn to Sin again.

Is it then some true Repentance
   That I feel for evil done?
No; 'tis horror of my sentence,
   'Tis the pangs of Hell begun.   100

By a thousand ills o'ertaken
   See me now quite sinking down;
'Till so lost and so forsaken,
   Sal is cast upon the town.

At the dusk of evening grey
   Forth I step from secret cell;
Roaming like a beast of prey,
   Or some hateful Imp of Hell.

Ah! how many youths so blooming
   By my wanton looks I've won;   110

Then by vices all confusing
    Left them ruin'd and undone!

Thus the cruel spider stretches
    Wide his web for every fly;
Then each victim that he catches
    Strait he poisons till he die.

Now no more by conscience troubled,
    Deep I plunge in every Sin:
True; my sorrows are redoubled,
    But I drown them all in Gin.   120

See me next with front so daring
    Band of ruffian Rogues among;
Fighting, cheating, drinking, swearing,
    And the vilest of the throng.

Mark that youngest of the thieves;
    Taught by Sal he ventures further;
What he filches Sal receives,
    'Tis for Sal he does the murther.

See me then attend my victim
    To the fatal Gallows Tree;   130
Pleas'd to think how I have nick'd him,
    Made him swing while I am free.

Jack I laughing see depart,
    While with Dick I drink and sing;
Soon again I'll fill the cart,
    Make this present Lover swing.

But while thus with guilt surprising,
    Sal pursues her bold career,
See God's dreadful wrath arising,
    And the day of vengeance near!   140

Fierce disease my body seizes,
    Racking pain afflicts my bones;
Dread of Death my spirit freezes,
    Deep and doleful are my groans.

Here with face so shrunk and spotted
    On the clay-cold ground I lie;
See how all my flesh is rotted,
    Stop, O Stranger, see me die!

Conscience, as my breath's departing,
    Plunges too his arrows deep,   150
With redoubled fury starting
    Like some Giant from his sleep.

In this Pit of Ruin lying,
    Once again before I die,
Fainting, trembling, weeping, fighting,
    Lord to thee I'll lift mine eye.

Thou can'st save the vilest Harlot,
    Grace, I've heard is free and full,
Sins that once were "red as scarlet"
    Thou can'st make as white as wool.[127]   160

Savior, whom I pierc'd so often,
    Deeper still my guilt imprint!
Let thy mighty Spirit soften
    This my harden'd heart of flint.

Vain, alas! is all my groaning,
    For I fear the die is cast;
True, thy blood is all atoning,
    But my day of Grace is past.

Savior! hear me or I perish!
    None who *lives* is quite undone;   170
Still a Ray of Hope I'll cherish
    'Till Eternity's begun.

MR. BRAGWELL AND HIS TWO DAUGHTERS
extracted from
THE TWO WEALTHY FARMERS
OR
The History of Mr. Bragwell and his two daughters

Mr. Bragwell and Mr. Worthy happened to meet last year at
Weyhill Fair.[128] They were glad to see each other as they had
but seldom met of late; Mr. Bragwell having removed some
years before from Mr. Worthy's neighbourhood, to a distant
village where he had bought an Estate.

Mr. Bragwell was a substantial Farmer and Grazier. He had
risen in the world by what worldly men call a run of good
fortune. He had also been a man of great industry; that is, he
had paid a diligent and constant attention to his own interest.
He understood business, and had a knack of turning almost
every thing to his own advantage. He had that sort of sense,
which good men call cunning, and knaves call wisdom. He was
too prudent ever to do any thing so wrong that the law could
take hold of him; yet he was not over scrupulous about the
morality of an action, when the prospect of enriching himself by
it was very great, and the chance of hurting his character was
small. The corn he sent home to his customers was not always
quite so good as the samples he had produced at Market; and he
now and then forgot to name some capital blemish in the horses
he sold at Fair. He scorned to be guilty of the petty frauds of
cheating in weights and measures, for he thought that was a
beggarly sin; but he valued himself on his skill in making a
bargain, and fancied it shewed his knowledge of the world to
take advantage of the ignorance of a dealer.

It was his constant rule to undervalue every thing he was
about to buy, and to overvalue every thing he was about to sell;

but as he prided himself on his character he avoided every thing that was very shameful, so that he was considered merely as a hard dealer, and a keen hand at a bargain. Now and then when he had been caught in pushing his own advantage too far, he contrived to get out of the scrape by turning the whole into a jest, saying it was a good take in, a rare joke, and that he had only a mind to divert himself with the folly of his neighbour who could be so easily imposed on.

Mr. Bragwell had one favourite maxim, namely, that a man's success in life was a sure proof of his wisdom; and that all failure and misfortune was the consequence of a man's own folly. As this opinion was first taken up by him from vanity and ignorance; so it was more and more confirmed by his own prosperity. He saw that he himself had succeeded greatly without either money or education to begin with, and he therefore now despised every Man, however excellent his character or talents might be, who had not the same success in life...He thought, for his part, that every man of sense could command success on his undertakings, and controul and dispose the events of his own life.

But though he considered those who had had less success than himself as no better than fools, yet he did not extend this opinion to Mr. Worthy, whom he looked upon not only as a good but a wise man. They had been bred up when children in the same house, but with this difference, that Worthy was the nephew of the master, and Bragwell the son of the Servant.

Bragwell's Father had been plowman in the family of Mr. Worthy's Uncle, a sensible man, who farmed a small estate of his own and who having no children, bred up young Worthy as his son, instructed him in the business of husbandry, and at his death left him his estate. The father of Worthy was a pious Clergyman, who lived with his brother the farmer, in order to help out a narrow income. He had bestowed much pains on the instruction of his Son...While he took care that he should be made an excellent Farmer, he filled up his leisure hours in improving his mind; so that young Worthy had read more good Books and understood them better than most men in his station.

His reading however had been chiefly confined to husbandry and Divinity, the two subjects which were of the most immediate importance to him.

The reader will see by this time that Mr. Bragwell and Mr. Worthy were likely to be as opposite to each other as two men could well be, who were nearly of the same age and condition, and who were neither of them without credit in the world. Bragwell indeed made far the greater figure for he liked to *cut a dash*, as he called it.[129] And while it was the study of Worthy to conform to his station, and to set a good example to those about him, it was the delight of Bragwell to vie in his way of life with men of larger fortune. He did not see how much this vanity raised the ill-will of his equals and the contempt of his betters.

His Wife was a notable stirring Woman, but vain, violent, and ambitious; very ignorant, and very high-minded. She had married Bragwell before he was worth a Shilling, and as she had brought him a good deal of money, she thought herself the grand cause of his rising in the world, and thence took occasion to govern him most completely. When ever he ventured to oppose her she took care to put him in mind "that he owed every thing to her that had it not been for her he might still have been stumping after a Plow tail, or serving Hogs in old Worthy's Farm-Yard, but that it was she who had made a Gentleman of him.[130] In order to set about making him a Gentleman she had begun by teazing him till he had turned away all his poor relations who worked in the Farm. She next drew him off from keeping company with his old acquaintance, and at last persuaded him to remove from the place where he had got his money. Poor Woman! she had not sense and virtue enough to see how honourable it is for a man to raise himself in the world by fair means, and then to help forward his poor relations and friends, engaging their services by his kindness, and endeavouring to keep want out of the family.

Mrs. Bragwell was an excellent mistress, according to her own notions of excellence, for no one could say that she ever lost an opportunity of scolding a servant, or was ever guilty of the weakness of overlooking a fault. Towards her two daughters her behaviour was far otherwise. In them she could see nothing but perfections; but her extravagant fondness for these girls was full as much owing to pride as to affection. She was bent on making a family, and having found out that she was too ignorant, and too much trained to the habits of getting money, ever to hope to make a figure herself, she looked to her daughters as the persons who were to raise the family of the Bragwells; And in this hope she foolishly submitted to any drudgery for their sakes, and to any impertinence from them.

The first wish of her heart was to set them above their neighbours; for she used to say, "what was the use of having substance, if her daughters might not carry themselves above girls who had nothing?" To do her justice, she herself would be about early and late to see that the business of the house was not neglected. She had been bred to great industry, and continued to work when it was no longer necessary, both from early habit, and the desire of heaping up money for her daughters. Yet her whole notion of gentility was that it consisted in being rich and idle, and though she was willing to be a drudge herself, she resolved to make her daughters gentlewomen. To be well dressed and to do nothing, or nothing which is of any use, was what she fancied distinguished people in genteel life. And this is too common a notion of a fine education among some people. They do not esteem things by their use but by their shew. They estimate the value of their children's education by the money it costs, and not by the knowledge and goodness it bestows. People of this stamp often take a pride in the expence of learning, instead of taking pleasure in the advantages of it. And the silly vanity of letting others see that they can afford any thing, often sets parents on letting their daughters learn not only things of no use, but things which may be really hurtful in their situation; either by setting them above their proper duties, or by taking up their time in a way inconsistent with them.

Mrs. Bragwell sent her daughters to a boarding School, where she wished them to hold up their heads as high as any body; to have more spirit than *to be put upon* by any one, never to be pitiful about money, but rather to shew that they could spend with the best; to keep company with the richest girls in the School and to make no acquaintance with Farmer's Daughters.

They came home at the usual age of leaving School, with a large portion of vanity grafted on their native ignorance. The vanity was added but the ignorance was not taken away. Of Religion they could not possibly learn any thing, since none was taught for at that place it was considered as a part of education which belonged only to Charity Schools. Of knowledge they had got just enough to laugh at their fond parents' rustic manners and vulgar language, and just enough taste to despise and ridicule every girl who was not as vainly dressed as themselves.

The Mother had been comforting herself for the heavy expence of their bringing up, by looking forward to the pleasure of seeing them become fine ladies, and to the pride of marrying them above their station.

Their Father hoped that they would be a comfort to him both in sickness and in health. He had had no learning himself, and could write but poorly, and owed what skill he had in figures to his natural turn for business. He hoped that his daughters after all the money he had spent on them would now write his letters and keep his accounts. And as he was now and then laid up with a fit of the gout, he was enjoying the prospect of having two affectionate children to nurse him.

When they came home however, he had the mortification to find, that though he had two smart showy ladies to visit him, he had neither dutiful daughters to nurse him, nor faithful stewards to keep his books. They neither soothed him by kindness when he was sick, nor helped him when he was busy. They thought the maid might take care of him in the gout as she did before. And as to their skill in cyphering he soon found to his cost that though they knew how to *spend* both Pounds, Shillings, and Pence, yet they did not know so well how to cast them up.

Mrs. Bragwell one day being very busy in making a great dinner for the neighbours, ventured to request her daughters to assist in making the pastry. They asked her scornfully "whether she had sent them to Boarding School to learn to cook; and added that they supposed she would expect them next to make puddings for the hay-makers." So saying they coolly marched off to their music. When the Mother found her girls were too polite to be of any use, she would take comfort in observing how her parlour was set out with their Fillagree and Flowers, their Embroidery and cut paper. They spent the morning in bed, the noon in dressing, the evening at the Spinnet, and the night in reading Novels.

With all these fine qualifications it is easy to suppose that as they despised their sober duties, they no less despised their plain neighbours. When they could not get to a horse race, a petty ball, or a strolling play with some company as idle and as smart as themselves, they were driven for amusement to the Circulating Library. Jack, the plow-boy, on whom they had now put a livery jacket, was employed half his time in trotting backwards and forwards with the most wretched trash the little neighbouring book shop could furnish. The choice was often left to Jack, who could not read, but who had general orders to bring all the new things, and a great many of them.

Things were in this state, or rather growing worse, for idleness and vanity are never at a stand; when these two wealthy farmers, Bragwell and Worthy met at Weyhill Fair, as was said before. After many hearty salutations had passed between them, it was agreed that Mr. Bragwell should spend the next day with his old friend, whose house was not many miles distant, which Bragwell invited himself to do in the following manner, "we have not had a comfortable day's chat for years, said he, and as I am to look at a drove of lean beasts in your neighbourhood, I will take a bed at your house, and we will pass the evening in debating as we used to do. You know I always loved a bit of an argument, and am reckoned not to make the worst figure at our club: I had not, to be sure, such good learning as you had, because your father was a Parson, and you got it for nothing. But I can bear my part pretty well for all that. When any man talks to me about his learning I ask if it has helped him to get a good estate; if he says no, then I would not give him a rush for it; for of what use is all the learning in the world if it does not make a man rich? But as I was saying I will come and see you to-morrow; but now don't let your wife put herself into a fuss for me. Don't alter your own plain way, for I am not proud I assure you, nor above my old friends, though I thank GOD, I am pretty well in the world...[131]

About the middle of the next day Mr. Bragwell reached Mr. Worthy's neat and pleasant dwelling. He found every thing in it the reverse of his own. It had not so many ornaments but it had more comforts. And when he saw his friend's good old fashioned arm chair in a warm corner, he gave a sigh to think how his own had been banished to make room for his daughter's Music. Instead of made flowers in glass cases, and a tea chest[132] and screens too fine to be used, and about which he was cautioned, and scolded as often as he came near them, he saw a neat shelf of good books for the service of the family, and a small medicine chest for the benefit of the poor.

Mrs. Worthy and her daughters had prepared a plain but neat and good dinner. The tarts were so excellent that Bragwell felt a secret kind of regret that his own daughters were too genteel to do any thing so very useful. Indeed he had been always unwilling to believe that any thing which was very proper and very necessary, could be so extremely vulgar and unbecoming as his daughters were always declaring it to be. And his late experience of the little comfort he found at home, inclined him now still more strongly to suspect that things were not so right as he had been made to suppose. But it was in vain to speak; for his daughters constantly stopped his mouth by a favorite saying of theirs, "better to be out of the world than out of the fashion."

Soon after dinner the women went out to their several employments, and Mr. Worthy being left alone with his guest the following discourse took place.

Bragwell. You have a couple of sober, pretty looking girls, Worthy; but I wonder they don't tiff off[133] a little more. Why my girls have as much fat and flour on their heads as would half maintain my reapers in suet pudding.

Worthy. Mr. Bragwell, in the management of my family, I don't consider what I might afford only, though that is one great point; but I consider also what is needful and becoming in a man of my station, for there are so many useful ways of laying out money, that I feel as if it were a sin to spend one unnecessary shilling. Having had the blessing of a good education myself, I have been able to give the like advantage to my daughters. One of the best lessons I have taught them is, to know themselves; and one proof that they have learnt this lesson is, that they are not above any of the duties of their station. They read and write well, and when my eyes are bad they keep my accounts in a very pretty manner. If I had put them to learn what you call *genteel things* these might either have been of no use to them, and so both time and money might have been thrown away; or they might have proved worse than nothing to them by leading them into wrong notions, and wrong company. Though we don't wish them to do the laborious parts of the dairy work; yet they always assist their Mother in the management of it. As to their appearance, they are every day nearly as you see them now, and on Sundays they are very neatly dressed, but it is always in a decent and modest way. There are no lappets, fringes, furbe-lows, and tawdry ornaments, fluttering about among my cheese and butter. And I should feel no vanity but much mortification if a stranger seeing Farmer Worthy's daughters at Church, should ask who those fine ladies were.

Bragwell. Now I own I should like to have such a question asked concerning my daughters. I like to make people stare and envy. It makes one feel one-self somebody. But as to yourself, to be sure you best know what you can afford. And indeed there is some difference between your daughters and the Miss Bragwells.

Worthy. For my part, before I engage in any expence, I always ask myself these two short questions, First – Can I afford it? – Secondly, Is it proper for me?

Bragwell. Do you so? Now I own I ask myself but one. For if I find can afford it, I take care to make it proper for me. If I can pay for a thing, no one has a right to hinder me from having it.

Worthy. Certainly. But a man's own prudence and sense of duty, ought to prevent him from doing an improper thing, as effectually as if there were somebody to hinder him.

Bragwell. Now I think a man is a fool who is hindered from having any thing he has a mind to; unless, indeed he is in want of money to pay for it. I'm no friend to debt. A poor man must want on.

Worthy. But I hope my children have learnt not to want any thing which is not proper for them. They are very industrious, they attend to business all day; and in the evening they sit down to their work and a good book. I think they live in the fear of GOD. I trust they are humble and pious, and I am sure they seem cheerful and happy. If I am sick, it is pleasant to see them dispute which shall wait upon me, for they say the maid cannot do it so tenderly as themselves. –

This part of the discourse staggered Bragwell. Vain as he was, he could not help feeling what a difference a religious and a worldly education made on the heart, and how much the former regulated even the natural temper. Another thing which surprised him was, that these girls living a life of domestic piety, without any public diversions should be so very cheerful and happy. While his own daughters who were never contradicted, and were indulged with continual amusements, were always sullen and ill-tempered. That they who were more humoured should be less grateful and happy, disturbed him much. He envied Worthy the tenderness of his children, though he would not own it, but turned it off thus:

Bragwell. But my girls are too smart to make mopes of, that is the truth. Though ours is such a lonely village, it is wonderful to see how soon they get the fashions. What with the descriptions in the Magazines, and the pictures in the pocket Books, they have them in a twinkling, and out do their patterns all to nothing. I used to take in the County Journal, because it was useful enough to see how Oats went, the time of high water, and the price of Stocks. But when my ladies came home forsooth, I was soon wheedled out of that, and forced to take a London paper, that tells a deal about caps and feathers, and all the trumpery of the quality. When I want to know what hops are a bag, they are snatching the paper to see what violet soap is a pound. And as to the dairy, they never care how Cow's milk goes, as long as they can get some stuff which they call Milk of Roses.

Worthy. But do your daughters never read?

Bragwell. Read! I believe they do too. Why our Jack the Plow-boy, spends half his time in going to a shop in our Market town, where they let out books to read with marble covers. And they sell paper with all manner of colours on the edges, and gim cracks, and powder-puffs, and wash-balls, and cards without any pips, and every thing in the world that's genteel and of no use.[134] 'Twas but t'other day I met Jack with a basket full of these books, so having some time to spare, I sat down to see a little what they were about.

Worthy. Well, I hope you there found what was likely to improve your daughters, and teach them the true use of time.

Bragwell. O, as to that, you are pretty much out. I could make neither head nor tail of it. It was neither fish, flesh, nor good red-herring: it was all about my Lord, and Sir Harry and the Captain. But I never met with such nonsensical fellows in my life. Their talk was no more like that of my old landlord, who was a Lord you know, nor the Captain of our fencibles,[135] than chalk is like cheese. I was fairly taken in at first and began to think I had got hold of a *godly* book, for there was a deal about "hope and despair, and heaven, and Angels, and torments, and everlasting happiness." But when I got a little on, I found there was no meaning in all these words, or if any, 'twas a bad meaning. "Misery" perhaps only meant a disappointment about a bit of a letter: and "everlasting happiness" meant two people talking nonsense together for five minutes. In short I never met with such a pack of lies. The people talk such gibberish as no folks in their sober senses ever talked; and the things that happen to them are not like the things that ever happen to any of my acquaintance. They are at home one minute, and beyond sea the next. Beggars today, and Lords tomorrow. Waiting-maids in the morning, and Duchesses at night. You and I, Master Worthy have worked hard many years, and think it very well to have scraped a trifle of money together, you a few hundreds I suppose, and I a few thousands. But one would think

every man in these books, had the Bank of England in his
'scrutore.[136] Then there is another thing which I never met with
in true life. We think it pretty well you know, if one has got one
thing, and another has got another. I will tell you how I mean.
You are reckoned sensible, our Parson is learned, the Squire is
rich, I am rather generous, one of your daughters is pretty, and
both mine are genteel. But in these books, (except here and
there one, whom they make worse than Satan himself) every
man and woman's child of them, are all wise, and witty, and
generous, and rich, and handsome, and genteel. No body is
middling, or good in one thing, and bad in another, like my live
acquaintance. But tis all up to the skies, or down to the dirt. I
had rather read Tom Hickathrift, or Jack the Giant Killer.[137]

Worthy. You have found out, Mr. Bragwell, that many of these
books are ridiculous, I will go further, and say that to me they
appear wicked also. And I should account the reading of them a
great mischief, especially to people in middling and low life, if I
only took into the account the great loss of time such reading
causes, and the aversion it leaves behind for what is more
serious and solid. But this, though a bad part, is not the worst.
These books give false views of human life. They teach a
contempt for humble and domestic duties; for industry, frugal-
ity, and retirement. Want of youth and beauty is considered as
ridiculous. Plain people like you and me, are objects of contempt. Parental authority is set at nought. Nay plots and contrivances against parents and guardians, fill half the volumes. They
make love as the great business of human life, and even teach
that it is impossible to be regulated or restrained, and to the
indulgence of this passion, every duty is therefore sacrificed. A
country life, with a kind mother, or a sober aunt, is described as
a state of intolerable misery. And one would be apt to fancy
from their painting, that a good country house is a prison, and
a worthy father the gaoler. Vice is set off with every ornament
which can make it pleasing and amiable; while virtue and piety
are made ridiculous by tacking to them something that is silly,
or absurd. Crimes which would be considered as hanging matter
at the Old Bailey, are here made to take the appearance of

virtue, by being mixed with some wild flight of unnatural generosity. Those crying sins, ADULTERY, GAMING, DUELS, and SELF-MURDER,[138] are made so familiar, and the wickedness of them is so disguised, that even innocent girls get to lose their abhorrence, and to talk with complacency, *of things which should not be so much as named by them.*

I should not have said so much on this mischief, (continued Mr. Worthy,) from which I dare say, great folks fancy people in our station are safe enough, if I did not know, and lament that this corrupt reading is now got down even among some of the lowest class. And it is an evil which is spreading every day. Poor industrious girls, who get their bread by the needle, or the loom, spend half the night in listening to these books. Thus the labour of one girl is lost,[139] and the minds of the rest are corrupted; for though their hands are employed in honest industry, which might help to preserve them from a life of sin, yet their hearts are at that very time polluted by scenes and descriptions which are too likely to plunge them into it. And I think I don't go too far when I say that the vain and shewy manner in which young women who have to work for their bread, have taken to dress themselves, added to the poison they draw from these books, contribute together to bring them to destruction, more than almost any other cause. Now tell me, do not you think these wild books will hurt your daughters?

Bragwell. Why I do think they are grown full of schemes and contrivances and whispers, that's the truth on't. Every thing is a secret. They always seem to be on the look-out for something, and when nothing comes on't, then they are sulky and disappointed. They will not keep company with their equals. They despise trade and farming, and I own, I'm for the stuff. I should not like for them to marry any, but a man of substance, if he was ever so smart. Now they will hardly sit down with a substantial country dealer. But if they hear of a recruiting party in our Market Town, on goes the finery – off they are. Some flimsy excuse is patched up. They want something at the book Shop or the Millener's because I suppose there is a chance that some Jackanapes of an Ensign[140] may be there buying Sticking plaister.

In short I do grow a little uneasy, for I should not like to see all I have saved thrown away on a Knapsack.

So saying they both rose, and walked out to view the Farm. Mr. Bragwell affected greatly to admire the good order of every thing he saw; but never forgot to compare it with something larger and handsomer or better of his own. It was easy to see that self was his standard of perfection in every thing. All he himself possessed gained some increased value in his eyes from being his; and in surveying the property of his friend, he derived food for his vanity, from things which seemed least likely to raise it. Every appearance of comfort, of success, of merit in any thing which belonged to Mr. Worthy, led him to speak of some superior advantage of his own, of the same kind. And it was clear that the chief part of the satisfaction he felt in walking over the farm of his friend, was caused by thinking how much larger his own was...

Mr. Bragwell when he returned home from his visit to Mr. Worthy...seemed...to feel less satisfaction in the idle gentility of his own daughters, since he had been witness to the simplicity, modesty, and usefulness of those of Mr. Worthy. And he could not help seeing that the vulgar violence of his wife did not produce so much family happiness at home as the humble piety and quiet diligence of Mrs. Worthy produced in the house of his friend...

At length the time came when Mr. Worthy had promised to return his visit...Worthy arrived at his friend's house on the Saturday, time enough to see the house and garden, and grounds of Mr. Bragwell, by daylight...During supper the young ladies sat in disdainful silence, not deigning to bestow the smallest civility on so plain a man as Mr. Worthy. They left the room with their Mamma as soon as possible; being impatient to get away to ridicule their father's old-fashioned friend.

The Dance; or, the *Christmas Merry-making.*

As soon as they were gone, Mr. Worthy asked Bragwell how his family comforts stood, and how his daughters, who, he said, were really fine young women, went on. "O, as to that," replied

Bragwell, "pretty much like other men's handsome daughters, I suppose, that is, wise and worse. I really begin to apprehend that their fantastical notions have gained such a head, that after all the money I have scraped together, I shall never get them well married. Betsey has just lost as good an offer as any girl could desire, young Wilson, an honest, substantial grazier as any in the county. He not only knows every thing proper for his station, but is pleasing in his behaviour, and a pretty scholar into the bargain; he reads history books and voyages, of a winter's evening, to his infirm father, instead of going to the card assembly in our town; neither likes drinking nor sporting, and is a sort of favourite with our Parson, because he takes in the weekly numbers of a fine Bible with Cuts,[141] and subscribes to the Sunday School, and makes a fuss about helping the poor, in these dear times, as they call them, but I think they are good times for *us*, Mr. Worthy. Well, for all this, Betsey only despised him, and laughed at him; but as he is both handsome and rich, I thought she might come round at last; and so I invited him to come and stay a day or two at Christmas, when we have always a little sort of merry-making here. But it would not do. He scorned to talk that palavering stuff which she has been used to in the marble covered books I told you of. He told her, indeed, that it would be the happiness of his heart to live with her, which, I own, I thought was as much as could be expected of any man. But Miss had no notion of marrying one who was only desirous of living with her. No, no, forsooth, her lover must declare himself ready to die for her, which honest Wilson was not such a fool as to offer to do. In the afternoon, however, he got a little into her favour by making out a Rebus[142] or two in the Lady's Diary, and she condescended to say, she did not think Mr. Wilson had been so good a scholar, but he soon spoilt all again. We had a bit of a hop[143] in the evening. The young man, though he had not much taste for those sort of gambols, yet thought he could foot it a little in the old-fashioned way. So he asked Betsey to be his partner. But when he asked what dance they should call, Miss drew up her head, and, in a strange gibberish, said she should dance nothing but a *Minuet de la Cour*, and ordered him to call it; Wilson stared, and honestly told her she must call it herself, for he could neither spell nor pronounce such outlandish words. I burst out a laughing, and told him, I supposed it was something like questions and commands; and if so, that was much merrier than dancing. Seeing her partner standing stock still, and not knowing how to get out of the scrape, the girl began by herself, and fell to swimming, and sinking, and capering, and flourishing, and posturing, for all the world just like the man on the slack rope at our fair.[144] But seeing Wilson standing like a stuck pig, and we all laughing at her, she resolved to wreak her malice upon him; so, with a look of rage and disdain, she advised him to go down country bumpkin[145] with the dairy maid, who would make a much fitter partner, as well as wife, for him, than she could do. 'I am quite of your mind, Miss,' said he, with more spirit than I thought was in him; 'you may make a good partner for a dance, but you would make a sad one to go through life with. I will take my leave of you, Miss, with this short story. I had lately a pretty large concern in hay-jobbing, which took me to London. I waited a good while in the Hay-market for my dealer, and, to pass away the time, I stepped into a sort of singing play-house there, where I was grieved to the heart to see young women painted and dizened out, and capering away just as you have been doing. I thought it bad enough in them, and wondered the quality could be entertained with such indecent mummery. But little did I think to meet with the same paint, finery, and posturing tricks in a farm-house. I will never marry a woman who despises me, nor the station in which I should place her, and so I take my leave.' Poor girl! how she *was* provoked! to be publicly refused, and turned off, as it were, by a grazier! But it was of use to some of the other girls, who have not held up their heads quite so high since, nor painted quite so red, but have condescended to speak to their equals...

Some Account of a Sunday in Mr. Bragwell's Family.

Mr. Worthy had been for so many years used to the sober ways of his own well-ordered family, that he greatly disliked to pass a Sunday in any house of which religion was not the governing principle. Indeed, he commonly ordered his affairs, and regulated his journies, with an eye to this object. "To pass a Sunday in an irreligious family," said he, "is always unpleasant, often unsafe. I seldom find I can do them any good, and they may, perhaps, do me some harm. At least, I am giving a sanction to their manner of passing it, if I pass it in the same manner. If I reprove them, I subject myself to the charge of singularity and of being 'righteous over-much;' if I do *not* reprove them, I confirm and strengthen them in evil. And whether I reprove them or not, I certainly partake of their guilt, if I spend it as they do."

He had, however, so strong a desire to be useful to Mr. Bragwell, that he at length determined to break through his common practice, and pass the Sunday at his house. Mr. Worthy was surprised to find that though the Church bell was going, the breakfast was not ready, and expressed his wonder how this should be the case in so industrious a family. Bragwell made some awkward excuses. He said his wife worked her servants so hard all the week, that even she, as notable as she was, a little relaxed from the strictness of her demands on Sunday mornings; and he owned that in a general way no one was up early enough for Church. He confessed that his wife commonly spent the morning in making puddings, pies, and cakes, to last through the week; as Sunday was the only leisure time she and her maids had. Mr. Worthy soon saw an uncommon bustle in the house. All hands were busy. It was nothing but baking, and boiling, and frying, and roasting, and running, and scolding, and eating. The boy was kept from Church to clean the plate, the man to gather the fruit, the mistress to make the cheese-cakes, the maids to dress the dinner, and the young ladies to dress themselves.

The truth was, Mrs. Bragwell, who had heard much of the order and good management of Mr. Worthy's family, but who looked down with disdain upon them as far less rich than herself, was resolved to indulge her vanity on the present occasion. She was determined to be even with Mrs. Worthy, in whose praises Bragwell had been so loud, and felt no small pleasure in the hope of making her guest uneasy, when he should be struck dumb with the display both of her skill and her wealth. Mr. Worthy was, indeed, struck to behold as large a dinner as he had been used to see at a Justice's meeting. He, whose frugal and pious wife had accustomed him only to such a plain Sunday's dinner as could be dressed without keeping any one from church, when he surveyed the loaded table of his friend, instead of feeling that envy which these grand preparations were meant to raise, felt nothing but disgust at the vanity of his friend's wife, mixed with much thankfulness for the piety and simplicity of his own.

After having made the dinner wait a long time, the Miss Bragwells marched in, dressed as if they were going to the Assize Ball: they looked very scornfully at having been so hurried, though they had been dressing ever since they got up; and their fond father, when he saw them so fine, forgave all their impertinence, and cast an eye of triumph on Mr. Worthy, who felt he had never loved his own humble daughters so well as at that moment.

In the afternoon, the whole party went to church. To do them justice, it was, indeed, their common practice once a day, when the weather was good and the road was neither dusty nor dirty, when the minister did not begin too early, when the young ladies had not been disappointed of their new bonnets on the Saturday night, and when they had no smart company in the house who rather wished to stay at home. When this last was the case, which, to say the truth, happened pretty often, it was thought a piece of good manners to conform to the humour of the guests. Mr. Bragwell had this day forborne to ask any of his usual company; well knowing that their vain and worldly conversation would only serve to draw on him some new reprimand from his guest.

Mrs. Bragwell and her daughters picked up, as usual, a good deal of acquaintance at church. Many compliments passed, and much of the news of the week was retailed before the service began. They waited with impatience for the lessons as a licensed season for whispering, and the subject begun during the lessons was finished while they were singing. The young ladies made an appointment for the afternoon with a friend in the next pew, while their Mamma took the opportunity of enquiring the character of a Dairy Maid, which she observed with a compliment to her own good management, would save time on a week day.

Mr. Worthy, who found himself quite in a new world, returned home with his friend alone. In the evening he ventured to ask Bragwell, if he did not, on a Sunday night, at least, make it a custom to read and pray with his family. Bragwell told him, he was sorry to say he had no family at home, else he should like to do it for the sake of example. But as his servants worked hard all the week, his wife was of opinion that they should then have a little holiday. Mr. Worthy pressed it home upon him, if the utter neglect of his servants' principles was not likely to make a heavy article in his final account; and asked him if he did not believe that the too general liberty of meeting together, jaunting, and diverting themselves on Sunday evenings, was not often found to produce the worst effects on the morals of servants and the good order of families? "I put it to your conscience," said he, "Mr. Bragwell, whether Sunday, which was meant as a blessing and a benefit, is not, as it is commonly kept, turned into the most mischievous part of the week, by the selfish kindness of masters, who, not daring to set their servants about any public work, allot them that day to follow their own devices, that they themselves may with more rigour refuse them a little indulgence and a reasonable holiday, in the working part of the week, which a good servant has now and then a fair right to expect..."

Mr. Bragwell owned that Sunday had produced many mischiefs in his own family. That the young men and maids, having no eye upon them, frequently went to improper places with other servants, turned adrift like themselves. That in these parties the poor girls were too frequently led astray, and the men got to public houses and fives-playing. But it was none of his business to watch them. His family only did as others do;

indeed, it was his wife's concern; and as she was so good a manager on other days, that she would not spare them an hour to visit a sick father or mother, it would be hard, she said, if they might not have Sunday afternoon to themselves, and she could not blame them for making the most of it. Indeed, she was so indulgent in this particular, that she often excused the men from going to church, that they might serve the beasts,[146] and the maids, that they might get the milking done before the holiday part of the evening came on. She would not, indeed, hear of any competition between doing *her* work and taking their pleasure; but when the difference lay between their going to church and taking their pleasure, he must say that for his wife, she always inclined to the good-natured side of the question. She is strict enough in keeping them sober; because drunkenness is a costly sin, and, to do her justice, she does not care how little they sin at her expence.

"Well," said Mr. Worthy, "I always like to examine both sides fairly, and to see the different effects of opposite practices; now, which plan produces the greatest share of comfort to the master, and of profit to the servants in the long run? Your servants, 'tis likely, are very much attached to you; and very fond of living where they get their own way in so great a point."

"O," as to that, replied Bragwell, "you are quite out. My house is a scene of discord, mutiny, and discontent. And though there is not a better manager in England than my wife, yet she is always changing her servants; so that every quarter-day is a sort of Gaol Delivery at my house;[147] and when they go off, as they often do, at a moment's warning, to own the truth, I often give them money privately that they may not carry my wife before the Justice to get their wages."

"I see," said Mr. Worthy "that all your worldly compliances do not procure you even worldly happiness. As to my own family, I take care to let them see that their pleasure is bound up with their duty, and that what they may call my strictness, has nothing in view but their safety and happiness. By this means I commonly gain their love as well as secure their obedience. I know that, with all my care, I am liable to be disappointed, from the corruption that is in the world through sin. But whenever this happens, so far from encouraging me in remissness, it only serves to quicken my zeal. If by God's blessing my servant turns out a good Christian, I have been an humble instrument in his hand of saving a soul committed to my charge."

Mrs. Bragwell came home, but brought only one of her daughters with her; the other, she said, had given them the slip, and was gone with a young friend, and would not return for a day or two. Mr. Bragwell was greatly displeased; as he knew that young friend had but a slight character, and kept bad acquaintances. Mrs. Bragwell came in, all hurry and bustle, saying, if her family did not go to bed with the Lamb on Sundays, when they had nothing to do, how could they rise with the Lark on Mondays, when so much was to be done.

Mr. Worthy had this night much matter for reflection. "We need not," said he, "go into the great world to look for dissipation and vanity. We can find both in a farm-house. As for me and my house," continued he, "we will serve the Lord every day, but especially on Sundays. It is the day which the Lord hath made; hath made for himself; we will rejoice in it, and consider the religious use of it, not only as a duty, but as a privilege." The next morning Mr. Bragwell and his friend set out early for the Golden Lion...

Mr. Bragwell got home in high spirits...As soon as he came in...his wife...burst into a violent fit of passion..."It is all over: we want no more money. You are a ruined man! A wicked creature, scraping and working as we have done for her!" Bragwell trembled, but durst not ask what he dreaded to hear. His wife spared him the trouble, by crying out, as soon as her rage permitted, – "Polly is gone off!" Poor Bragwell's heart sunk within him; he grew sick and giddy, and as his wife's rage swallowed up her grief, so, in his grief, he almost forgot his anger...

Mr. Worthy, who though much concerned, was less discomposed now called to mind, that the young lady had not returned with her mother and sister the night before: he begged Mrs.

Bragwell to explain this sad story. She, instead of soothing her husband, fell to reproaching him. "It is all your fault," said she: "you were a fool for your pains. If I had had my way, the girls would never have kept company with any but men of substance." "Mrs. Bragwell," said Worthy, "if she has chosen a bad man, it would be still a misfortune, even though he had been rich." "O, that would alter the case," said she; "*a fat sorrow is better than a lean one.* But to marry a beggar." Here Miss Betsey, who stood sullenly by, put in a word, and said, "her sister, however, had not disgraced herself by having married a Farmer or a Tradesman; she had, at least, made choice of a Gentleman." "What marriage! what Gentleman?" cried the afflicted father. "Tell me the worst!" He was now informed that his darling daughter was gone off with a strolling player, who had been acting in the neighbouring villages lately. Miss Betsey again put in, saying, "he was no stroller, but a gentleman in disguise, who only acted for his own diversion." "Does he so?" said the now furious Bragwell, "then he shall be transported for mine." At this moment a letter was brought him from his new son-in-law, who desired his leave to wait upon him, and implore his forgiveness. He owned he had been shopman to a haberdasher, but thinking his person and talents ought not to be thrown away upon trade, and being also a little behind hand, he had taken to the stage with a view of making his fortune. That he had married Miss Bragwell entirely for love, and was sorry to mention so paltry a thing as money, which he despised, but that his wants were pressing, his landlord, to whom he was in debt, having been so vulgar as to threaten to send him to prison. He ended with saying, "I have been obliged to shock your daughter's delicacy, by confessing my unlucky real name: I believe I owe part of my success to my having assumed that of Augustus Frederick Theodosius. She is inconsolable at this confession, which, as you are now my father, I must also make to you, and subscribe myself, with many blushes, by the vulgar name of your dutiful son,   TIMOTHY INCLE."

"Oh!" cried the afflicted father, as he tore the letter in a rage, "Miss Bragwell married to a strolling actor! How shall I bear it?"

"Why, I would not bear it at all," cried the enraged mother. "I would never see her; I would never forgive her. I would let her starve at one corner of the barn, while that rascal, with all those Pagan, Popish names, was ranting away at the other." "Nay," said Miss Betsey, "if he is only a shopman, and if his name be really Timothy Incle, I would never forgive her neither. But who would have thought it by his looks, and by his monstrous genteel behaviour."

"Come, come," said Mr. Worthy, "were he really an honest haberdasher, I should think there was no other harm done, except the disobedience of the thing. Mr. Bragwell, this is no time to blame you, or hardly to reason with you. I feel for you sincerely. I ought not, perhaps, just at present, to reproach you for the mistaken manner in which you have bred up your daughters, as your error has brought its punishment along with it. You now see, because you now feel, the evil of a false education. It has ruined your daughter; your whole plan has led to some such end. The large sums you spent to qualify them as you thought for a high station, could do them nothing but harm, while your habits of life properly confined them to company of a lower station.[148] While they were better drest than the daughters of the first gentry they were worse taught, as to real knowledge, than the daughters of your plowmen.[149] Their vanity has been raised by excessive finery, and kept alive by excessive flattery. Every evil temper has been fostered by indulgence. Their pride has never been controlled. Their self-will has never been turned.[150] Their idleness has laid them open to every temptation, and their abundance has enabled them to gratify every desire. Their time, that precious talent, has been entirely wasted. Every thing they have been taught to do is of no use, while they are utterly unacquainted with all which they ought to have known. I deplore Miss Polly's false step. That she should have married a run-away shopman, turned stroller, I truly lament. But for what better husband was she qualified? For the wife of a Farmer, she was too idle; for the wife of a Tradesman, she was too expensive; for the wife of a Gentleman, she was too ignorant. You yourself was most to blame. You expected her to act wisely, though you never taught her that *fear of God which is the beginning of wisdom...*"[151]

Mrs. Bragwell attempted several times to interrupt Mr. Worthy, but her husband would not permit it. He felt the force of all his friend said, and encouraged him to proceed. Mr. Worthy thus went on: "It grieves me to say how much your own indiscretion has contributed even to bring on your present misfortune. You gave your countenance to this very company of strollers, though you knew they are acting in defiance to the laws of the land, to say no worse.[152] They go from town to town, and barn to barn, stripping the poor of their money, the young of their innocence, and all of their time. Do you remember with how much pride you told me that you had bespoke *The Bold Stroke for a Wife*, for the benefit of this very Mr. Frederic Theodosius? To this pernicious ribaldry you not only carried your own family, but wasted I know not how much money in treating your workmen's wives and children, in these hard times too, when they have scarcely bread to eat, or a shoe on their feet. And all this only that you might have the absurd pleasure of seeing those flattering words, *By Desire of Mr. Bragwell*, stuck up in Print at the Public-house, on the Blacksmith's shed, at the Turnpike-gate, and on the Barn-door."

Mr. Bragwell acknowledged, that his friend's rebuke was but too just, and he looked so very contrite as to raise the pity of Mr. Worthy, who, in a mild voice, thus went on: "What I have said is not so much to reproach you with the ruin of one daughter, as from a desire to save the other. Let Miss Betsey go home with me. I do not undertake to be her gaoler, but I will be her friend. She will find in my daughters kind companions, and in my wife a prudent guide. I know she will dislike us at first, but I do not despair in time of convincing her that a sober, humble, useful, pious life, is as necessary to make us happy on earth, as it is to fit us for heaven."

Poor Miss Betsey, though she declared it would be *frightful dull*, and *monstrous vulgar*, and *dismal melancholy*, yet was she so terrified at the discontent and grumbling which she would have to endure at home, that she sullenly consented. She had none of that filial tenderness which led her to wish to stay and soothe and comfort her afflicted father. All she thought about was to get out of the way of her mother's ill humour, and to carry so much finery with her as to fill the Miss Worthies with envy and respect. Poor girl! She did not know that envy was a feeling they never indulged; and that fine clothes were the last thing to draw their respect. Mr. Worthy took her home next day. When they reached his house, they found there young Wilson, Miss Betsey's old admirer. She was much pleased at this, and resolved to treat him well. But her good or ill treatment now signified but little. This young Grazier reverenced Mr. Worthy's character, and...had been thinking what a happiness it would be to marry a young woman bred up by such a father. He had heard much of the modesty and discretion of both the daughters, but his inclination now determined him in favour of the elder.

Mr. Worthy, who knew him to be a young man of good sense and sound principles, allowed him to become a visitor at his house, but deferred his consent to the marriage till he knew him more thoroughly. Mr. Wilson, from what he saw of the domestic piety of this family, improved daily both in the knowledge and practice of religion; and Mr. Worthy soon formed him into a most valuable character. During this time Miss Bragwell's hopes had revived, but though she appeared in a new dress almost every day, she had the mortification of being beheld with great indifference by one whom she had always secretly liked. Mr. Wilson married before her face a girl who was greatly her inferior in fortune, person, and appearance, but who was humble, frugal, meek, and pious. Miss Bragwell now strongly felt the truth of what Mr. Wilson had once told her, that a woman may make an excellent partner for a dance, who would make a very bad companion for life.

Hitherto Mr. Bragwell and his daughters had only learnt to regret their folly and vanity, as it had produced them mortification in this life; whether they were ever brought to a more serious sense of their errors, may be seen in a future part of this history.

Good Resolutions

Mr. Bragwell was so much afflicted at the disgraceful marriage of his daughter who ran off with Timothy Incle, the
strolling player, that he never fully recovered his spirits...Mr.
Bragwell was one of those people, who, even if they would be
thought to bear with tolerable submission such trials as appear
to be sent more immediately from Providence, yet think they
have a sort of right to rebel at every misfortune which befalls
them through the fault of a fellow creature; as if our fellow-
creatures were not the agents and instruments by which Providence often sees fit to try or to punish us. This imprudent
daughter Bragwell would not be brought to see or forgive, nor
was the degrading name of Mrs. Incle ever allowed to be
pronounced in his hearing. He had loved her with an excessive
and undue affection, and while she gratified his vanity by her
beauty and finery, he deemed her faults of little consequence;
but when she disappointed his ambition by a disgraceful marriage, all his natural affection only served to increase his resentment. Yet, though he regretted her crime less than his own
mortification, he never ceased in secret to lament her loss. She
soon found out she was undone, and wrote in a strain of bitter
repentance to ask his forgiveness. She owned that her husband,
whom she had supposed to be a man of fashion in disguise, was
a low person in distressed circumstances. She implored that her
father, though he refused to give her husband that fortune for
which alone it was now too plain he had married her, would at
least allow her some subsistence, for that Mr. Incle was much in
debt, and she feared in danger of a gaol. The father's heart was
half melted at this account, and his affection was for a time
awakened. But Mrs. Bragwell opposed his sending her any
assistance. She always made it a point of duty never to forgive;
"for she said it only encouraged those who had done wrong
once to do worst next time; for her part, she had never yet been
guilty of so mean and pitiful a weakness as to forgive any one;
for to pardon an injury always shewed either want of spirit to
feel it, or want of power to resent it. She was resolved she
would never squander the money for which she had worked

early and late on a baggage who had thrown herself away on a beggar, while she had a daughter single who might yet raise her family by a great match." I am sorry to say that Mrs. Bragwell's anger was not owing to the undutifulness of the daughter, or the worthlessness of the husband; poverty was in her eyes the grand crime. The doctrine of forgiveness, as a religious principle, made no more a part of Mr. Bragwell's system than of his wife's; but in natural feeling, particularly for this offending daughter, he much exceeded her.

In a few months the youngest Miss Bragwell desired leave to return home from Mr. Worthy's. She had, indeed, only consented to go thither as a less evil of the two, than staying in her father's house after her sister's elopement. But the sobriety and simplicity of Mr. Worthy's family were irksome to her. Habits of vanity and idleness were become so rooted in her mind, that any degree of restraint was a burthen; and though she was outwardly civil, it was easy to see that she longed to get away. She resolved, however, to profit by her sister's faults, and made her parents easy by assuring them she never would throw herself away on a *man who was worth nothing*. Encouraged by these promises, which were all that her parents thought they could in reason expect, her father allowed her to come home.

...the very day...there happened to be a grand ball at the next town on account of the assizes. An assize ball is a scene to which gentlemen and ladies periodically resort to celebrate the crimes and calamities of their fellow-creatures by dancing and music, and to divert themselves with feasting and drinking, while unhappy wretches are receiving sentence of death.

To this Ball Miss Bragwell went, dressed out with a double portion of finery, pouring out on her own head the whole bandbox of feathers and flowers her sister had left behind her. While she was at the ball her father formed many plans of religious reformation; he talked of lessening his business, that he might have more leisure for devotion; though not *just now* while the markets were so high; and began to think of sending a handsome subscription to the infirmary; though, on second thoughts, he concluded he need not be *in a hurry*, but leave it in his will; but to give, and repent, and reform, were three things he was bent upon. But when his daughter came home at night, so happy and so fine, and telling how "she had danced with 'Squire Squeeze the great Corn-Contractor, and how many fine things he had said to her, Mr. Bragwell felt the old spirit of the world return in its full force. A marriage with Mr. Dashall Squeeze, the contractor, was beyond his hopes; for Mr. Squeeze was supposed from a very low beginning to have got rich during the war. Mr. Squeeze had picked up as much of the history of his partner between the dances as he desired, he was convinced there would be no money wanting, for Miss Bragwell, who was now looked on as an only child, must needs be a great fortune, and Mr. Squeeze was too much used to advantageous contracts to let this slip. As he was gaudily dressed, and possessed all the arts of vulgar flattery, Miss Bragwell eagerly caught at his proposal to wait on her father next day. Squeeze was quite a man after Bragwell's own heart, a genius at getting money, a fine dashing fellow at spending it. He told his wife that this was the very sort of man for his daughter; for he got money like a jew, and spent it like a prince; but whether it was fairly got or wisely spent, he was too much a man of the world to inquire. Mrs. Bragwell was not so run away with by appearances, but that she desired her husband to be careful, and make quite sure it was the right Mr. Squeeze and no impostor. But being assured that Betsey would certainly keep her carriage, she never gave herself one thought with what sort of man she was to ride in it. To have one of her daughters to drive in her own coach filled up all her ideas of human happiness. The marriage was celebrated with great splendour, and Mr. and Mrs. Squeeze set off for London, where they had a house.

Mr. Bragwell now tried to forget that he had any other daughter, and...finding he was likely to have a grandchild, he became more worldly and ambitious than ever; thinking this a just pretence for adding house to house and field to field; and there is no stratagem by which men more deceive themselves, than when they make even unborn children a pretence for that rapine, or that hoarding of which their own covetousness is the true motive. Whenever he ventured to write to Mr. Worthy about the wealth, the gaiety, and the grandeur of Mr. and Mrs. Squeeze, that faithful friend honestly reminded him of the vanity and uncertainty of worldly greatness, and the error he had been guilty of in marrying his daughter before he had taken time to enquire into the real character of the man, saying, that he could not help foreboding that the happiness of a match made at a ball might have an untimely end. Though Mr. Bragwell had paid down a larger fortune than was prudent, for fear Mr. Squeeze should fly off, yet he was surprised to receive very soon a pressing letter from him, desiring him to advance a considerable sum, as he had the offer of an advantageous purchase, which he must lose for want of money. Bragwell was staggered, and refused to comply, but his wife told him he must not be shabby to such a gentleman as 'Squire Squeeze; for that she heard on all sides such accounts of their grandeur, their feasts, their carriages, and their liveries, that she and her husband ought even to deny themselves comforts to oblige such a generous son, who did all this in honour of their daughter; besides, if he did not send the money soon, they must be obliged to lay down their coach, and then she should never be able to shew her face again. At length Mr. Bragwell lent him the money on his bond: he knew Squeeze's income was large, for he had carefully enquired into this particular, and for the rest he took his word. Mrs. Squeeze also got great presents from her mother, by representing to her how expensively they were forced to live to keep up their credit, and what honor she was conferring on the family of the Bragwells, by spending their money in such grand company. "You can't imagine, dear mother," continued she, "how charmingly we live – I lye a-bed almost all day, and am up all night; but it is never dark for all that, for we burn such numbers of candles all at once, that the sun would be of no use at all in London. – Then I am so happy, for we are never quiet a moment, Sundays or working-days, nay, I should not know which was which, only that we have most pleasure on a Sunday, because it is the only day on which people have nothing to do but divert themselves. – Then the great folks are all so kind, and so good, they have not a bit of pride, for they will come and eat and drink, and win my money, just as if I was their equal, and if I have got but a cold, they are so very unhappy that they send to know how I do, and though I suppose they can't rest till the footman has told them, yet they are so polite, that if I have been dying they seem to have forgot it next time we meet, and not to know but they have seen me the day before. Oh! they are true friends; and for ever smiling, and so fond of one another, that they like to meet and enjoy one another's company by hundreds, and always think the more the merrier."

The style of her letters, however, altered in a few months. She owned that though things went on gayer and grander than ever, yet she hardly ever saw her husband, except her house was full of company, and cards or dancing was going on; that he was often so busy abroad he could not come home all night, that he always borrowed the money her mother sent her when he was going out on this nightly business; and that the last time she had asked *him* for money he cursed and swore, and bid her apply to the old farmer and his rib, who were made of money. This letter Mrs. Bragwell concealed from her husband.

At length on some change in public affairs, Mr. Squeeze, who had made an overcharge of some thousand pounds in one article, lost his contract, he was found to owe a large debt to government, and his accounts must be made up immediately. This was impossible, he had not only spent his large income without making any provision for his family, but had contracted heavy debts by gaming and other vices. His creditors poured in upon him. He wrote to Bragwell to borrow another sum; but without hinting at the loss of his Contract. These repeated demands made Bragwell so uneasy, that instead of sending him the money, he resolved to go himself secretly to London, and judge by his own eyes how things were going on, as his mind strangely misgave him. He got to Mr. Squeeze's house about eleven at night, and knocked gently, concluding that they must needs be gone to bed. But what was his astonishment to find the hall was full of men; he pushed through in spite of them, though to his great surprise they insisted on knowing his name. This affronted him: he refused, saying, "I am not ashamed of my name, it will pass for thousands in any market in the west of England." What was his amazement to see every room as full of card-tables and of fine gentlemen and ladies as it would hold; all was so light, and so gay, and so festive, and so grand, that he reproached himself for his suspicions, thought nothing too good for them, and resolved secretly to give Squeeze another five hundred pounds to help to keep up so much grandeur and happiness. At length seeing a footman he knew, he asked him where were his master and mistress, for he could not pick them out among the company. The man said that his master had just sent for his lady up stairs, and he believed that he was not well. Mr. Bragwell said he would go up himself and look for his daughter, as he could not speak so freely to her before all that company. He went up and knocked at the chamber door, and its not being opened, made him push it with some violence. He heard a bustling noise within, and again made a fruitless attempt to open the door. At this the noise increased, and Mr. Bragwell was struck to the heart at the sound of a pistol from within. He now kicked so violently against the door that it burst open, when the first sight he saw was his daughter falling to the ground in a fit, and Mr. Squeeze dying by a shot from a pistol which was dropping out of his hand. Mr. Bragwell was not the only person whom the sound of the pistol had alarmed. The servants, the company, all heard it, and all ran up to this scene of horror. Those who had the best of the game took care to bring up their tricks in their hands, having had the prudence to leave the very few who could be trusted to watch the stakes, while those who had a prospect of losing, profited by the confusion and threw up their cards. All was dismay and terror. Some ran for a surgeon, others examined the dying man, some removed Mrs. Squeeze to her bed, while poor Bragwell could neither see nor hear, nor do any thing. One of the company took up a letter which lay open upon the table, addressed *to Mr. Bragwell*, they read it, hoping it might explain the horrid mystery. It was as follows:

"Sir, Fetch home your daughter, I have ruined her, myself,

and the child to which she every hour expects to be a mother. I
have lost my contract. My debts are immense. You refuse me
money. I must die then; but I will die like a man of spirit. They
wait to take me to prison, I have two executions in my house;
but I have ten card-tables in it. I would die as I have lived. I
invited all this company, and have drunk hard since dinner to
get primed for the dreadful deed. My wife refuses to write to
you for another thousand, and she must take the consequences.
Vanity has been my ruin: it has caused all my crimes. Whoever is
resolved to live beyond his income is liable to every sin. He can
never say to himself thus far shalt thou go, and no farther.
Vanity led me to commit acts of rapine, that I might live in
splendour; vanity makes me commit self-murder, because I will
not live in poverty. The new philosophy[153] says, that death is an
eternal sleep; but the new philosophy lies. Do you take heed: I
am past repentance – Farewell. DASHALL SQUEEZE."

The dead body was removed, and Mr. Bragwell remaining
almost without speech or motion, the company began to think
of retiring, much out of humour at having their party so
disagreeably broken up: they comforted themselves, however,
that as it was *so early*, for it was now scarcely twelve, they could
finish their evening at another party or two; so completely do
habits of *pleasure*, as it is called, harden the heart, and steel it,
not only against virtuous impressions, but against natural feelings. Now it was that those who had nightly rioted at the
expence of these wretched people were the first to abuse them.
Not an offer of assistance was made to this poor forlorn woman;
not a word of kindness or of pity, nothing but censure was now
heard. "Why must these upstarts ape people of quality?" though
as long as these upstarts could feast them, their vulgarity and
their bad character had never been produced against them. "As
long as thou dost well unto thyself, men shall speak good of
thee." One guest, who, unluckily, had no other house to go to,
coolly said, "Squeeze might as well as have put off shooting
himself till the morning."

As every thing in the house was seized, Mr. Bragwell prevailed on his miserable daughter, weak as she was, next morning

to set out with him for the country. His acquaintance with polite life was short, but he had seen a great deal in a little time. They had a slow and a sad journey. In about a week, Mrs. Squeeze lay-in of a dead child, she herself languished a few days, and then died; and the afflicted parents saw the two darling objects of their ambition, for whose sakes they had made *too much haste to be rich*,[154] carried to the land where all things are forgotten. Mrs. Bragwell's grief, like her other passions, was extravagant, and poor Bragwell's sorrow was rendered so bitter by self reproach, that he would quite have sunk under it had he not thought of his old expedient in distress, that of sending for Mr. Worthy to comfort him...

Mr. Worthy attended his afflicted friend to the funeral of his unhappy daughter and her babe. The solemn service, the committing his late gay and beautiful daughter to darkness, to worms, and to corruption; the sight of the dead infant, for whose sake he had resumed all his schemes of vanity and covetousness, when he thought he had got the better of them, the melancholy conviction that all human prosperity ends in *ashes to ashes and dust to dust*,[155] had brought down Mr. Bragwell's soul into something of that humble frame in which Mr. Worthy had wished to see it. As soon as they returned home, he was beginning to seize the favourable moment for fixing these serious impressions, when they were unseasonably interrupted by the parish officer, who came to ask Mr. Bragwell what he was to do with a poor dying woman, who was travelling the country with her child, and was taken in a fit under the church-yard wall? "At first they thought she was dead," said the man; "but finding she still breathed, they have carried her into the work-house till she could give some account of herself." Mr. Bragwell told the man he was at that time too much overcome by sorrow to attend to business, but he would give him an answer to-morrow. "But, my friend," said Mr. Worthy, "the poor woman may die tonight: your mind is indeed not in a frame for worldly business, but there is no sorrow too great to forbid our attending the calls of duty. An act of christian charity will not disturb, but improve the seriousness of your spirit, and though you

cannot dry your own tears, God may in great mercy, permit you
to dry those of another. This may be one of those occasions for
which I told you life was worth keeping. Do let us see this
woman." Bragwell was not in a state either to consent or refuse,
and his friend drew him to the workhouse, about the door of
which stood a crowd of people. "She is not dead," said one: "she
moves her head." "But she wants air," said all of them, while
they all, according to custom, pushed so close upon her that it
was impossible she should get any. A fine boy of two or three
years old stood by her, crying, "Mammy is dead, mammy is
starved." Mr. Worthy made up to the poor woman, holding his
friend by the arm: to give her air he untied a large black bonnet
which hid her face, when Mr. Bragwell at that moment casting
his eyes on her, saw in this poor stranger the face of his own
run-away daughter, Mrs. Incle. He groaned, but could not
speak, and as he was turning away to conceal his anguish, the
little boy fondly caught hold of his hand, lisping out, – "O stay
and give mammy some bread." His heart yearned towards the
child, he grasped his little hand in his, while he sorrowfully said
to Mr. Worthy, "it is too much, send away the people. It is my
dear naughty child: *my punishment is greater than I can bear.*" Mr.
Worthy desired the people to go and leave the stranger to them;
but by this time she was no stranger to any of them. Pale and
meagre as was her face, and poor and shabby as was her dress
the proud and flaunting Miss Polly Bragwell was easily known
by every one present. They went away, but with the mean
revenge of little minds, they paid themselves by abuse, for all the
airs and insolence they had once endured from her. "Pride must
have a fall," said one. "I remember when she was too good to
speak to a poor body; where are her flounces and furbelows
now? It is come home to her at last. Her child looks as if he
would be glad of the worst bit she formerly denied us."

In the mean time Mr. Bragwell had sunk into an old wicker
chair which stood behind, and groaned out, "Lord forgive my
hard heart! Lord subdue my proud heart, create a clean heart,
renew a right spirit within me." This was perhaps, the first word
of genuine prayer he had ever offered up in his whole life.

Worthy overheard it and his heart rejoiced; but this was not a time for talking, but doing. He asked Bragwell what was to be done with the unfortunate woman, who now seemed to recover fast, but she did not see them, for they were behind. She embraced her boy, and faintly said – my child, what shall we do? *I will arise and go to my father, and say unto him, father, I have sinned against heaven and before thee.*[156]...The boy then sprung from his mother, and ran to Bragwell, saying, "Do be good to mammy." Mrs. Incle looking round, now perceived her father, she fell at his feet, saying, "O forgive your guilty child, and save your innocent one from starving." Bragwell sunk down by her, and prayed God to forgive both her and himself in terms of genuine sorrow. To hear words of real penitence and heart-felt prayer from this once high-minded father and vain daughter, was music to Worthy's ears, who thought this moment of outward misery was the only joyful one he had ever spent in the Bragwell family. He was resolved not to interfere, but to let the father's own feelings work out the way in which he was to act. Bragwell said nothing, but slowly led to his own house, holding the little boy by the hand, and pointing to Worthy to assist the feeble steps of his daughter, who once more entered her father's doors, but the dread of seeing her mother quite overpowered her. Mrs. Bragwell's heart was not changed, but sorrow had weakened her powers of resistance, and she rather suffered her daughter to come in, than gave her a kind reception. As soon as she was a little recovered, Mr. Bragwell desired his daughter to tell him how she happened to be at that place just at that time.

In a weak voice she began, "my tale, Sir, is short, but mournful." Now, I am very sorry that my Readers must wait for this short but mournful tale till next month.

Mrs. Incle's Story

"I left your house, my dear father," said Mrs. Incle, "with a heart full of vain triumph. I had no doubt but my husband was a great man who had put on that disguise to obtain my hand. Judge then what I felt to find that he was a needy impostor, who wanted my money, but did not care for me. This discovery, though it mortified did not humble me. I had neither affection to bear with the man who had deceived me, nor religion to improve by the disappointment. I have found that change of circumstances does not change the heart, till God is pleased to do it. My misfortune only taught me to rebel more against him. I thought God unjust, I accused my father, I was envious of my sister, I hated my husband; but never once did I blame myself. My husband picked up a wretched subsistence by joining himself to any low scheme of idleness that was going on. He would follow a mountebank, carry a dice-box, or fiddle at a fair. He was always taunting me for that gentility on which I so much valued myself. 'If I had married a poor working girl,' said he 'she could now have got her bread; but a fine lady without money is a burden to her husband and a plague to society.' Every trial which affection might have made lighter, we doubled by animosity; at length my husband was detected in using false dice, he fought with his accuser, both were seized by a press-gang, and sent to sea. I was now left to the wide world, and miserable as I had thought myself before, I soon found there were higher degrees of misery. I was near my time, without bread for myself, or hope for my child. I set out on foot in search of the village where I had heard my husband say his friends lived. It was a severe trial to my proud heart to stoop to those low people; but hunger is not delicate, and I was near perishing. My husband's parents received me kindly, saying, that "though they had nothing but what they earned by their labour, yet I was welcome to share their hard fare, for they trusted that God who sent mouths would send meat also." They gave me a small room and many necessaries, which they denied themselves."

"Oh, my child!" interrupted Bragwell, "every word cuts me to the heart. These poor people gladly gave thee of their little, while thy rich parents left thee to starve."

"How shall I own," continued Mrs. Incle, "that all this goodness could not soften my heart, for God had not yet touched it. I received all their kindness as a favour done to them. When my father brought me home any little dainty, and my mother kindly dressed it for me, I would not condescend to eat it with them, but devoured it sullenly in my little garret alone; suffering them to fetch and carry every thing I wanted. As my haughty behaviour was not likely to gain their affection, it was plain they did not love me; and as I had no notion that there were any other motives to good actions but fondness, or self-interest, I was puzzled to know what could make them so kind to me, for of the powerful and constrained law of christian charity I was quite ignorant. To cheat the weary hours, I looked about for some books, and found, among a few others of the same cast, *Doddridge's Rise and Progress of Religion*.[157] But all those sort of books were addressed to *sinners*; now as I knew I was not a sinner, I threw them away in disgust. Indeed they were ill suited to a taste formed by novels, to which reading I chiefly trace my ruin, for, vain as I was, I should never have run away had not my heart been tainted by those pernicious books.

"At length my little George was born. This added to the burden I had brought on this poor family, but it did not diminish their kindness, and we continued to share their scanty fare without any upbraiding on their part, or any gratitude on mine. Even this poor baby did not soften my heart; I wept over him indeed day and night, but they were tears of despair: I was always idle, and wasted those hours in sinful murmurs at his fate, which I should have employed in trying to maintain him. Hardship, grief, and impatience, at length brought on a fever. Death seemed now at hand, and I felt a gloomy satisfaction in the thought of being rid of my miseries, to which I fear was added a sullen joy, to think that you, Sir, and my mother, would be plagued to hear of my death when it would be too late, and in this your grief I anticipated a gloomy sort of revenge. But it pleased my merciful God not to let me thus perish in my sins. My poor mother-in-law sent for a good clergyman, who pointed out to me the danger of dying in that hard and unconverted state so forcibly, that I shuddered to find on what a dreadful precipice I stood. He prayed with me and for me so earnestly, that at length God, who is sometimes pleased to magnify his own glory in awakening those who are dead in trespasses and sins, was pleased, of his free grace, to open my blind eyes, and soften my stony heart. I saw myself a sinner, and prayed to be delivered from the wrath of God, in comparison of which the poverty and disgrace I now suffered appeared as nothing. Instead of reproaching Providence, or blaming my parents, or abusing my husband, I now learnt to condemn myself, to adore that God who had not cut me off in my ignorance, to pray for pardon for the past, and grace for the time to come. I now desired to submit to penury and hunger in this world, so that I might but live in the fear of God in this world, and enjoy his favour in the world to come. I now learnt to compare my present light sufferings as the consequence of my own sin, with those bitter sufferings of my Saviour which he endured for my sake, and I was ashamed of murmuring; but self-ignorance, conceit, and vanity, were so rooted in me that my progress was very gradual, and I had the sorrow to feel how much the power of long bad habits keeps down the growth of religion in the heart. I was so ignorant of divine things, that I hardly knew words to frame a prayer; but when I got acquainted with the psalms, I there learnt how to pour out the fulness of my heart, while in the Gospel I rejoiced to see what great things God had done for my soul.

"I now took down once more from the shelf *Doddridge's Rise and Progress*; and, oh! with what new eyes did I read it! I now saw clearly, that not only the thief and the drunkard, the murderer and the adulterer, are sinners, for that I knew before, but I found that the unbeliever, the selfish, the proud, the worldly-minded, all in short, who live without God in the world, are sinners. I did not now apply the reproofs I met with to my husband, or my father, or other people, as I used to do, but brought them home to myself. In this book I traced, with strong emotions and close self-application, the sinner through all his course; his first awakening, his convictions, repentance, joys, sorrows, backsliding and recovery, despondency, and delight, to a triumphant death-bed; and God was pleased to make it a chief instrument in bringing me to himself. Here it is," continued Mrs. Incle, untying her little bundle, and taking out a book, "accept it, my dear father, and I will pray that God may bless it to you, as He has done to me.

"When I was able to come down, I past[158] my time with these good old people, and soon won their affection. I was surprised to find they had very good sense, which I never had thought poor people could have; but indeed worldly persons do not know how much religion, while it mends the heart enlightens the understanding also. I now regretted the evenings I had wasted in my solitary garret, when I might have passed them in reading the Bible with these good folks. This was their refreshing cordial after a weary day, which sweetened the pains of want and age. I expressed my surprise that my unfortunate husband, the son of such pious parents, should have turned out so ill: the poor old man said, with tears, 'I fear we have been guilty of the sin of Eli: our love was of the wrong sort.[159] Alas! like him, *we honoured our son more than God*, and God has smitten us for it. We shewed him what was right, but through a false indulgence, we did not correct him for what was wrong. We were blind to his faults. He was a handsome boy, with sprightly parts; we took too much delight in those outward things. He soon got above our management, and became vain, idle, and extravagant, and when we sought to restrain him it was then too late. We humbled ourselves before God; but he was pleased to make our sin become its own punishment. Timothy grew worse and worse, till he was forced to abscond for a misdemeanor, after which we never saw him, but have often heard of him changing from one idle way of life to another, *Unstable as water*;[160] he has been a footman, a soldier, a shopman, and a strolling actor. With deep sorrow we trace back his vices to our ungoverned fondness; that lively and sharp wit, by which he has been able to carry on such a variety of wild schemes, might, if we had used him to bear reproof in his youth, have enabled him to have done great service for God and his country. But our flattery made him wise in his own conceit. We indulged our own vanity, and have destroyed his soul.'"

Here Mr. Worthy stopped Mrs. Incle, saying, that "whenever he heard it lamented that the children of pious parents often turned out so ill, he could not help thinking that there must be frequently something of this sort of error in the bringing them up: he knew, indeed, some instances to the contrary, but he believed, that from Eli the Priest, to Incle the Labourer, much more than half the failures of this sort might be traced to some mistake, or vanity, or bad judgment, or sinful indulgence in the parents."

"I now looked about," continued Mrs. Incle, "in order to see in what I could assist my poor mother, regretting, more heartily than she did that I knew no one thing that was of any use. I was so desirous of humbling myself before God and her, that I offered even to try to wash." – "You wash!" exclaimed Bragwell, starting up with great emotion: "Heaven forbid that with such a fortune and education Miss Bragwell should be seen at a washing-tub." This vain father, who could bear to hear of her distresses and her sins, could not bear to hear of her washing. Mr. Worthy stopped him, saying, "As to her fortune, you know you refused to give her any; and as to her education, you see it had not taught her how to do any thing better. I am sorry you do not see in this instance the beauty of Christian humility. For my own part, I set a greater value on such an active proof of it than on a whole volume of professions."

Mrs. Incle went on: "What to do to get a penny I knew not. Making of filigree or fringe, or card purses, or cutting out paper, or dancing and singing, was of no use in our village. The shopkeeper indeed would have taken me, if I had known any thing of accounts; and the clergyman could have got me a nursery-maid's place if I could have done good plain work. I made some awkward attempts to learn to spin and knit, when my mother's wheel or knitting lay by, but I spoilt both through my ignorance. At last I luckily thought upon the fine netting I used to make for my trimmings, and it struck me that I might turn this to some little account. I procured some twine, and worked early and late to make nets for fishermen, and cabbage-nets.[161] I was so pleased that I had at last found an opportunity to shew my good will by this mean work, that I regretted my little George was not big enough to contribute his share to our support by travelling about to sell my nets."

"Cabbage nets!" exclaimed Bragwell, "There is no bearing

this. Cabbage-nets! My grandson hawk cabbage-nets! How could you think of such a scandalous thing?" "Sir," said Mrs. Incle, mildly, "I am now convinced that nothing is scandalous which is not wicked. Besides, we were in want; and necessity, as well as piety, would have reconciled me to this mean trade." Mr. Bragwell groaned, and bade her go on.

"In the mean time, my little George grew a fine boy; and I adored the goodness of God, who, in the sweetness of maternal love, had given me a reward for many sufferings. Instead of indulging a gloomy distrust about the fate of this child, I resigned him to the will of God. Instead of lamenting because he was not likely to be rich, I was resolved to bring him up with such notions as might make him contented to be poor. I thought, if I could subdue all vanity and selfishness in him, I should make him a happier man than if I had thousands to bestow on him, and I trusted that I should be rewarded for every painful act of present self-denial by the future virtue and happiness of my child. Can you believe it, my dear father, my days now past[162] not unhappily? I worked hard all day, and that alone is a source of happiness beyond what the idle can guess. After my child was asleep at night, I read the Bible to my parents, whose eyes now began to fail them. We then thanked God over our frugal supper of potatoes, and talked over the holy men of old, the saints, and the martyrs, who would have thought our homely fare a luxury. We compared our peace, and liberty, and safety, with their bonds, and imprisonment, and tortures; and should have been ashamed of a murmur. We then joined in prayer, in which my absent parents and my husband were never forgotten and went to rest in charity with the whole world, and at peace in our own souls."

"Oh, my forgiving child!" interrupted Mr. Bragwell, sobbing; "and didst thou really pray for thy unnatural father, and lie down in rest and peace? Then let me tell thee thou wast better off than thy mother and I were – but no more of this – go on."

"Whether my father-in-law had worked beyond his strength, in order to support me and my child, I know not, but he was taken dangerously ill. While he lay in this state, we received an account that my husband was dead in the West Indies of the yellow fever, which has carried off such numbers of our countrymen;[163] we all wept together, and prayed that his awful death might quicken us in preparing for our own. This shock, joined to the fatigue of nursing her sick husband, soon brought my poor mother to death's door. I nursed them both, and felt a satisfaction in giving them all I had to bestow, my attendance, my tears, and my prayers. I who was once so nice and so proud, so disdainful in the midst of plenty, and so impatient under the smallest inconvenience, was now enabled to glorify God by my activity and my submission. After having watched by these poor people the whole night, I sat down to breakfast on my dry crust and coarse dish of tea, without a murmur; my greatest grief was, lest I should bring away the infection to my dear boy. I prayed to know what it was my duty to do between my dying parents and my helpless child. 'To take care of the sick and aged' seemed to be the answer. So I offered up my child to him who is the father of the fatherless, and he spared him to me.

"The cheerful piety with which these good people breathed their last proved to me, that the temper of mind with which the pious poor commonly meet death is the grand compensation made them by providence for all the hardships of their inferior condition. If they have had few joys and comforts in life already, and have still fewer hopes in store, is not all fully made up to them by their being enabled to leave this world with stronger desires of heaven, and without those bitter regrets after the good things of this life, which add to the dying tortures of the worldly rich? To the forlorn and destitute death is not so terrible as it is to him who *sits at ease in his possessions*, and who fears that this night his soul shall be required of him."

Mr. Bragwell felt this remark more deeply than his daughter meant he should. He wept, and bade her proceed.

"I followed my departed parents to the same grave, and wept over them, but not as one who had no hope. They had neither houses nor lands to leave me, but they left me their Bible, their blessing, and their example, of which I humbly trust I shall feel the benefits when all the riches of this world shall have an end.

Their few effects, consisting of some poor household goods, and some working-tools, hardly sufficed to pay their funeral expences. I was soon attacked with the same fever, and saw myself, as I thought, dying the second time; my danger was the same, but my views were changed. I now saw eternity in a more awful light than I had done, when I wickedly thought death might be gloomily called upon as a refuge from every common trouble. Though I had still reason to be humbled on account of my sin, yet, through the grace of God, I saw Death stripped of his sting and robbed of his terrors, *through him who loved me, and gave himself for me.*

"I recovered however, and was chiefly supported by the kind clergyman's charity. When I felt myself nourished and cheered by a little tea or broth, which he daily sent me from his own slender provision, my heart smote me to think how I had daily sat down at home to a plentiful dinner, without any sense of thankfulness for my own abundance, or without inquiring whether my poor sick neighbours were starving, and I sorrowfully remembered, that what my poor sister and I used to waste through daintiness would now have comfortably fed myself and child. Believe me, my dear mother, a labouring man who has been brought low by a fever might often be restored to his work some weeks sooner, if on his recovery he was nourished and strengthened by a good bit from a farmer's table. Less than is often thrown to a favourite spaniel would suffice, so that the expence would be almost nothing to the giver, while to the receiver it would bring health, and strength, and comfort.

"By the time I was tolerably recovered, I was forced to leave the house. I had no human prospect of subsistence. I humbly asked of God to direct my steps, and to give me entire obedience to his will. I then cast my eyes mournfully on my child, and though prayer had relieved my heart of a load which without it would have been intolerable, my tears flowed fast, while I cried out in the bitterness of my soul, *How many hired servants of my father have bread enough, and to spare, and I perish with hunger.*[164] This text appeared a kind of answer to my prayer, and gave me courage to make one more attempt to soften you in my favour.

I resolved to set out directly to find you, to confess my disobedience, and to beg a scanty pittance with which I and my child might be meanly supported in some distant country, where we should not disgrace our more happy relations. We set out and travelled as fast as my weak health and poor George's little feet and ragged shoes would permit. I brought a little bundle of such work and necessaries as I had left, by selling which we subsisted on the road." "I hope," interrupted Bragwell, "there were no cabbage-nets in it?" "At least," said her mother, "I hope you did not sell them near home." "No, I had none left," said Mrs. Incle, "or I should have done it. I got many a lift in a waggon for my child and my bundle, which was a great relief to me. And here I cannot help saying, I wish drivers would not be too hard in their demands if they help a poor sick traveller on a mile or two, it proves a great relief to weary bodies and naked feet; and such little cheap charities may be considered as *the cup of cold water*, which, if given on right grounds, *shall not lose its reward*."[165] Here Bragwell sighed, to think that when mounted on his fine bay mare, or driving his neat chaise, it had never once crossed his mind that the poor way worn foot traveller was not equally at his ease, or that shoes were a necessary accommodation. Those who want nothing are apt to forget how many there are who want every thing. – Mrs. Incle went on, "I got to this village about seven this evening, and while I sat on the church yard wall to rest and meditate how I should make myself known at home, I saw a funeral; I enquired whose it was, and learnt it was my sister's. This was too much for me. I sunk[166] down in a fit, and knew nothing that happened to me from that moment till I found myself in the workhouse with my father and Mr. Worthy."

Here Mrs. Incle stopped. Grief, shame, pride, and remorse, had quite overcome Mr. Bragwell. He wept like a child, and said he hoped his daughter would pray for him, for that he was not in a condition to pray for himself, though he found nothing else could give him any comfort. His deep dejection brought on a fit of sickness: "O!" said he, "I now begin to feel an expression in the sacrament which I used to repeat without thinking it had any meaning, *the remembrance of my sins is grievous*, the burden of them is *intolerable*.[167] O it is awful to think what a sinner a man may be, and yet retain a decent character! How many thousands are in my condition, taking to themselves all the credit of their prosperity, instead of giving God the glory! Heaping up riches to their hurt, instead of dealing their bread to the hungry. O let those who hear of the Bragwell family, never say that *vanity is a little sin*. In me it has been the fruitful parent of a thousand sins, selfishness, hardness of heart, forgetfulness of God. In one of my sons vanity was the cause of rapine, injustice, extravagance, ruin, self-murder. Both my daughters were undone by vanity, though it only wore the more harmless shape of dress, idleness, and dissipation. The husband of my daughter Incle it destroyed, by leading him to live above his station, and to despise labour. Vanity ensnared the souls even of his pious parents, for while it led them to wish to see their son in a better condition, it led them to allow him such indulgences as were unfit for his own. O you who hear of us, humble yourselves under the mighty hand of God. Resist high thoughts. If you set a value on finery, look into that grave; behold the mouldering body of my Betsey, who now says to *Corruption, thou art my father, and to the worm, thou art my mother and my sister*.[168] Look at the bloody and brainless head of her husband. O Mr. Worthy, how does Providence mock at human foresight! I have been greedy of gain, that the son of Mr. Squeeze might be a great man; he is dead; while the child of Timothy Incle, whom I had doomed to beggary, will be my heir. Mr. Worthy, to you I commit this boy's education. Teach him to value his immortal soul more, and the good things of this life less, than I have done. Bring him up in the fear of God, and in the government of his passions. Teach him that unbelief and pride are at the root of all sin. "I have found this to my cost. I trusted in my riches; I said, tomorrow shall be as this day and more abundant. I did not remember that *for all these things God would bring me to judgment*. I am not sure that I believed in a judgment."

Bragwell at length grew better but he never recovered his spirits. The conduct of Mrs. Incle through life was that of an humble Christian. She sold all her sister's finery, which her father had given her, and gave the money to the poor, saying, it did not become one who professed penitence to return to the gaieties of life. Mr. Bragwell did not oppose this; not that he had fully acquired a just notion of the self-denying spirit of religion, but having a head not very clear at making distinctions, he was never able, after the sight of Squeeze's mangled body, to think of gaiety and grandeur, without thinking at the same time of a pistol and bloody brains; for as his first introduction into gay life had presented him with all these objects at one view, he never afterwards could separate them in his mind. He even kept his fine beaufet of plate always shut, because it brought to his mind the grand unpaid-for sideboard that he had seen laid out for Mr. Squeeze's supper, to the remembrance of which he could not help tacking the idea of debts, prisons, executions, and self-murder.

Mr. Bragwell's heart had been so buried in the love of the world, and evil habits were become so rooted in him, that the progress he made in religion was slow; yet he earnestly prayed and struggled against sin and vanity; and when his unfeeling wife declared she could not love the boy unless he was called by their name instead of Incle, Mr. Bragwell would never consent, saying he stood in need of every help against pride. He also got the letter which Squeeze wrote just before he shot himself framed and glazed; this he hung up in his chamber, and made it a rule to go and read it as often as he found his heart disposed to VANITY.

STRICTURES
ON THE
MODERN SYSTEM
OF
FEMALE EDUCATION.
WITH
A VIEW OF THE PRINCIPLES AND CONDUCT PREVALENT
AMONG WOMEN OF RANK AND FORTUNE
[1799]

INTRODUCTION.

It is a singular injustice which is often exercised towards women, first to give them a very defective Education, and then to expect from them the most undeviating purity of conduct; – to train them in such a manner as shall lay them open to the most dangerous faults, and then to censure them for not proving faultless. Is it not unreasonable and unjust, to express disappointment if our daughters should, in their subsequent lives, turn out precisely that very kind of character for which it would be evident to an unprejudiced by-stander that the whole scope and tenor of their instruction had been systematically preparing them?

Some reflections on the present erroneous system are here with great deference submitted to public consideration. The Author is apprehensive that she shall be accused of betraying the interests of her sex by laying open their defects: but surely, an earnest wish to turn their attention to objects calculated to promote their true dignity, is not the office of an enemy: so to expose the weakness of the land as to suggest the necessity of internal improvement, and to point out the means of effectual defence, is not treachery, but patriotism.

Again, it may be objected to this little work, that many errors
are here ascribed to women which by no means belong to them
exclusively, and that it has seemed to confine to the sex those
faults which are common to the species: but this is in some
measure unavoidable. In speaking on the qualities of one sex the
moralist is somewhat in the situation of the Geographer, who is
treating on the nature of one country: – the air, soil, and
produce of the land which he is describing, cannot fail in many
essential points to resemble those of other countries under the
same parallel; yet it is his business to descant on the one without
adverting to the other: and though in drawing his map he may
happen to introduce some of the neighbouring coast, yet his
principal attention must be confined to that country he pro-
poses to describe, without taking into account the resembling
circumstances of the adjacent shores.

It may be objected also that the opinion here suggested on
the state of manners among the higher classes of our countrywomen, may seem to controvert the just encomiums of modern
travellers, who unanimously concur in ascribing a decided
superiority to the ladies of this country over those of every
other. But such is the state of manners in most of those
countries with which the comparison has been made, that the
comparative praise is almost an injury to *English* women. To be
flattered for excelling those whose standard of excellence is very
low, is but a degrading kind of commendation; for the value of
all praise derived from superiority depends on the worth of the
competitor. The character of British ladies, with all the
unparalled[169] advantages they possess, must never be determined by a comparison with the women of other nations, but by
what they themselves might be if all their talents and unrivalled
opportunities were turned to the best account.

Again, it may be said, that the Author is less disposed to
expatiate on excellence than error: but the office of the historian
of human manners is not panegyric, but delineation. Were the
end in view eulogium and not improvement, eulogium would
have been far more gratifying, nor would just objects for praise
have been difficult to find. Even in her own limited sphere of

observation, the Author is herself acquainted with much excellence in the class of which she treats; – with women who,
possessing learning which would be thought extensive in the
other sex, set an example of deep humility to their own; –
women who, distinguished for wit and genius, are eminent for
domestic qualities; – who, excelling in the fine arts, have carefully enriched their understandings; – who, enjoying great afflu-
ence, devote it to the glory of God; – who, possessing elevated
rank, think their noblest style and title is that of a Christian. –

That there is also much worth which is little known, she is
persuaded; for it is the modest nature of goodness to exert itself
quietly, while a few characters of the opposite cast seem, by the
rumour of their exploits, to fill the world; and by their noise to
multiply their numbers. For it will generally be found in any
bustle for notice, that the minority, by occupying the fore-
ground, so seize the public attention and monopolize the public
talk, that *they* appear to be the great body: a few active spirits,
provided their activity take the wrong turn and support the
wrong cause, seem to fill the scene; and a few disturbers of
order, who have the talent of thus exciting a false idea of their
multitudes by their mischiefs, actually gain strength and swell
their numbers, by this fallacious arithmetic.

But the present work is no more intended for a panegyric on
those purer characters who, acting from higher motives, seek
not human praise, than for a satire on the avowedly licentious,
who, acting from no motives but the impulse of the moment or
the predominance of fashion, dislike no censure, so it may serve
to rescue them from neglect or oblivion.

...the Strictures on Modern Education in the first of these
Volumes, and on the Habits of polished Life in the second, will
not be found so repugnant to truth, and reason, and common
sense, as may on a first view be supposed...

BATH,
March 14, 1799.

CHAP. I.

*Address to women of rank and fortune, on the effects of their influence on
society. — Suggestions for the exertion of it in various instances.*

Among the talents for the application of which women of the
higher class will be peculiarly accountable, there is one, the
importance of which they can scarcely rate too highly. This
talent is influence...and when one considers the variety of
mischiefs which an ill-directed influence has been known to
produce, one is led to reflect with the most sanguine hope on
the beneficial effects to be expected from the same powerful
force when exerted in its true direction.

The general state of civilized society depends more than those
are aware, who are not accustomed to scrutinize into the springs
of human action, on the prevailing sentiments and habits of
women, and on the nature and degree of the estimation in
which they are held. Even those who admit the power of female
elegance on the manners of men, do not always attend to the
influence of female principles on their character. In the former
case, indeed, women are apt to be sufficiently conscious of their
power, and not backward in turning it to account. But there are
nobler objects to be effected by the exertion of their powers;
and unfortunately, ladies, who are often unreasonably confident
where they ought to be diffident, are sometimes capriciously
diffident just when they ought to feel where their true importance lies; and, feeling, to exert it. To use their boasted power
over mankind to no higher purpose than the gratification of
vanity or the indulgence of pleasure, is the degrading triumph of
those fair victims to luxury, caprice, and despotism, whom the
laws and the religion of the voluptuous prophet of Arabia
exclude from light, and liberty, and knowledge; and it is humbling to reflect, that in those countries in which fondness for the
mere persons of women is carried to the highest excess, *they are
slaves*; and that their moral and intellectual degradation increases

in direct proportion to the adoration which is paid to mere external charms.[170]

But I turn to the bright reverse of this mortifying scene; to a country where our sex enjoys the blessings of liberal instruction, of reasonable laws, of a pure religion, and all the endearing pleasures of an equal, social, virtuous, and delightful intercourse: I turn to them with a confident hope, that women, thus richly endowed with the bounties of Providence, will not content themselves with polishing, when they are able to reform; with entertaining, when they may awaken; and with captivating for a day, when they may bring into action powers of which the effects may be commensurate with eternity.

In this moment of alarm and peril,[171] I would call on them with a "warning voice," which should stir up every latent principle in their minds, and kindle every slumbering energy in their hearts; I would call on them to come forward, and contribute their full and fair proportion towards the saving of their country. But I would call on them to come forward, without departing from the refinement of their character, without derogating from the dignity of their rank, without blemishing the delicacy of their sex: I would call them to the best and most appropriate exertion of their power, to raise the depressed tone of public morals, to awaken the drowsy spirit of religious principle, and to re-animate the dormant powers of active piety. They know too well how imperiously they give the law to manners, and with how despotic a sway they fix the standard of fashion. But this is not enough; this is a low mark, a prize not worthy of their high and holy calling. For, on the use which women of the superior class may be disposed to make of that power delegated to them by the courtesy of custom, by the honest gallantry of the heart, by the imperious controul of virtuous affections, by the habits of civilized states, by the usages of polished society; on the use, I say, which they shall hereafter make of this influence, will depend, in no low degree, the well-being of those states, and the virtue and happiness, nay perhaps the very existence of that society.

At this period, when our country can only hope to stand by

opposing a bold and noble *unanimity* to the most tremendous
confederacies against religion and order, and governments,
which the world ever saw; what an accession would it bring to
the public strength, could we prevail on beauty, and rank, and
talents, and virtue, confederating their several powers, to come
forward with a patriotism at once firm and feminine for the
general good! I am not sounding an alarm to female warriors, or
exciting female politicians: I hardly know which of the two is
the most disgusting and unnatural character. Propriety is to a
woman what the great Roman orator says action is to an orator;
it is the first, the second, the third requisite.[172] A woman may
be knowing, active, witty, and amusing; but without propriety
she cannot be amiable. Propriety is the centre in which all the
lines of duty and of agreeableness meet. It is to character what
proportion is to figure, and grace to attitude. It does not depend
on any one perfection; but it is the result of general excellence.
It shews itself by a regular, orderly, undeviating course; and
never starts from its sober orbit into any splendid eccentricities;
for it would be ashamed of such praise as it might extort by any
aberrations from its proper path. It renounces all commendation
but what is characteristic; and I would make it the criterion of
true taste, right principle, and genuine feeling, in a woman,
whether she would be less touched with all the flattery of
romantic and exaggerated panegyric, than with that beautiful
picture of correct and elegant propriety, which Milton draws of
our first mother, when he delineates

> 'Those thousand decencies which daily flow
> From all her words and actions.'[173]

Even the influence of religion is to be exercised with discretion. A female Polemic wanders almost as far from the limits
prescribed to her sex, as a female Machiavel or warlike
Thalestris.[174] Fierceness and bigotry have made almost as few
converts as the sword, and both are peculiarly ungraceful in a
female...

I am persuaded, if many a one, who is now disseminating
unintended mischief, under the dangerous notion that there is
no harm in any thing short of positive vice; and under the false

colours of that indolent humility, "What good can I do?" could be brought to see in its collected force the annual aggregate of the random evil she is daily doing, by constantly throwing a *little* casual weight into the wrong scale, by mere inconsiderate and unguarded chat, she would start from her self complacent dream. If she could conceive how much she may be diminishing the good impressions of *young* men; and if she could imagine how little amiable levity or irreligion make her appear in the eyes of those who are older and abler, (however loose their own principles may be,) she would correct herself in the first instance, from pure good nature; and in the second, from worldly prudence and mere self-love. But on how much higher ground would she restrain herself, if she habitually took into account the important doctrine of consequences; and if she reflected that the lesser but more habitual corruptions make up by their number, what they may seem to come short of by their weight; then perhaps she would find that among the higher class of women, *inconsideration* is adding more to the daily quantity of evil than almost all the more ostensible causes put together.

There is an instrument of inconceivable force, when it is employed against the interests of christianity. It is not reasoning, for that may be answered; it is not learning, for luckily the infidel is not seldom ignorant; it is not invective, for we leave so coarse an engine to the hands of the vulgar; it is not evidence, for happily we have that all on our side. It is RIDICULE, the most deadly weapon in the whole arsenal of impiety, and which becomes an almost unerring shaft, when directed by a fair and fashionable hand. No maxim has been more readily adopted, or is more intrinsically false, than that which the fascinating eloquence of a noble sceptic of the last age contrived to render so popular, that "ridicule is the test of truth."[175] It is no test of truth itself; but of their firmness who assert the cause of truth, it is indeed a severe test. This light, keen, missile weapon, the irresolute, unconfirmed Christian, will find it harder to withstand, than the whole heavy artillery of infidelity united.

A young man of the better sort, just entered upon the world with a certain share of good dispositions and right feelings, not ignorant of the evidences, nor destitute of the principles of Christianity; without parting with his respect for religion, he sets out with the too natural wish of making himself a reputation, and of standing well with the fashionable part of the female world. He preserves for a time a horror of vice, which makes it not difficult for him to resist the grosser corruptions of society; he can as yet repel profaneness; nay he can withstand the banter of a club. He has sense enough to see through the miserable fallacies of the new philosophy, and spirit enough to expose its malignity.[176] So far he does well, and you are ready to congratulate him on his security. You are mistaken: the principles of the ardent, and hitherto promising adventurer are shaken, just in that very society, where, while he was looking for pleasure, he doubted not of safety. In the society of certain women of good fashion and no ill fame, he makes shipwreck of his religion. He sees them treat with levity or derision subjects which he has been used to hear named with respect. He could confute an argument, he could unravel a sophistry; but he cannot stand a laugh. A sneer, not at the truth of religion, for that perhaps they do not disbelieve, but at its gravity, its unseasonableness, its dulness, puts all his resolution to flight. He feels his mistake, and struggles to recover his credit; in order to which, he adopts the gay affectation of trying to seem worse than he really is; he goes on to say things which he does not believe, and to deny things which he does believe; and all to efface the first impression, and to recover a reputation which he has committed to *their* hands, on whose report he knows he shall stand or fall, in those circles in which he is ambitious to shine.

That cold compound of irony, irreligion, selfishness, and sneer, which make up what the French (from whom we borrow the thing as well as the word) so well express by the term *persiflage*, has of late years made an incredible progress in blasting the opening buds of piety in young persons of fashion.[177] A cold pleasantry, a temporary cant word, the jargon of the day, for the "great vulgar" have their jargon, blight the first promise of seriousness. The ladies of *ton* have certain watch-words, which may be detected as indications of this spirit. The clergy are spoken of under the contemptuous appellation of *The Parsons*. Some ludicrous association is infallibly combined with every idea of religion. If a warm-hearted youth has ventured to name with enthusiasm some eminently pious character, his glowing ardour is extinguished with a laugh; and a drawling declaration that the person in question is really a mighty *harmless* good creature, is uttered in a tone which leads the youth secretly to vow, that whatever else he may be, he will never be a good harmless creature.

Nor is ridicule more dangerous to true piety than to true taste. An age which values itself on parody, burlesque, irony, and caricature, produces little that is sublime, either in genius or in virtue; but they *amuse*, and we live in an age which *must* be amused, though genius, feeling, truth, and principle, be the sacrifice. Nothing chills the ardours of devotion like a frigid sarcasm; and, in the season of youth, the mind should be kept particularly clear of all light associations...

There was a time when a variety of epithets were thought necessary to express various kinds of excellence, and when the different qualities of the mind were distinguished by appropriate and discriminating terms; when the words venerable, learned, sagacious, profound, acute, pious, ingenious, elegant, agreeable, wise or witty, were used as specific marks of distinct characters. But the legislators of fashion have of late years thought proper to comprise all merit in one established epithet, and it must be confessed to be a very desirable one as far as it goes. This epithet is exclusively and indiscriminately applied wherever commendation is intended. The word *pleasant* now serves to combine and express all moral and intellectual excellence. Every individual, from the gravest professors of the gravest profession, down to the trifler who is of no profession at all, must earn the epithet of *pleasant*, or must be contented to be nothing; but must be consigned over to ridicule, under the vulgar and inexpressive cant word of a *bore*.[178] This is the mortifying designation of many a respectable man, who, though of much worth and much ability, cannot perhaps clearly make out his letters patent to the title of *pleasant*. But, according to this modern classification, there is no intermediate state, but all are comprised within the ample bounds of one or other of these two terms.

We ought to be more on our guard against this spirit of ridicule, because, whatever may be the character of the present day, its faults do not spring from the redundancies of great qualities, or the overflowings of extravagant virtues. It is well if more correct views of life, a more regular administration of laws, and a more settled state of society, have helped to restrain the excesses of the heroic ages, when love and war were considered as the great and sole business of human life. Yet, if that period was marked by a romantic extravagance, and the present by an indolent selfishness, our superiority is not so triumphantly decisive, as, in the vanity of our hearts, we may be ready to imagine.

I do not wish to bring back the frantic reign of chivalry, nor to reinstate women in that fantastic empire in which they then sat enthroned in the hearts, or rather in the imaginations of men. Common sense is an excellent material of universal application, which the sagacity of latter ages has seized upon, and rationally applied to the business of common life. But let us not forget, in the insolence of acknowledged superiority, that it was religion and chastity, operating on the romantic spirit of those times, which established the despotic sway of woman; and though she now no longer looks down on her adoring votaries, from the pedestal to which an absurd idolatry had lifted her, yet let her remember that it is the same religion and chastity which once raised her to such an elevation, that must still furnish the noblest energies of her character.

While we lawfully ridicule the absurdities which we have abandoned, let us not plume ourselves on that spirit of novelty which glories in the opposite extreme. If the manners of the period in question were affected, and if the gallantry was unnatural, yet the tone of virtue was high; and let us remember that constancy, purity, and honour, are not ridiculous in themselves, though they may unluckily be associated with qualities which are so; and women of delicacy would do well to reflect, when descanting on those exploded manners, how far it be decorous to deride with too broad a laugh, attachments which could subsist on remote gratifications; or grossly to ridicule the taste which led the admirer to sacrifice pleasure to respect, and inclination to honour; to sneer at that purity which made self-denial a proof of affection, to call in question the sound understanding of him who preferred the fame of his mistress to his own indulgence.

One cannot but be struck with the wonderful contrast exhibited to our view, when we contemplate the manners of the two periods in question. In the former, all the flower of Europe smit with a delirious gallantry; all that was young and noble, and brave and great, with a fanatic frenzy and preposterous contempt of danger, traversed seas, and scaled mountains, and compassed a large portion of the globe, at the expence of ease, and fortune, and life, for the unprofitable project of rescuing, by force of arms, from the hands of infidels, the sepulchre of that Saviour, whom, *in the other period*, their posterity would think it the height of fanaticism so much as to name in good company: whose altars they desert, whose temples they neglect; and though in more than one country at least they still call themselves by his name, yet too many consider it rather as a political than a religious distinction; too many, it is to be feared, contemn his precepts; still more are ashamed of his doctrines, and not a few reject his sacrifice.

But in an age when inversion is the order of the day, the modern idea of improvement does not consist in altering, but extirpating.[179] We do not reform, but subvert. We do not correct old systems, but demolish them, fancying that when every thing shall be new it will be perfect. Not to have been wrong, but to have been at all, is the crime. Excellence is no longer considered as an experimental thing which is to grow gradually out of observation and practice, and to be improved by the accumulating additions brought by the wisdom of successive ages. *Our* wisdom is not a child perfected by gradual growth, but a goddess which starts at once, full grown, mature, armed cap-a-pee, from the heads of our modern thunderers.[180] Or rather, if I may change the illusion, a perfect system is *now* expected inevitably to spring at once, like the fabled bird of Arabia, from the ashes of its parent, and can receive its birth no other way but by the destruction of its predecessor.[181]

Instead of clearing away what is redundant, pruning what is cumbersome, supplying what is defective, and amending what is wrong, we adopt the indefinite rage for radical reform of Jack, who, in altering Lord Peter's* coat, shewed his zeal by crying out, "Tear away, brother Martin, for the love of heaven; never mind, so you do but tear away."[182]

This tearing system has unquestionably rent away some valuable parts of that strong, rich, native stuff which formed the antient texture of British manners. That we have gained much I am persuaded; that we have lost nothing I dare not therefore affirm. And though it fairly exhibits a mark of our improved judgment to ridicule the fantastic notions of love and honour in the heroic ages; let us not rejoice that that spirit of generosity in sentiment, and of ardour in piety, the exuberancies of which were then so inconvenient, are now sunk as unreasonably low. That revolution of manners which the unparalleled wit and genius of Don Quixote so happily effected, by abolishing extravagances the most absurd and pernicious, was so far imperfect, that the virtues which he never meant to expose, fell into disrepute with the absurdities which he did; and it is become the turn of the present taste to attach in no small degree that which is ridiculous to that which is heroic. Some modern works of wit have assisted in bringing piety and some of the noblest virtues into contempt, by studiously associating them with oddity, childish simplicity, and ignorance of the world: and unnecessary pains have been taken to extinguish that zeal and ardour, which, however liable to excess and error, are yet the spring of whatever is great and excellent in the human character. The novel of Cervantes is incomparable; the Tartuffe of Moliere is unequalled; but true generosity and true religion will never lose any thing of their intrinsic value, because knight-errantry and hypocrisy are legitimate objects for satire.[183]

* Swift's "Tale of a Tub."

But to return from this too long digression, to the subject of female influence. Those who have not watched the united operation of vanity and feeling on a youthful mind, will not conceive how much less formidable the ridicule of all his own sex will be to a very young man, than that of those women to whom he has been taught to look up as the arbitresses of elegance. Such an one, I doubt not, might be able to work himself up, by the force of genuine christian principle, to such a pitch of true heroism, as to refuse a challenge, (and it requires more real courage to refuse a challenge than to accept one,) who would yet be in danger of relapsing into the dreadful pusillanimity of the world, when he is told that no woman of fashion will hereafter look on him but with contempt. While we have cleared away the rubbish of the Gothic ages, it were to be wished we had not retained the most criminal of all their institutions. Why chivalry should indicate a madman, while its leading object, the *single combat*, should designate a gentleman, has not yet been explained. Nay the original motive is lost, while the sinful practice is continued; for the fighter of the duel no longer *pretends* to be a glorious redresser of the wrongs of strangers; no longer considers himself as piously appealing to heaven for the justice of his cause; but from the slavish fear of unmerited reproach, often selfishly hazards the happiness of his nearest connections, and always comes forth in direct defiance of an acknowledged command of the Almighty. Perhaps there are few occasions on which female influence might be exerted to a higher purpose than in this, in which laws and conscience have hitherto effected so little; but while the duellist[184] (who perhaps becomes a duellist only because he was first a seducer) is welcomed with smiles; the more hardy youth, who, not because he fears man but God, declines a challenge; who is resolved to brave disgrace rather than commit sin, would be treated with cool contempt by those very persons to whose esteem he might reasonably look, as one of the rewards of his true and substantial fortitude.

But how shall it be reconciled with the decisions of principle, that delicate women should receive with complacency the successful libertine, who has been detected by the wretched father or the injured husband in a criminal commerce, the discovery of which has too justly banished the unhappy partner of his crime from virtuous society? Nay, if he happens to be very handsome, or very brave, or very fashionable, is there not sometimes a kind of dishonourable competition for his favour? But, whether his popularity be derived from birth, or parts, or person, or (what is often a substitute for all) from his having made his way into *good company*, women of distinction sully the sanctity of virtue by the too visible pleasure they sometimes express at the attentions of a popular libertine, whose voluble small talk they admire, and whose sprightly nothings they quote, and whom perhaps their very favour tends to prevent from becoming a better character, because he finds himself more acceptable as he is...

In animadverting farther on the reigning evils which the times more particularly demand that women of rank and influence should repress, Christianity calls upon them to bear their decided testimony against every thing which is notoriously contributing to the public corruption. It calls upon them to banish from their dressing-rooms, (and oh, that their influence could banish from the libraries of their sons and husbands!) that sober and unsuspected mass of mischief, which, by assuming the plausible names of Science, of Philosophy, of Arts, of Belles Lettres, is gradually administering death to the principles of those who would be on their guard, had the poison been labelled with its own pernicious title. Avowed attacks upon revelation are more easily resisted, because the malignity is advertised. But who suspects the destruction which lurks under the harmless or instructive names of *General History*, *Natural History*, *Travels*, *Voyages*, *Lives*, *Encyclopedias*, *Criticism*, *and Romance*?[185] Who will deny that many of these works contain much admirable matter; brilliant passages, important facts, just descriptions, faithful pictures of nature, and valuable illustrations of science? But while "the dead fly lies at the bottom," the whole will exhale a corrupt and pestilential stench.

Novels, which used chiefly to be dangerous in one respect,

are now become mischievous in a thousand. They are continually shifting their ground, and enlarging their sphere, and
are daily becoming vehicles of wider mischief. Sometimes they
concentrate their force, and are at once employed to diffuse
destructive politics, deplorable profligacy, and impudent infidelity. Rousseau was the first popular dispenser of this
complicated drug, in which the deleterious infusion was
strong, and the effect proportionably fatal.[186] For he does not
attempt to seduce the affections but through the medium of
the principles. He does not paint an innocent woman, ruined,
repenting, and restored; but with a far more mischievous
refinement, he annihilates the value of chastity, and with
pernicious subtlety attempts to make his heroine appear almost
more amiable without it. He exhibits a virtuous woman, the
victim not of temptation but of reason, not of vice but of
sentiment, not of passion but of conviction; and strikes at the
very root of honour by elevating a crime into a principle. With
a metaphysical sophistry the most plausible, he debauches the
heart of woman, by cherishing her vanity in the erection of a
system of male virtues, to which, with a lofty dereliction of
those that are her more peculiar and characteristic praise, he
tempts her to aspire; powerfully insinuating, that to this
splendid system chastity does not necessarily belong: thus
corrupting the judgment and bewildering the understanding, as
the most effectual way to inflame the imagination and deprave
the heart.

The rare mischief of this author consists in his power of
seducing by falsehood those who love truth, but whose minds
are still wavering, and whose principles are not yet formed. He
allures the warm-hearted to embrace vice, not because they
prefer vice, but because he gives to vice so natural an air of
virtue: and ardent and enthusiastic youth, too confidently
trusting in their integrity and in their teacher, will be undone,
while they fancy they are indulging in the noblest feelings of
their nature. Many authors will more infallibly complete the
ruin of the loose and ill-disposed; but perhaps (if I may change
the figure) there never was a net of such exquisite art and

inextricable workmanship, spread to entangle innocence and ensnare inexperience, as the writings of Rousseau: and, unhappily, the victim does not even struggle in the toils, because part of the delusion consists in imagining that he is set at liberty.

Some of our recent popular publications have adopted all the mischiefs of this school, and the principal evil arising from them is, that the virtues they exhibit are almost more dangerous than the vices. The chief materials out of which these delusive systems are framed, are characters who practise superfluous acts of generosity, while they are trampling on obvious and commanded duties; who combine sentiments of honour with actions the most flagitious; a high-tone of self-confidence, with a perpetual breach of self-denial: pathetic apostrophes to the passions, but no attempt to resist them. They teach that no duty exists which is not prompted by feeling: that impulse is the main spring of virtuous actions, while laws and principles are only unjust restraints; the former imposed by arbitrary men, the latter by the absurd prejudices of timorous and unenlightened conscience. In some of the most splendid of these characters, compassion is erected into the throne of justice, and justice degraded into the rank of plebeian virtues. Creditors are defrauded, while money due to them is lavished in dazzling acts of charity to some object that affected their senses; which fits of charity are made the sponge of every sin, and the substitute of every virtue: the whole indirectly tending to intimate how very *benevolent people are who are not Christians*. From many of these compositions, indeed, Christianity is systematically, and always virtually excluded; for the law and the prophets and the gospel *can* make no part of a scheme in which this world is looked upon as all in all; in which poverty and misery are considered as evils arising solely from human governments, and not from the dispensations of God: this poverty is represented as the greatest of evils, and the restraints which tend to keep the poor honest, as the most flagrant injustice. The gospel can have nothing to do with a system in which sin is reduced to a little human imperfection, and Old Bailey crimes are softened down into a few engaging weaknesses; and in which the turpitude of all the vices a man himself commits, is done away by his *candour* in tolerating all the vices committed by others.[187]

But the most fatal part of the system to that class whom I am addressing is, that even in those works which do not go all the lengths of treating marriage as an unjust infringement on liberty, and a tyrannical deduction from general happiness; yet it commonly happens that the hero or heroine, who has practically violated the letter of the seventh commandment,[188] and continues to live in the allowed violation of its spirit, is painted as so amiable and so benevolent, so tender or so brave; and the temptation is represented as so *irresistible*, (for all these philosophers are fatalists,) the predominant and cherished sin is so filtered and purged of its pollutions, and is so sheltered and surrounded, and relieved with shining qualities, that the innocent and impressible young reader is brought to lose all horror of the awful crime in question, in the complacency she feels for the engaging virtues of the criminal.

But there is a new and strong demand for the exertion of that power I am humbly endeavouring to direct to its true end. Those ladies who take the lead in society are loudly called upon to act as the guardians of public taste as well as public virtue, in an important instance. They are called upon to oppose with the whole weight of their influence, the irruption of those swarms of publications that are daily issuing from the banks of the Danube; which, like their ravaging predecessors of the darker ages, though with far other arms, are over-running civilized society. Those readers, whose purer taste has been formed on the correct models of the old classic school, see with indignation and astonishment the Vandals once more overpowering the Greeks and Romans. They behold our minds, with a retrograde but rapid motion, hurried back to the reign of "chaos and old night," by wild and mis-shapen superstitions; in which, with that *consistency* which forms so striking a feature of the new philosophy, those who deny the immortality of the soul are the most eager to introduce the machinery of ghosts; and by terrific and unprincipled compositions, which unite the taste of the Goths with the morals of Bagshot.*

> Gorgons, and hydras, and chimeras dire![190]

The writings of the French infidels were some years ago circulated in England with uncommon industry, and with some effect: but the good sense and good principles of the far greater part of our countrymen resisted the attack, and rose superior to the trial.[191] Of the doctrines and principles here alluded to, the dreadful consequences, not only in the unhappy country where they originated and were almost universally adopted, but in every part of Europe where they have been received, have been such as to serve as a beacon to surrounding nations, if any warning can preserve them from destruction. In this country the subject is now so well understood, that every thing which issues from the *French* press is received with jealousy; and a work, on the first appearance of its exhibiting the doctrines of Voltaire and his associates, is rejected with indignation.

But let us not on account of this victory repose in confident security. The modern apostles of infidelity and immorality, little less indefatigable in dispersing their pernicious doctrines than the first apostles were in propagating gospel truths, have only changed their weapons, but they have by no means desisted from the attack. To destroy the principles of Christianity in this island, appears at the present moment to be their grand aim. Deprived of the assistance of the French press, they are now attempting to attain their object under the close and more artificial veil of German literature. Conscious that religion and morals will stand or fall together, their attacks are sometimes levelled against the one and sometimes against the other. With occasional strong professions of attachment to both of them, the feelings and the passions of the reader are engaged on the side of some one particular vice, or some one objection to revealed religion. Poetry as well as prose, romance as well as history;

---

* The newspapers announce that Schiller's Tragedy of the Robbers, which inflamed the young nobility of Germany to inlist themselves into a band of highwaymen to rob in the forests of Bohemia, is *now acting in England by persons of quality!*[189]

writings on philosophical as well as political subjects, have thus
been employed to instil the principles of *Illuminatism*, while
incredible pains have been taken to obtain able translations of
every book which was supposed could be of use in corrupting
the heart, or misleading the understanding.[192] In many of these
translations, the stronger passages, which, though well received
in Germany, would have excited disgust in England, are wholly
omitted, in order that the mind may be more certainly, though
more slowly prepared for the full effect of the poison at another
period.

Let not those to whom these pages are addressed deceive
themselves, by supposing this to be a fable; and let them inquire
most seriously whether I speak the truth, when I assert that the
attacks of infidelity in Great Britain are at this moment principally directed against the female breast. Conscious of the influence of women in civil society, conscious of the effect which
female infidelity produced in France, they attribute the ill
success of their attempts in this country to their having been
hitherto chiefly addressed to the male sex. They are now
sedulously labouring to destroy the religious principles of
women, and in too many instances they have fatally succeeded.
For this purpose not only novels and romances have been made
the vehicles of vice and infidelity, but the same allurement has
been held out to the women of our country, which was
employed by the original tempter to our first parent – Knowledge. Listen to the precepts of the new German enlighteners,
and you need no longer remain in that situation in which
Providence has placed you! Follow their examples, and you shall
be permitted to indulge in all those gratifications which custom,
not religion, has too far overlooked in the male sex!

We have hitherto spoken only of the German *writings*; but
because there are multitudes who never read, equal pains have
been taken to promote the same object through the medium of
the stage: and this weapon is, of all others, that against which it
is at the present moment, the most important to warn my
countrywomen. As a specimen of the German drama, it may not
be unseasonable to offer a few remarks on the admired play of

the *Stranger*.[193] In this piece the character of an adulteress, which, in all periods of the world, ancient as well as modern, in all countries heathen as well as Christian, has hitherto been held in detestation, and has never been introduced but to be reprobated, is for the first time presented to our view in the most pleasing and fascinating colours. The heroine is a woman who forsook a husband, the most affectionate and the most amiable, and lived for some time in the most criminal commerce with her seducer. Repenting at length of her crime, she buries herself in retirement. The talents of the poet during the whole piece are exerted in attempting to render this woman the object, not only of the compassion and forgiveness, but of the esteem and affection, of the audience. The injured husband, convinced of his wife's repentance, forms a resolution, which every man of true feeling and christian piety will probably approve. He forgives her offence, and promises her through life his advice, protection, and fortune, together with every thing which can alleviate the misery of her situation, but refuses to replace her in the situation of his wife. But this is not sufficient for the *German* author. His efforts are employed, and it is to be feared but too successfully, in making the audience consider the husband as an unrelenting savage, while they are led by the art of the poet anxiously to wish to see an adulteress restored to that rank of women who have not violated the most solemn covenant that can be made with man, nor disobeyed one of the most positive laws which has been enjoined by God.

About the same time that this first attempt at representing an adulteress in an exemplary light was made by a German dramatist, which forms an æra in manners; a direct vindication of adultery was for the first time attempted by a *woman*, a professed admirer and imitator of the German suicide Werter. The Female Werter, as she is styled by her biographer,[194] asserts, in a work, intitled "The Wrongs of Woman," that adultery is justifiable, and that the restrictions placed on it by the laws of England constitute part of the *wrongs of woman*.[195]

But let us take comfort. These fervid pictures are not yet generally realised. These atrocious principles are not yet adopted into common practice. Though corruptions seem to be pouring in upon us from every quarter, yet there is still left among us a discriminating judgement. Clear and strongly marked distinctions between right and wrong still subsist ...thanks to the surviving efficacy of a holy religion, to the operation of virtuous laws, and to the energy and unshaken integrity with which these laws are *now* administered, and still more perhaps to a standard of morals which continues in force, when the principles which sanctioned it are no more; this crime, in the female sex at least, is still held in just abhorrence; if it be practised, it is not honourable; if it be committed, it is not justified; we do not yet affect to palliate its turpitude; as yet it hides its abhorred head in lurking privacy; and reprobation hitherto follows its publicity.

But on YOUR exerting your influence, with just application and increasing energy, may, in no small degree, depend whether this corruption shall still continue to be resisted. For, from admiring to adopting, the step is short, and the progress rapid; and it is in the moral as in the natural world, the motion, in the case of minds as well as of bodies, is accelerated on a nearer approach to the centre to which they are tending.

...There are certain women of good fashion who practise irregularities not consistent with the strictness of virtue; while their good sense and knowledge of the world make them at the same time keenly alive to the value of reputation. They want to retain their indulgences, without quite forfeiting their credit; but finding their fame fast declining, they artfully cling, by flattery and marked attentions, to a few persons of more than ordinary character; and thus, till they are driven to let go their hold, continue to prop a falling fame.

On the other hand, there are not wanting women of distinction, of very correct general conduct, and of no ordinary sense and virtue, who, confiding with a high mind on what they too confidently call *the integrity of their own hearts*; anxious of deserving a good fame on the one hand, by a life free from reproach, yet secretly too desirous on the other of securing a worldly and fashionable reputation; while their general associates are persons of honour, and their general resort places of safety; yet allow themselves to be occasionally present at the midnight orgies of revelry and gaming, in houses of no honourable estimation; and thus help to keep up characters, which, without their sustaining hand, would sink to their just level of reprobation and contempt. While they are holding out this plank to a drowning reputation, rather, it is to be feared, to shew their own strength than to assist another's weakness, they value themselves, perhaps, on not partaking of the worst parts of the amusements which may be carrying on; but they sanction them by their presence; they lend their countenance to corruptions they should abhor, and their example to the young and inexperienced, who are looking about for some such sanction to justify them in what they were before inclined to do, but were too timid to have done without the protection of such unsullied names. Thus these respectable characters, without looking to the general consequences of their indiscretion, are thoughtlessly employed in breaking down, as it were, the broad fence, which should ever separate two very different sorts of society, and are becoming a kind of unnatural link between vice and virtue.

But the great object to which you, who are, or may be mothers, are more especially called, is the education of your children. If we are responsible for the use of influence in the case of those over whom we have no definite right; in the case of our children we are responsible for the exercise of acknowledged *power:* a power wide in its extent, indefinite in its effects, and inestimable in its importance. On you, depend in no small degree the principles of the whole rising generation. To your direction the daughters are almost exclusively committed; and to a certain age, to you also is consigned the mighty privilege of forming the hearts and minds of your infant sons...

CHAP. II.

On the education of women. – The prevailing system tends to establish the errors which it ought to correct. – Dangers arising from an excessive cultivation of the arts.

It is far from being the object of this slight work to offer a regular plan of female education, a task which has been often more properly assumed by far abler writers; *but* it is intended rather to suggest a few remarks on the existing mode, which, though it has had many panegyrists, appears to be defective, not only in certain particulars, but as a general system. There are indeed numberless honourable exceptions to an observation which will be thought severe; yet the author questions if it be not the natural and direct tendency of the prevailing and popular system, to excite and promote those very defects, which it ought to be the main end and object of Christian instruction to remove; whether, instead of directing this important engine to attack and destroy vanity, selfishness, and inconsideration, that triple alliance in league against female virtue; the combined powers of instruction are not sedulously confederated in confirming their strength, and establishing their empire?

If indeed the *material* substance; if the body and limbs, with the organs and senses, be really the more valuable objects of attention, then there is little room for animadversion and improvement. But if the immaterial and immortal mind; if the heart, "out of which are the issues of life," be the main concern; if the great business of education be to implant ideas, to communicate knowledge, to form a correct taste and a sound judgment, to resist evil propensities, and, above all, to seize the favourable season for infusing principles and confirming habits; if education be a school to fit us for life, and life be a school to fit us for eternity; if such, I repeat it, be the chief work and grand ends of education, it may then be worth inquiring how far these ends are likely to be effected by the prevailing system?...

Since...there is a season when the youthful must cease to be young, and the beautiful to excite admiration; to grow old gracefully is, perhaps, one of the rarest and most valuable arts which can be taught to woman. It is for this sober season of life that education should lay up its rich resources. However disregarded they may hitherto have been, they will be wanted now. When admirers fall away, and flatterers become mute, the mind will be driven to retire into itself, and if it will find no entertainment at home, it will be driven back again upon the world with increased force. Yet forgetting this, do we not seem to educate our daughters, exclusively, for the transient period of youth, when it is to maturer life we ought to advert? Do we not educate them for a crowd, forgetting that they are to live at home? for the world, and not for themselves? for show, and not for use? for time, and not for eternity?...

Not a few of the evils of the present day arise from a new and perverted application of terms; among these perhaps, there is not one more abused, misunderstood, or misapplied, than the term *accomplishments*. This word in its original meaning, signifies *completeness, perfection*. But I may safely appeal to the observation of mankind, whether they do not meet with swarms of youthful females, issuing from our boarding schools, as well as emerging from the more private scenes of domestic education, who are introduced into the world, under the broad and universal title of *accomplished young ladies*, of *all* of whom it cannot very truly and correctly be pronounced, that they illustrate the definition by a completeness which leaves nothing to be added, and a perfection which leaves nothing to be desired.

This phrenzy of accomplishments, unhappily, is no longer restricted within the usual limits of rank and fortune; the middle orders have caught the contagion, and it rages with increasing violence, from the elegantly dressed but slenderly portioned curate's daughter, to the equally fashionable daughter of the little tradesman, and of the more opulent, but not more judicious farmer.[196] And is it not obvious that as far as this epidemical mania has spread, this valuable part of society declines in usefulness, as it rises in its unlucky pretensions to elegance. And this revolution of the manners of the middle class has so far altered the character of the age, as to be in danger of rendering obsolete the heretofore common saying, "that most worth and virtue are to be found in the middle station?" For I do not scruple to assert, that in general, as far as my little observation has extended, this class of females, in what relates both to religious knowledge and to practical industry, falls short both of the very high and the very low. Their new course of education, and the habits of life, and elegance of dress connected with it, peculiarly unfits them for the active duties of their own very important condition; while, with frivolous eagerness and second-hand opportunities, they run to snatch a few of those showy acquirements which decorate the great. This is done apparently with one or other of these views; either to make their fortune by marriage, or to qualify them to become teachers of others: hence the abundant multiplication of superficial wives, and of incompetent and illiterate governesses. The use of the pencil, the performance of exquisite but unnecessary works, the study of foreign languages and of music, require (with some exceptions, which should always be made in favour of great natural genius) a degree of leisure which belongs exclusively to affluence.* One use of learning languages is, not that we may know what the terms which express the articles of our dress and our table are called in French or Italian; not that we may think over a few ordinary phrases in English, and then translate them, without one foreign idiom; for he who cannot *think* in a language cannot be said to understand it: but the great use of acquiring any foreign language is, either that it enables us occasionally to converse with foreigners unacquainted with any other, or that it is a key to the literature of the country to which it belongs; and those humbler females, the chief part of whose time is required for domestic offices, are little likely to fall in the way of foreigners; and so far from enjoying opportunities for the acquisition of foreign literature, have seldom time to possess

* Those among the class in question, whose own good sense leads them to avoid these mistaken pursuits, cannot be offended at a reproof which does not belong to them.

themselves of all that valuable knowledge, which the books of their own country so abundantly furnish; and the acquisition of which would be so much more useful and honourable than the paltry accessions they make, by hammering out the meaning of a few passages in a tongue they but imperfectly understand, and of which they are likely to make no use.

It would be well if the reflection how eagerly this redundancy of accomplishments is seized on by their inferiors, were to operate as in the case of other absurd fashions, which the great can seldom be brought to renounce from any other considera- tion than they are adopted by the vulgar.

But, to return to that more elevated, and, on account of their more extended influence only, that important class of females, to whose use this little work is more immediately dedicated. Some popular authors, on the subject of female instruction, had for a time established a fantastic code of artificial manners. They had refined elegance into insipidity, frittered down delicacy into frivolousness, and reduced manner into *minauderie*.[197] But "to lisp and to amble and to nick-name God's creatures,"[198] has nothing to do with true gentleness of mind; and to be silly makes no necessary part of softness. Another class of cotemporary[199] authors turned all the force of their talents to excite *emotions*, to inspire *sentiment*, and to reduce all moral excellence into *sym-pathy* and *feeling*. These softer qualities were elevated at the expence of principle; and young women were incessantly hear- ing unqualified sensibility extolled as the perfection of their nature; till those who really possessed this amiable quality, instead of directing, and chastising, and restraining it, were in danger of fostering it to their hurt, and began to consider themselves as deriving their excellence from its excess; while those less interesting damsels, who happened not to find any of this amiable sensibility in their *hearts*, but thought it creditable to have it somewhere, fancied its seat was in the *nerves*; and here indeed it was easily found or feigned; till a false and excessive display of feeling became so predominant, as to bring in ques- tion the actual existence of that true tenderness, without which, though a woman may be worthy, she can never be amiable.

Fashion then, by one of her sudden and rapid turns, instantaneously struck out sensibility and the affectation from the standing list of female perfections; and, by a quick touch of her magic wand, shifted the scene, and at once produced the bold and independent beauty, the intrepid female, the hoyden, the huntress, and the archer; the swinging arms, the confident address, the regimental, and the four-in-hand.[200] Such self-complacent heroines made us ready to regret their softer predecessors, who had aimed only at pleasing the other sex, while these aspiring fair ones struggled for the bolder renown of rivalling them. The project failed; for, whereas the former had sued for admiration, the latter challenged, seized, compelled it; but the men, as was natural, continued to prefer the more modest claimant to the sturdy competitor.

It would be well if we, who have the advantage of contemplating the errors of the two extremes, were to look for truth where she is commonly to be found, in the plain and obvious middle path, equally remote from each excess; and, while we bear in mind that helplessness is not delicacy, let us also remember that masculine manners do not necessarily include strength of character nor vigour of intellect. Should we not reflect also, that we are neither to train up Amazons nor Circassians,[201] but to form Christians? that we have to educate not only rational but accountable beings? and, remembering this, should we not be solicitous to let our daughters learn of the well-taught, and associate with the well-bred? In training them, should we not carefully cultivate intellect, implant religion, and cherish modesty? then, whatever is delicate in manners, would be the natural result of whatever is just in sentiment, and correct in principle: then the decorums, the proprieties, the elegancies, and even the graces, as far as they are simple, pure, and honest, would follow as an almost inevitable consequence...

Whether we have made the best use of the errors of our predecessors, and of our own numberless advantages, and whether the prevailing system be really consistent with sound policy or with Christian principle, it may be worth our while to inquire.

Would not a stranger be led to imagine by a view of the reigning mode of female education, that human life consisted of one universal holiday, and that the grand contest between the several competitors was, who should be most eminently qualified to excel, and carry off the prize, in the various shows and games which were intended to be exhibited in it?...

What would the polished Addison, who thought that one great end of a lady's learning to dance was, that she might know how to sit still gracefully;[202] what would even the pagan historian* of the great Roman conspirator, who could commemorate it among the defects of his hero's *accomplished* mistress, "that she was too good a singer and dancer for a virtuous woman;" what would these refined critics have said, had they lived as we have done, to see the art of dancing lifted into such importance, that it cannot with any degree of safety be confided to one instructor, but a whole train of successive masters are considered as absolutely essential to its perfection? What would these accurate judges of female manners have said, to see a modest young lady first delivered into the hands of a military sergeant to instruct her in the feminine art of marching? and when this delicate acquisition is attained, to see her transferred to a professor who is to teach her the Scotch steps; which professor, having communicated his indispensable portion of this indispensable art, makes way for the professor of French dances; and all perhaps in their turn, either yield to, or have the honour to co-operate with a finishing master; each probably receiving a stipend which would make the pious curate or the learned chaplain rich and happy?[204]

The science of music, which used to be communicated in so competent a degree by one able instructor, is now distributed among a whole band. A young lady now requires, not a master, but an orchestra. And my country readers would accuse me of exaggeration were I to hazard enumerating the variety of musical teachers who attend in the same family; the daughters of

* Sallust.[203]

which are summoned, by at least as many instruments as the subjects of Nebuchadnezzar, to worship the idol which fashion has set up. They would be incredulous were I to produce real instances, in which the delighted mother has been heard to declare, that the visits of masters of every art, followed each other in such close and rapid succession during the whole London residence, that her girls had not a moment's interval to look into a book; nor could she contrive any method to introduce one, till she happily devised the scheme of reading to them herself for half an hour while they were drawing, by which means no time was lost.[205]

Before the evil is past redress, it will be prudent to reflect that in all polished countries an entire devotedness to the fine arts has been one grand source of the corruption of the women; and so justly were these pernicious consequences appreciated by the Greeks, among whom these arts were carried to the highest possible perfection, that they seldom allowed them to be cultivated to a very exquisite degree by women of great purity of character. And if the ambition of an elegant British lady should be fired by the idea that the accomplished females of those polished states were the admired companions of the philosophers, the poets, the wits, and the artists of Athens; and their beauty or talents the favourite subjects of the muse, the lyre, the pencil, and the chissel; that their pictures and statues furnished the most consummate models of Grecian art: if, I say, the accomplished females of our day are panting for similar renown, let their modesty chastise their ambition, by recollecting that these celebrated women are not to be found among the chaste wives and the virtuous daughters of the Aristides's, the Agis's, and the Phocions;[206] but that they are to be looked for among the Phrynes, the Lais's, the Aspasias, and the Glyceras.[207] I am persuaded the Christian female, whatever be her talents, will renounce the desire of any celebrity when attached to impurity of character, with the same noble indignation with which the virtuous biographer of the above-named heroes renounced all dishonest fame, by exclaiming, "I had rather it should be said there never was a Plutarch, than that they should say Plutarch was malignant, unjust, or envious."*

And while this corruption, brought on by an excessive cultivation of the arts, has contributed its full share to the decline of states, it has always furnished an infallible symptom of their impending fall. The satires of the most penetrating and judicious of the Roman poets, corroborating the testimonies of the most accurate of their historians, abound with invectives against the depravity of manners, introduced by the corrupt habits of female education. The bitterness and gross indelicacy of some of these satirists (too gross to be either quoted or referred to) make little against their authority in these points; for how shocking must those corruptions have been, and how obviously offensive their causes, which could have appeared so highly disgusting to minds not likely to be scandalized by slight deviations from decency! The famous ode of Horace,[208] attributing the vices and disasters of his country to the same cause, might, were it quite free from the above objections, be produced, I will not presume to say as an exact picture of the existing manners of this country; but may I not venture to say, as a prophecy, the fulfilment of which cannot be very remote? It may however be observed, that the modesty of the Roman matron, and the chaste demeanour of her virgin daughters, which amidst the stern virtues of the state were as immaculate and pure as the honour of the Roman citizen, fell a sacrifice to the luxurious dissipation brought in by their Asiatic conquests; after which the females were soon taught a complete change of character. They were instructed to accommodate their talents of pleasing to the more vitiated tastes of the other sex; and began to study every grace and every art which might captivate the exhausted hearts, and excite the wearied and capricious inclinations of the men: till by a rapid and at length complete enervation, the Roman character lost its signature, and through a quick succession of slavery, effeminacy, and vice, sunk into that degeneracy of

* No censure is levelled at the exertions of real genius, which is as valuable as it is rare; but at the absurdity of that system which is erecting *the whole sex* into artists.

which some of the modern Italian states serve to furnish a too just specimen.

It is of the essence of human things that the same objects which are highly useful in their season, measure, and degree, become mischievous in their excess, at other periods, and under other circumstances. In a state of barbarism, the arts are among the best reformers; and they go on to be improved themselves, and improving those who cultivate them, till, having reached a certain point, those very arts which were the instruments of civilization and refinement, become instruments of corruption and decay; enervating and depraving in the second instance as certainly as they refined in the first. They become agents of voluptuousness. They excite the imagination; and the imagination thus excited, and no longer under the government of strict principle, becomes the most dangerous stimulant of the passions; promotes a too keen relish for pleasure, teaching how to multiply its sources, and inventing new and pernicious modes of artificial gratification.

May the author be allowed to address to our own country and our own circumstances, to both of which they seem peculiarly applicable, the spirit of that beautiful apostrophe of the most polished poet of antiquity to the most victorious nation? "Let us leave to the inhabitants of conquered countries the praise of carrying to the very highest degree of perfection, sculpture and the sister arts; but let *this* country direct her own exertions to the art of governing mankind in equity and peace, of shewing mercy to the submissive, and of abasing the proud among surrounding nations."[209]

CHAP. III.
External improvement. – Children's balls. – French governesses.

Let me not however, be misunderstood. The customs which fashion has established, when not in opposition to what is right, should unquestionably be pursued in the education of ladies.

Piety maintains no natural war with elegance, and Christianity would be no gainer by making her disciples unamiable. Religion does not forbid that the exterior be made to a certain degree the object of attention. But the admiration bestowed, the sums expended, and the time lavished on arts which add little to the intrinsic value of life, should have limitations. While these arts should be admired, let them not be admired above their just value: while they are practised, let it not be to the exclusion of higher employments: while they are cultivated, let it be to amuse leisure, not to engross life...

"To every thing there is a season, and a time for every purpose under heaven," said the wise man; but he said it before the invention of baby-balls.[210] This modern device is a sort of triple conspiracy against the innocence, the health, and the happiness of children; thus, by factitious amusements, to rob them of a relish for the simple joys, the unbought delights, which naturally belong to their blooming season, is like blotting out spring from the year. To sacrifice the true and proper enjoyments of sprightly and happy children, is to make them pay a dear and disproportionate price for their artificial pleasures. They step at once from the nursery to the ball-room; and, by a preposterous change of habits, are thinking of dressing themselves, at an age when they used to be dressing their dolls. Instead of bounding with the unrestrained freedom of little wood-nymphs over hill and dale, their cheeks flushed with health, and their hearts overflowing with happiness, these gay little creatures are shut up all the morning, demurely practising the *pas grave*, and transacting the serious business of acquiring a new step for the evening, with more cost of time and pains than it would have taken them to acquire twenty new ideas.

Thus they lose the amusements which naturally belong to their smiling period, and unnaturally anticipate those pleasures (such as they are) which would come in, too much of course, on their introduction into fashionable life. The true pleasures of childhood are cheap and natural; for every object teems with delight to eyes and hearts new to the enjoyment of life; nay, the hearts of healthy children abound with a general disposition to mirth and joyfulness, even without a specific object to excite it; like our first parent, in the world's first spring, when all was new, and fresh, and gay about him,

> they live and move,
> And feel that they are happier than they know.[211]

Only furnish them with a few simple and harmless materials, and a little, but not too much, leisure, and they will manufacture their own pleasures with more skill, and success, and satisfaction, than they will receive from all that your money can purchase. Their bodily recreations should be such as will promote their health, quicken their activity, enliven their spirits, whet their ingenuity, and qualify them for their mental work. But, if you begin thus early to create wants, to invent gratifications, to multiply desires, to waken dormant sensibilities, to stir up hidden fires, you are studiously laying up for your children a store of premature caprice and irritability, and discontent.

While childhood preserves its native simplicity, every little change is interesting, every gratification is a luxury; a ride or a walk will be a delightful amusement to a child in her natural state; but it will be dull and tasteless to a sophisticated little creature, nursed in these forced and costly and vapid pleasures. Alas! that we should throw away this first grand opportunity of working into a practical habit the moral of this important truth, that the chief source of human discontent is to be looked for, not in our real but in our factitious wants; not in the demands of nature, but in the artificial cravings of desire!

When one sees the growing zeal to crowd the midnight ball with these pretty fairies, one would be almost tempted to fancy it was a kind of pious emulation among the mothers to cure their infants of a fondness for vain and foolish pleasures, by tiring them out by this premature familiarity with them; and that they were actuated by something of the same principle, which led the Spartans to introduce their sons to scenes of riot, that they might conceive an early disgust at vice! or possibly, that they imitated those Scythian[212] mothers who used to plunge their new-born infants into the flood, thinking none to be worth saving who could not stand this early struggle for their lives: the greater part indeed, as it might have been expected, perished; but the parents took comfort, that if many were lost, the few who escaped would be the stronger for having been thus exposed.

To behold lilliputian coquettes, projecting dresses, studying colours, assorting ribbands and feathers, their little hearts beating with hopes about partners and fears about rivals; to see their fresh cheeks pale after the midnight supper, their aching heads and unbraced nerves, disqualifying the little languid beings for the next day's task, and to hear the grave apology, "that it is owing to the wine, the crowd, the heated room of the last night's ball;" all this, I say, would really be as ludicrous, if the mischief of the thing did not take off from the merriment of it, as any of the ridiculous and preposterous disproportions in the diverting travels of Captain Lemuel Gulliver.

Under a just impression of the evils which we are sustaining from the principles and the practices of *modern* France, we are apt to lose sight of those deep and lasting mischiefs which so long, so regularly, and so systematically, we have been importing from the same country, though in another form and under another government. In one respect, indeed, the first were the more formidable, because we embraced the ruin without suspecting it; while we defeat the malignity of the latter, by detecting the turpitude and defending ourselves against it. This is not the place to descant on that levity of manners, that contempt of the Sabbath, that fatal familiarity with loose principles, and those relaxed notions of conjugal fidelity, which have often been transplanted into this country by women of fashion, as a too common effect of a long residence in that: but it is peculiarly suitable to my subject to advert to another domestic mischief derived from the same foreign extraction: I mean, the risks that have been run, and the sacrifices which have been made, in order to furnish our young ladies with the means of acquiring the French language in the greatest possible purity. Perfection in this accomplishment has been so long established as the supreme object; so long considered as the predominant excellence to which all other excellencies must bow down, that it would be hopeless to attack a law which fashion has immutably decreed, and which has received the stamp of long prescription. We must therefore be contented with expressing a wish, that this indispensable perfection could have been attained at the expence of sacrifices less important. It is with the greater regret I animadvert on this and some other prevailing practices, as they are errors into which the wise and respectable have, through want of consideration, or rather through want of firmness to resist the tyranny of fashion, sometimes fallen. It has not been unusual when mothers of rank and reputation have been asked how they ventured to intrust their daughters to foreigners, of whose principles they know nothing, except that they were Roman Catholics, to answer, "That they had taken care to be secure on that subject, for that it had been stipulated that the question of religion should never be agitated between the teacher and the pupil." This, it must be confessed, is a most desperate remedy; it is like starving to death, to avoid being poisoned. And one cannot help trembling for the event of that education, from which religion, as far as the governess is concerned, is thus formally and systematically excluded. Surely it would not be exacting too much to suggest at least that an attention no less scrupulous should be exerted to insure the character of our children's instructor for piety and knowledge, than is thought necessary to ascertain that she has nothing *patois* in her dialect.

I would rate a correct pronunciation and an elegant phraseology at their just price, and I would not rate them low; but I would not offer up principle as a victim to sounds and accents. And the matter is now made more easy; for whatever disgrace it might once have brought on an English lady to have had it suspected from her accent that she had the misfortune, not to be born in a neighbouring country; some recent events may serve to reconcile her to the suspicion of having been bred in her own: a country, to which, (with all its faults, which are many!) the whole world is looking up with envy and admiration, as the seat of true glory and of comparative happiness: a country, in which the exile, driven out by the crimes of his own, finds a home! a country, to obtain the protection of which it was claim enough to be unfortunate; and no impediment to have been the subject of her direst foe![213] a country, which in this respect, humbly imitating the Father of compassion, when it offered mercy to a suppliant enemy, never conditioned for merit, nor insisted on the virtues of the miserable as a preliminary to its own bounty!

CHAP. IV.

Comparison of the mode of female education in the last age with the present.

To return, however, to the subject of general education. A young lady may excel in speaking French and Italian, may repeat a few passages from a volume of extracts; play like a professor, and sing like a syren; have her dressing-room decorated with her own drawings, tables, stands, screens, and cabinets; nay, she may dance like Sempronia*[214] herself, and yet may have been very badly educated. I am far from meaning to set no value whatever on any or all of these qualifications; they are all of them elegant, and many of them properly tend to the perfecting of a polite education. These things in their measure and degree, may be done, but there are others which should not be left undone. Many things are becoming, but "one thing is needful."[215] Besides, as the world seems to be fully apprized of the value of whatever tends to embellish life, there is less occasion here to insist on its importance.

But, though a well bred young lady may lawfully learn most of the fashionable arts, yet it does not seem to be the true end of education to make women of fashion *dancers, singers, players,*

* See Catiline's Conspiracy.

painters, actresses, sculptors, gilders, varnishers, engravers, and *embroiderers*. Most men are commonly destined to some profession, and their minds are consequently turned each to its respective object. Would it not be strange if they were called out to exercise their profession, or to set up their trade, with only a little general knowledge of the trades of all other men, and without any previous definite application to their own peculiar calling? The profession of ladies, to which the bent of *their* instruction should be turned, is that of daughters, wives, mothers, and mistresses of families. They should be therefore trained with a view to these several conditions, and be furnished with a stock of ideas, and principles, and qualifications ready to be applied and appropriated, as occasion may demand, to each of these respective situations: for though the arts which merely embellish life must claim admiration; yet when a man of sense comes to marry, it is a companion whom he wants, and not an artist. It is not merely a creature who can paint, and play, and dress, and dance; it is a being who can comfort and counsel him; one who can reason and reflect, and feel, and judge, and discourse, and discriminate; one who can assist him in his affairs, lighten his cares, soothe his sorrows, strengthen his principles, and educate his children.

Almost any ornamental talent is a good thing, when it is not the best thing a woman has. And the writer of this page is intimately acquainted with several ladies who, excelling most of their sex in the art of music, but excelling them also in prudence and piety, find little leisure or temptation, amidst the delights and duties of a large and lovely family, for the exercise of this talent, they regret that so much of their own youth was wasted in acquiring an art which can be turned to so little account in married life; and are now conscientiously restricting their daughters in the portion of time allotted to its acquisition...

That injudicious practice, therefore, cannot be too much discouraged, of endeavouring to create talents which do not exist in nature. *That their daughters shall learn every thing*, is so general a maternal maxim, that even unborn daughters, of

whose expected abilities and conjectured faculties, it is presumed, no very accurate judgment can previously be formed,
are yet predestined to this universality of accomplishments. This
comprehensive maxim, thus almost universally brought into
practice, at once weakens the general powers of the mind, by
drawing off its strength into too great a variety of directions;
and cuts up time into too many portions, by splitting it into
such an endless multiplicity of employments...The care taken to
prevent *ennui* is but a creditable plan for promoting self-
ignorance. We run from one occupation to another (I speak of
those arts to which little intellect is applied) with a view to
lighten the pressure of time; above all to save us from our own
thoughts; whereas, were we thrown a little more on our own
hands, we might at last be driven, by way of something to do, to
try to get acquainted with our own hearts; and though our being
less absorbed by this busy trifling and frivolous hurry, might
render us somewhat more sensible of the tædium of life, might
not this very sensation tend to quicken our pursuit of a better?...

Among the boasted improvements of the present age, none
affords more frequent matter of peculiar exultation, than the
manifest superiority in the employments of the young ladies of
our time over those of the good housewives of the last century.
The present are employed in learning the polite arts, or in
acquiring liberal accomplishments; while the others wore out
their days in adorning the mansion-house with hangings of
hideous tapestry and disfiguring tent-stitch. Most chearfully do
I allow to the reigning modes their boasted superiority; for
certainly there is no piety in bad taste. Still, granting all the
deformity of the exploded ornaments, one advantage attended
them: the walls and floors were not vain of their decorations;
and it is to be feared, that the little person sometimes is. The
flattery bestowed on the old employments, for probably even
they had their flatterers, furnished less aliment and less gratification to vanity, and was less likely to impair the delicacy of
modesty, than the exquisite cultivation of *personal* accomplishments or personal decorations; and every mode which keeps
down vanity and keeps back *self*, has at least a moral use: and

while one admires the elegant fingers of a young lady, busied in working or painting her ball dress, one cannot help suspecting that her alacrity may be a little stimulated by the animating idea *how very well she shall look in it...*

Let me be allowed to repeat, that I mean not with preposterous praise to descant on the ignorance or the prejudices of past times, nor absurdly to regret that vulgar system of education which rounded the little circle of female acquirements within the limits of the sampler and the receipt book. Yet if a preference almost exclusive was then given to what was merely useful, a preference almost equally exclusive also is now assigned to what is merely ornamental. And it must be owned, that if the life of a young lady, formerly, too much resembled the life of a confectioner, it now too much resembles that of an actress; the morning is all rehearsal, and the evening is all performance: and those who are trained in this regular routine, who are instructed in order to be exhibited, soon learn to feel a sort of impatience in those societies in which their kind of talents are not likely to be brought into play: the task of an auditor becomes dull to her, who has been used to be a performer...And unluckily, while the age is become so knowing and so fastidious, that if a young lady does not play like a public performer, no one thinks her worth attending to, yet if she does so excel, some of the soberest of the admiring circle feel a strong alloy to their pleasure, on reflecting at what a vast expence of time this perfection must probably have been acquired...

CHAP. VI.

Filial obedience not the character of the age. — A comparison with the preceding age in this respect. — Those who cultivate the mind advised to study the nature of the soil. — Unpromising children often make strong characters. — Teachers too apt to devote their pains almost exclusively to children of parts.

Among the real improvements of modern times, and they are not a few, it is to be feared that the growth of filial obedience cannot be included. Who can forbear observing and regretting in a variety of instances, that not only sons but daughters have adopted something of that spirit of independence, and disdain of control, which characterise the times? And is it not obvious that domestic manners are not slightly tinctured with the hue of public principles? The *rights of man* have been discussed, till we are somewhat wearied with the discussion.[216] To these have been opposed with more presumption than prudence, *the rights of woman*.[217] It follows according to the natural progression of human things, that the next stage of that irradiation which our enlighteners are pouring in upon us will produce grave descants on the *rights of children*.

This revolutionary spirit in families suggests the remark that among the faults with which it has been too much the fashion of recent times to load the memory of the incomparable Milton, one of the charges brought against his private character (for with his political character we have here nothing to do) has been, that he was so severe a father as to have compelled his daughters, after he was blind, to read aloud to him for his sole pleasure Greek and Latin authors of which they did not understand a word. But this is in fact nothing more than an instance of the strict domestic regulations of the age in which Milton lived; and should not be brought forward as a proof of the severity of his individual temper...[218]

Is the author then inculcating the harsh doctrine of parental

austerity? By no means. It drives the gentle spirit to artifice, and
the rugged to despair. It generates deceit and cunning, the most
hopeless and hateful in the whole catalogue of female failings.
Ungoverned anger in the teacher, and inability to discriminate
between venial errors and premeditated offence, though they
may lead a timid creature to hide wrong tempers, or to conceal
bad actions, will not help her to subdue the one or to correct
the other. Severity will drive terrified children to seek, not for
reformation, but for impunity. A readiness to forgive them
promotes frankness. And we should, above all things, encourage
them to be frank, in order to come at their faults. They have not
more faults for being open, they only *discover* more.

Discipline, however, is not cruelty, and restraint is not severity. We must strengthen the feeble while we repel the bold. The
cultivator of the human mind must, like the gardener, study
diversities of soil. The skilful labourer knows that even where
the surface is not particularly promising, there is often a rough
strong ground which will amply repay the trouble of breaking it
up; and we are often most taken with a soft surface, though it
conceal a shallow depth, because it promises present reward and
little trouble. But strong and pertinacious tempers, of which
perhaps obstinacy is the leading vice, under skilful management
often turn out steady and sterling characters; while from softer
clay a firm and vigorous virtue is but seldom produced...

But while I would deprecate harshness, I would inforce
discipline; and that not merely on the ground of religion, but of
happiness also. One reason not seldom brought forward by
tender but mistaken mothers, as an apology for their unbounded
indulgence, especially to weakly children, is, that they probably
will not live to enjoy the world when grown up, and that,
therefore they would not abridge the little pleasure they may
enjoy at present. But a slight degree of observation would prove
that this is an error in judgment as well as in principle. For,
omitting any considerations respecting their future welfare, and
entering only into their immediate interests; it is an indisputable
fact that children who know no control, whose faults encounter
no contradiction, and whose humours experience constant

indulgence, grow more irritable and capricious, invent wants, create desires, lose all relish for the pleasures which they know they may reckon upon; and become perhaps more miserable than even those children, who labour under the more obvious and more commiserated misfortune of suffering under the tyranny of unkind parents.

An early habitual restraint is peculiarly important to the future character and happiness of women. They should when very young be inured to contradiction. Instead of hearing their bon-mots treasured up and repeated to the guests till they begin to think it dull, when they themselves are not the little heroines of the theme, they should be accustomed to receive but little praise for their vivacity or their wit, though they should receive just commendation for their patience, their industry, their humility, and other qualities which have more worth than splendour. They should be led to distrust their own judgment; they should learn not to murmur at expostulation; but should be accustomed to expect and to endure opposition. It is a lesson with which the world will not fail to furnish them; and they will not practise it the worse for having learnt it the sooner. It is of the last importance to their happiness in life that they should early acquire a submissive temper and a forbearing spirit. They must even endure to be thought wrong sometimes, when they cannot but feel they are right. And while they should be anxiously aspiring to do well, they must not expect always to obtain the praise of having done so...

There is a custom among teachers which is not the more right for being common; they are apt to bestow an undue proportion of pains on children of the best capacity, as if only geniuses were worthy of attention. They should reflect that in moderate talents carefully cultivated, we are perhaps to look for the chief happiness and virtue of society...Besides while we are conscientiously instructing children of moderate capacity, it is a comfort to reflect that if no labour will raise them to a high degree in the scale of intellectual excellence, yet they may be led on to perfection in that road in which "a way-faring man though simple, shall not err."[219] And when a mother feels disposed to repine that her family is not likely to exhibit a groupe of future wits and growing beauties, let her console herself by looking abroad into the world, where she will quickly perceive that the monopoly of happiness is not engrossed by beauty, nor that of virtue by genius.

A girl who has docility will seldom be found to want understanding sufficient for all the purposes of a useful, a happy, and a pious life. And it is as wrong for parents to set out with too sanguine a dependence on the figure their children are to make in life, as it is unreasonable to be discouraged at every disappointment. Want of success is so far from furnishing a motive for relaxing their energy, that it is a reason for redoubling it. Let them suspect their own plans, and reform them; let them distrust their own principles, and correct them...

It is one grand object to give the young probationer just and sober views of the world on which she is about to enter. Instead of making her bosom bound at the near prospect of emancipation from her instructors; instead of teaching her young heart to dance with premature flutterings as the critical winter draws near in which *she is to come out*:[220] instead of raising a tumult in her busy imagination at the approach of her first *grown up ball*, endeavour to convince her that the world will not turn out to be that scene of unvarying and never-ending delights which she has perhaps been led to expect, not only from the sanguine temper and warm spirits natural to youth, but from the value she has seen put on those showy accomplishments which have too probably been fitting her for her exhibition in life. Teach her that this world is not a stage for the display of superficial talents, but for the strict and sober exercise of fortitude, temperance, meekness, faith, diligence, and self-denial; of her due performance of which Christian graces, Angels will be the spectators, and God the judge. Teach her that human life is not a splendid romance, spangled over with brilliant adventures, and enriched with extraordinary occurrences, and diversified with wonderful incidents; lead her not to expect that life will abound with scenes which will call shining qualities and great powers into perpetual action; and for which if she acquit herself well she will

be rewarded with proportionate fame and certain commendation. But apprize her that human life is a true history, many
passages of which will be dull, obscure, and uninteresting; some
perhaps tragical; but that whatever gay incidents and pleasing
scenes may be interspersed in the progress of the piece, yet
finally "one event happeneth to all;" to all there is one awful and
infallible catastrophe. Apprize her that the estimation which
mankind forms of merit is not always just, nor its praise exactly
proportioned to desert; that the world weighs actions in far
different scales from "the balance of the sanctuary," and esti-
mates worth by a far different standard from that of the gospel;
apprize her that while her best intentions may be sometimes
calumniated, and her best actions misrepresented, she will be
liable to receive commendation on occasions wherein her conscience will tell her she has not deserved it.

Do not however give her a gloomy and discouraging picture
of the world, but rather seek to give her a just and sober view of
the part she will have to act in it. And humble the impetuosity
of hope, and cool the ardour of expectation, by explaining to
her that this part, even in her best estate, will probably consist
in a succession of petty trials, and a round of quiet duties...

Say not that these just and sober views will cruelly wither her
young hopes, and deaden the innocent satisfactions of life. It is
not true. There is, happily, an active spring in the mind of youth
which bounds with fresh vigour, and uninjured elasticity, from
any such temporary depression. It is not meant that you should
darken her prospect, so much as that you should enlighten her
understanding to contemplate it. And though her feelings,
tastes, and passions, will all be against you, if you set before her
a faithful delineation of life, yet it will be something to get her
judgment on your side. It is no unkind office to assist the short
view of youth with the aids of long-sighted experience, to
enable them to discover spots in the brightness of that life which
dazzles them in prospect, though it is probable they will after all
choose to believe their own eyes rather than the offered glass.

CHAP. VII.

On female study, and initiation into knowledge. – Error of cultivating the imagination to the neglect of the judgment. – Books of reasoning recommended.

As this little work by no means assumes the character of a general scheme of education, the author...has been so far from thinking it necessary to enter into the enumeration of those books which are useful in general instruction, that she has forborne to mention any. With such books the rising generation is far more copiously and ably furnished than any preceding period has been; and, out of an excellent variety the judicious instructor can hardly fail to make such a selection as shall be beneficial to the pupil...

Will it not be ascribed to a captious singularity if I venture to remark that real knowledge and real piety, though they have gained in many instances, have suffered in others from that profusion of little, amusing, sentimental books with which the youthful library overflows? Abundance has its dangers as well as scarcity. In the first place may not the multiplicity of these alluring little works increase the natural reluctance to those more dry and uninteresting studies, of which after all, the rudiments of every part of learning *must* consist? And, secondly, is there not some danger (though there are many honourable exceptions) that some of those engaging narratives may serve to infuse into the youthful heart a sort of spurious goodness, a confidence of virtue? And that the benevolent actions with the recital of which they abound, when they are not made to flow from any source but feeling, may tend to inspire a self-complacency, a self-gratulation, a "stand by, for I am holier than thou?"[221] May they not help to infuse a love of popularity and an anxiety for praise, in the place of that simple and unostentatious rule of doing whatever good we do, *because it is the will of God?* The universal substitution of this principle would tend to purify the worldly morality of many a popular little story. And there are few dangers which good parents will more carefully guard against than that of giving their children a mere political piety; that sort of religion which just goes to make people more respectable, and to stand well with the world.*

There is a certain precocity of mind which is helped on by these superficial modes of instruction; for frivolous reading will produce its correspondent effect, in much less time than books of solid instruction; the imagination being liable to be worked upon, and the feelings to be set a going, much faster than the understanding can be opened and the judgment enlightened. A talent for conversation should be the result of education, not its precursor; it is a golden fruit when suffered to ripen gradually on the tree of knowledge; but if forced in the hot-bed of a circulating library,[223] it will turn out worthless and vapid in proportion as it was artificial and premature. Girls who have been accustomed to devour frivolous books, will converse and write with a far greater appearance of skill as to style and sentiment at twelve or fourteen years old, than those of a more advanced age who are under the discipline of severer studies; but the former having early attained to that low standard which had been held out to them, became stationary; while the latter, quietly progressive, are passing through just gradations to a higher strain of mind; and those who early begin with talking and writing like women, commonly end with thinking and acting like children.

The swarms of *Abridgements*, *Beauties*, and *Compendiums*, which form too considerable a part of a young lady's library, may be considered in many instances as an infallible receipt for making a superficial mind. The *names* of the renowned characters in history thus become familiar in the mouths of those who can

---

* An ingenious (and in many respects useful) French Treatise on Education,[222] has too much encouraged this political piety; by sometimes considering religion as a thing of human convention; as a thing creditable rather than commanded: by erecting the doctrine of expediency in the place of Christian simplicity; and wearing away the spirit of truth, by the substitution of occasional deceit, equivocation, subterfuge, and mental reservation.

Selections from Strictures on Female Education

neither attach to the idea of the person, the series of his actions, nor the peculiarities of his character. A few fine passages from the poets (passages perhaps which derived their chief beauty from their position and connection) are huddled together by some extract-maker, whose brief and disconnected patches of broken and discordant materials, while they inflame young readers with the vanity of reciting, neither fill the mind nor form the taste: and it is not difficult to trace back to their shallow sources the hackney'd quotations of certain *accomplished* young ladies, who will be frequently found not to have come legitimately by any thing they know: I mean, not to have drawn it from its true spring, the original works of the author from which some *beauty-monger* has severed it. Human inconsistency in this, as in other cases, wants to combine two irreconcileable things; it strives to unite the reputation of knowledge with the pleasures of idleness, forgetting that nothing that is valuable can be obtained without sacrifices, and that if we would purchase knowledge we must pay for it the fair and lawful price of time and industry.

This remark is by no means of general application; there are many valuable works which from their bulk would be almost inaccessible to a great number of readers, and a considerable part of which may not be generally useful. Even in the best written books there is often superfluous matter; authors are apt to get enamoured of their subject, and to dwell too long on it: every person cannot find time to read a longer work on any subject, and yet it may be well for them to know something on almost every subject; those therefore, who abridge voluminous works judiciously, render service to the community. But there seems, if I may venture the remark, to be a mistake in the *use* of abridgments. They are put systematically into the hands of youth, who have, or ought to have leisure for the works at large; while abridgments seem more immediately calculated for persons in more advanced life, who wish to recal something they had forgotten; who want to restore old ideas rather than acquire new ones; or they are useful for persons immersed in the business of the world who have little leisure for voluminous reading. They are excellent to refresh the mind, but not competent to form it.

Perhaps there is some analogy between the mental and bodily conformation of women. The instructor therefore should imitate the physician. If the latter prescribe bracing medicines for a body of which delicacy is the disease, the former would do well to prohibit relaxing reading for a mind which is already of too soft a texture, and should strengthen its feeble tone by invigorating reading.

By softness, I cannot be supposed to mean imbecility of understanding, but natural softness of heart, with that indolence of spirit which is fostered by indulging in seducing books and in the general habits of fashionable life.

I mean not here to recommend books which are immediately religious, but such as exercise the reasoning faculties, teach the mind to get acquainted with its own nature, and to stir up its own powers. Let not a timid young lady start if I should venture to recommend to her, after a proper course of preparation, to swallow and digest such strong meat, as Watts's or Duncan's little book of Logic, some parts of Mr. Locke's Essay on the Human Understanding, and Bishop Butler's Analogy.[224] Where there is leisure, and capacity, and an able counsellor, works of this nature might be profitably substituted in the place of so much English Sentiment, French Philosophy, Italian Poetry,[225] and fantastic German imagery and magic wonders. While such enervating or absurd books sadly disqualify the reader for solid pursuit or vigorous thinking, the studies here recommended would act upon the constitution of the mind as a kind of alternative, and, if I may be allowed the expression, would help to brace the intellectual stamina.

This is however by no means intended to exclude works of taste and imagination, which must always make the ornamental part, and of course a very considerable part of female studies. It is only suggested that they should not form them entirely. For what is called dry tough reading, independent of the knowledge it conveys, is useful as a habit and wholesome as an exercise. Serious study serves to harden the mind for more trying conflicts; it lifts the reader from sensation to intellect; it abstracts her from the world and its vanities; it fixes a wandering spirit, and fortifies a weak one; it divorces her from matter; it corrects that spirit of trifling which she naturally contracts from the frivolous turn of female conversation, and the petty nature of female employments; it concentrates her attention, assists her in a habit of excluding trivial thoughts, and thus even helps to qualify her for religious pursuits. Yes; I repeat it, there is to woman a Christian use to be made of sober studies; while books of an opposite cast, however unexceptionable they may be sometimes found in point of expression; however free from evil in its more gross and palpable shapes, yet by their very nature and constitution they excite a spirit of relaxation, by exhibiting scenes and ideas which soften the mind; they impair its general powers of resistance, and at best feed habits of improper indulgence, and nourish a vain and visionary indolence, which lays the mind open to error and the heart to seduction.

Women are little accustomed to close reasoning on any subject; still less do they inure their minds to consider particular parts of a subject; they are not habituated to turn a truth round and view it in all its varied aspects and positions; and this perhaps is one cause...of the too great confidence they are disposed to place in their opinions. Though their imagination is already too lively, and their judgment naturally incorrect; in educating them we go on to stimulate the imagination, while we neglect the regulation of the judgment. They already want ballast, and we make their education consist in continually crowding more sail than they can carry. Their intellectual powers being so little strengthened by exercise, makes every little business appear a hardship to them: whereas serious study would be useful, were it only that it leads the mind to the habit of conquering difficulties. But it is peculiarly hard to turn at once from the indolent repose of light reading, from the concerns of mere animal life, the objects of sense, or the frivolousness of chit chat; it is peculiarly hard, I say, to a mind so softened, to rescue itself from the dominion of self-indulgence, to resume its powers, to call home its scattered strength, to shut out every foreign intrusion, to force back a spring so unnaturally bent, and to devote itself to religious reading, reflection, or self-examination: whereas to an intellect accustomed to think at all the difficulty of thinking seriously is obviously lessened.

Far be it from me to desire to make scholastic ladies or female dialecticians; but there is little fear that the kind of books here recommended, if thoroughly studied, and not superficially skimmed, will make them pedants or induce conceit; for by shewing them the possible powers of the human mind, you will bring them to see the littleness of their own, and to get acquainted with the mind and to regulate it, does not seem the way to puff it up. But let her who is disposed to be elated with her literary acquisitions, check her vanity by calling to mind the just remark of Swift, "that after all her boasted acquirements, a woman will, generally speaking, be found to possess less of what is called learning than a common school-boy."[226]

Neither is there any fear that this sort of reading will convert ladies into authors. The direct contrary effect will be likely to be produced by the perusal of writers who throw the generality of readers at such an unapproachable distance. Who are those ever multiplying authors, that with unparalleled fecundity are over-stocking the world with their quick succeeding progeny? They are novel writers; the easiness of whose productions is at once the cause of their own fruitfulness, and of the almost infinitely numerous race of imitators to whom they give birth. Such is the frightful facility of this species of composition, that every raw girl while she reads, is tempted to fancy that she can also write. And as Alexander, on perusing the Iliad, found by congenial sympathy the image of Achilles in his own ardent soul, and felt himself the hero he was studying; and as Corregio, on first beholding a picture which exhibited the perfection of the Graphic art, prophetically felt all his own future greatness, and cried out in rapture, "And I too am a painter!"[227] so a thorough paced novel reading Miss, at the close of every tissue of hack-ney'd adventures, feels within herself the stirring impulse of corresponding genius, and triumphantly exclaims, "And I too am an author!" The glutted imagination soon overflows with the redundance of cheap sentiment and plentiful incident, and by a sort of arithmetical proportion, is enabled by the perusal of any three novels to produce a fourth; till every fresh production, like the progeny of Banquo, is followed by

Another, and another, and another!*[228]

Is a lady, however destitute of talents, education, or knowledge of the world, whose studies have been completed by a circulating library, in any distress of mind? the writing a novel suggests itself as the best soother of her sorrows! Does she labour under any depression of circumstances? writing a novel occurs as the readiest receipt for mending them! And she solaces herself with the conviction that the subscription which has been given to her importunity or her necessities, has been given to her genius. And this confidence instantly levies a fresh contribution for a succeeding work. Capacity, and cultivation are so little taken into the account, that writing a book seems to be now considered as the only sure resource which the idle and the illiterate have always in their power.

May I be indulged in a short digression to remark, though rather out of its place, that the corruption occasioned by these books has spread so wide, and descended so low, that not only among milliners, mantua-makers, and other trades where numbers work together, the labour of one girl is frequently sacrificed that she may be spared to read those mischievous books to the others;[229] but the Author has been assured by clergymen, who have witnessed the fact, that they are procured and greedily read in the wards of our Hospitals! an awful hint, that those who teach the poor to read, should not only take care to furnish them with principles which will lead them to abhor corrupt

---

* It is surely not necessary to state, that no disrespect can be here intended to those females of real genius and correct character, some of whose justly admired writings in this kind, are accurate histories of life and manners, and striking delineations of character. It is not *their* fault if their works have been attended with the consequences which usually attend good originals, that of giving birth to a multitude of miserable imitations.

books, but should also furnish them with such books as shall strengthen and confirm their principles.*

CHAP. XIII.

The practical use of female knowledge. — A comparative view of both sexes.

The chief end to be proposed in cultivating the understandings of women, is to qualify them for the practical purposes of life. Their knowledge is not often like the learning of men, to be reproduced in some literary composition, and never in any learned profession; but it is to come out in conduct. A lady studies, not that she may qualify herself to become an orator or a pleader; not that she may learn to debate, but to act. She is to read the best books, not so much to enable her to talk of them, as to bring the improvement she derives from them to the rectification of her principles, and the formation of her habits. The great uses of study are to enable her to regulate her own mind, and to be useful to others.

To woman therefore, whatever be her rank, I would recommend a predominance of those more sober studies, which, not having display for their object, may make her wise without vanity, happy without witnesses, and content without panegyrists; the exercise of which will not bring celebrity, but will improve usefulness. She should pursue every kind of study which will teach her to elicit truth; which will lead her to be intent upon realities; will give precision to her ideas; will make

---

* The above facts furnish no argument on the side of those who would keep the poor in ignorance. Those who cannot *read* can *hear*, and are likely to hear to worse purpose than those who have been better taught. And that ignorance furnishes no security for integrity either in morals or politics, the late revolts in more than one country, remarkable for the ignorance of the poor, fully illustrates. It is earnestly hoped that the above facts may tend to impress ladies with the importance of superintending the instruction of the poor, and of making it an indispensable part of their charity to give them moral and religious books.

an exact mind; every study which, instead of stimulating her sensibility, will chastise it; which will give her definite notions; will bring the imagination under dominion; will lead her to think, to compare, to combine, to methodise; which will confer such a power of discrimination that her judgment shall learn to reject what is dazzling if it be not solid; and to prefer, not what is striking, or bright, or new, but what is just. Every kind of knowledge which is rather fitted for home consumption than foreign exportation, is peculiarly adapted to women.[230]

It is because the superficial mode of their education furnishes them with a false and low standard of intellectual excellence, that women have sometimes become ridiculous by the unfounded pretensions of literary vanity: for it is not the really learned, but the smatterers, who have generally brought their sex into discredit, by an absurd affectation, which has set them on despising the duties of ordinary life. There have not indeed been wanting (but the character is not common) *précieuses ridicules*,[231] who, assuming a superiority to the sober cares which ought to occupy their sex, claim a lofty and supercilious exemption from the dull and plodding drudgeries

Of this dim speck called earth![232]

who have affected to establish an unnatural separation between talents and usefulness, instead of bearing in mind that talents are the great appointed instruments of usefulness; who act as if knowledge were to confer on woman a kind of fantastic sovereignty, which should exonerate her from female duties; whereas it is only meant the more eminently to qualify her for the performance of them...

For instance; ladies whose natural vanity has been aggravated by a false education, may look down on *œconomy*[233] as a vulgar attainment, unworthy of the attention of a highly cultivated intellect; but this is the false estimate of a shallow mind. Œconomy, such as a woman of fortune is called on to practise, is not merely the petty detail of small daily expences, the shabby curtailments and stinted parsimony of a little mind operating on

little concerns; but it is the exercise of a sound judgment
exerted in the comprehensive outline of order, of arrangement,
of distribution; of regulations by which alone well governed
societies, great and small, subsist. She who has the best regulated mind will, others things being equal, have the best regulated
family. As in the superintendence of the universe, wisdom is
seen in its *effects*; and as in the visible works of Providence, that
which goes on with such beautiful regularity is the result not of
chance but of design; so that management which seems the
most easy is commonly the consequence of the best concerted
plan. A sound œconomy is a sound understanding brought into
action; it is calculation realised; it is the doctrine of proportion
reduced to practice; it is foreseeing consequences and guarding
against them; it is expecting contingencies and being prepared
for them. The difference is that to a narrow minded vulgar
œconomist the details are continually present; she is over-
whelmed by their weight, and is perpetually bespeaking your
pity for her labours and your praise for her exertions: she is
afraid you will not see how much she is harassed. Little events,
and trivial operations engross her whole soul; while a woman of
sense, having provided for their probable recurrence, guards
against the inconveniences, without being disconcerted by the
casual obstructions which they offer to her general scheme.

Superior talents however are not so common, as, by their
frequency, to offer much disturbance to the general course of
human affairs; and many a lady who tacitly accuses herself of
neglecting her ordinary duties because she is a *genius*, will
perhaps be found often to accuse herself as unjustly as good St.
Jerome, when he laments that he was beaten by the angel for
being too Ciceronian in his style...

But the truth is, women who are so puffed up with the conceit
of talents as to neglect the plain duties of life, will not be found to
be women of the best abilities. And here may the author be
allowed the gratification of observing, that those women of real
genius and extensive knowledge, whose friendship have confer-
red honour and happiness on her own life, have been in general
eminent for œconomy, and the practice of domestic virtues.

A romantic girl with an affectation of sentiment, which her still more ignorant friends mistake for genius, (for in the empire of the blind the one-eyed are kings,) and possessing something of a natural ear, has perhaps, in her childhood exhausted all the images of grief, and love, and fancy, picked up in her desultory poetical reading in an elegy on a sick linnet, or a dead lap-dog; she begins thenceforward to be considered as a prodigy in her little circle; surrounded with flatterers, she has no opportunity of getting to know that her fame is derived not from her powers, but her position; and that when an impartial critic shall have made all the necessary deductions, such as, that – she is a neighbour, that she is a relation, that she is a female, that she is young, that she has had no advantages, that she is pretty, perhaps – when her verses come to be stripped of all their extraneous appendages, and the fair author is driven off her 'vantage ground of partiality, sex, and favour, she will commonly sink to the level of ordinary capacities; while those quieter women, who have meekly sat down in the humble shades of prose and prudence, by a patient perseverance in rational studies, rise afterwards much higher in the scale of intellect, and acquire a stock of sound knowledge for far better purposes. And though it may seem a contradiction, yet it will generally be found true, that girls who take to scribbling are the least studious. They early acquire a false confidence in their own unassisted powers; it becomes more gratifying to their natural vanity to be always pouring out their minds on paper, than to be drawing into them fresh ideas from richer sources.

They pant for the unmerited praise of fancy and of genius, while they disdain the commendation of judgment, knowledge, and perseverance, which is within their reach. To extort admiration they are accustomed to boast of an impossible rapidity of composing; and while they insinuate how little time their performances cost them, they intend you should infer how perfect they might have made them had they condescended to the drudgery of application. But instead of extolling these effusions for their facility, it would be kind in friends to blame them for their crudeness; and when the young pretenders are eager to prove in how short a time such a poem has been struck off; it would be well to regret that they have not taken a longer time, or forborne from writing at all; as in the former case the work would have been less defective, and in the latter, the writer would have discovered more humility and self-distrust.

A general capacity for knowledge, and the cultivation of the understanding at large, will always put a woman into the best state for directing her pursuits into those particular channels which her destination in life may afterwards require. But she should be carefully instructed that her talents are only a means to a still higher attainment, and that she is not to rest in them as an end; that merely to exercise them as instruments for the acquisition of fame and the promotion of pleasure is subversive of her delicacy as a woman, and contrary to the spirit of a Christian...

But there is one *human* consideration which would perhaps more effectually tend to damp in an aspiring woman the ardours of literary vanity (I speak not of real genius) than any which she will derive from motives of humility, or propriety, or religion; which is, that in the judgment passed on her performances, she will have to encounter the mortifying circumstance of having her sex always taken into account, and her highest exertions will probably be received with the qualified approbation *that it is really extraordinary for a woman*. Men of learning, who are naturally apt to estimate works in proportion as they appear to be the result of art, study, and institution, are apt to consider even the happier performances of the other sex as the spontaneous productions of a fruitful but shallow soil, and to give them the same sort of praise which we bestow on certain sallads, which often draw from us a sort of wondering commendation; not indeed as being worth much in themselves, but because by the lightness of the earth, and a happy knack of the gardener, these indifferent cresses spring up in a night, and therefore we are ready to wonder they are no worse.

As to men of sense they need be the less inimical to the improvement of the other sex, as they themselves will be sure to be gainers by it; the enlargement of the female understanding being the most likely means to put an end to those petty cavils and contentions for equality which female smatterers so anxiously maintain. I say smatterers, for between the first class of both sexes the question is much more rarely agitated; co-operation and not competition is indeed the clear principle we wish to see reciprocally adopted by those higher minds which really approximate the nearest to each other. The more a woman's understanding is improved, the more obviously she will discern that there can be no happiness in any society where there is a perpetual struggle for power; and the more her judgment is rectified, the more accurate views will she take of the station she was born to fill, and the more readily will she accommodate herself to it; while the most vulgar and ill-informed women are ever most inclined to be tyrants, and those always struggle most vehemently for power, who would not fail to make the worst use of it when attained. Thus the weakest reasoners are always the most positive in debate; and the cause is obvious, for *they* are unavoidably driven to maintain their pretensions by violence who want arguments and reasons to prove that they are in the right.

There is this singular difference between a woman vain of her wit, and a woman vain of her beauty, that the beauty while she is anxiously alive to her own fame, is often indifferent enough about the beauty of other women; and provided she herself is sure of your admiration, she does not insist on your thinking that there is another handsome woman in the world: while she who is vain of her genius, more liberal at least in her vanity, is jealous for the honour of her whole sex, and contends for the equality of their pretensions, in which she feels that her own are involved. The beauty vindicates her own rights, the wit the rights of women; the beauty fights for herself, the wit for a party; and while the more moderate beauty

would but be Queen for life,[234]

the wit struggles to abrogate the Salique law of intellect, and to enthrone a whole sex of Queens.[235]

At the revival of letters in the sixteenth and the following
century, the controversy about this equality was agitated with
more warmth than wisdom; and the process was instituted and
carried on, on the part of the female complainant, with an
acrimony which always raises a suspicion of the justice of any
cause. The novelty of that knowledge which was then bursting
out from the dawn of a long dark night, kindled all the ardours
of the female mind, and the ladies fought zealously for a portion
of that renown which the reputation of learning was beginning
to bestow. Besides their own pens, they had for their advocates
all those needy authors who had anything to hope from their
power, their riches, or their influence; and so giddy did some of
these literary ladies become by the adulation of their numerous
panegyrists, that through these repeated draughts of inebriating
praise, they grew to despise the equality for which they had
before contended, as a state below their merit and unworthy of
their acceptance. They now scorned to litigate for what they
already thought they so obviously possessed, and nothing short
of the palm of superiority was at length considered as adequate
to their growing claims. When court-ladies and princesses were
the candidates, they could not long want champions to support
their cause; by these champions female authorities were produced as if paramount to facts; quotations from these female
authors were considered as proofs, and their point-blank asser-
tions stood for solid reasons. In those parasites who offered this
homage to female genius, the homage was therefore the effect
neither of truth, nor of justice, nor of conviction. It arose rather
out of gratitude, or it was a reciprocation of flattery; it was
vanity, it was often distress, which prompted the praise; it was
the want of a patroness. When a lady, and especially as it then
often happened, when one who was noble or royal sat with
gratifying docility at the foot of a professor's chair; when she
admired the philosopher, or took upon her to protect the
theologian whom his rivals among his own sex were tearing to
pieces, what could the grateful professor or theologian do less in

return than make the apotheosis of her who had had the penetration to discern his merit and the spirit to reward it? Thus in fact it was not so much *her* vanity as his own that he was often flattering, though she was the dupe of her more deep and designing panegyrist.

But it is a little unlucky for the perpetuity of that fame which the encomiast had made over to his patroness, in the never-dying records of his verses and orations, that, in the revolution of a century or two the very names of the flattered are now almost as little known as the works of the flatterers. *Their memorial is perished with them.**...

But when the temple of Janus seemed to have been closed, or at worst the peace was only occasionally broken by a slight and random shot from the hand of some single straggler; it appears that though open rebellion had ceased, yet the female claim had not been renounced; it had only (if we may change the metaphor) lain in abeyance. The contest has recently been revived with added fury, and with multiplied exactions; for whereas the ancient demand was merely a kind of imaginary prerogative, a speculative importance, a mere titular right, a shadowy claim to a few unreal acres of Parnassian territory; the revived contention has taken a more serious turn, and brings forward political as well as intellectual pretensions: and among the innovations of this innovating period, the imposing term of *rights* has been produced to sanctify the claim of our female pretenders, with a view not only to rekindle in the minds of women a presumptuous vanity dishonourable to their sex, but produced with a view to excite in their hearts an impious discontent with the post which God has assigned them in this world.[237]

But *they* little understand the true interests of woman who would lift her from the important duties of her allotted station, to fill with fantastic dignity a loftier but less appropriate niche. Nor do they understand her true happiness, who seek to annihilate distinctions from which she derives advantages, and

* See Brantome, Père le Moine, Mons. Thomas, &c.[236]

to attempt innovations which would depreciate her real value. Each sex has its proper excellences, which would be lost were they melted down into the common character by the fusion of the new philosophy. Why should we do away distinctions which increase the mutual benefits and satisfactions of life? Whence, but by carefully preserving the original marks of difference stamped by the hand of the Creator, would be derived the superior advantage of mixed society? Have men no need to have their rough angles filed off, and their harshnesses and asperities smoothed and polished by assimilating with beings of more softness and refinement? Are the ideas of women naturally so very judicious, are their principles so invincibly firm, are their views so perfectly correct, are their judgments so completely exact, that there is occasion for no additional weight, no super-added strength, no increased clearness, none of that enlargement of mind, none of that additional invigoration which may be derived from the aids of the stronger sex? What identity could advantageously supercede an enlivening and interesting variety of character? Is it not then more wise as well as more honourable to move contentedly in the plain path which Providence has obviously marked out to the sex, and in which custom has for the most part rationally confirmed them, rather than to stray awkwardly, unbecomingly, and unsuccessfully in a forbidden road? to be the lawful possessors of a lesser domestic territory, rather than the turbulent usurpers of a wider foreign empire? to be good originals, rather than bad imitators? to be the best thing of one's own kind, rather than an inferior thing, even if it were of an higher kind? to be excellent women rather than indifferent men?

Is the author, then, undervaluing her own sex? – No. It is her zeal for their true *interests* which leads her to oppose their imaginary *rights*. It is her regard for their happiness which makes her endeavour to cure them of a feverish thirst for a fame. A little Christian humility worth all the wild metaphysical discussion which has unsettled the peace of vain women, and forfeited the respect of reasonable men. And the most elaborate definition of ideal rights, and the most hardy measures for attaining them, are of less value in the eyes of an amiable woman, than "that meek and quiet spirit, which is in the sight of God of great price."[238]

Natural propensities best mark the designations of Providence as to their application. The fin was not more clearly bestowed on the fish that he should swim, nor the wing given to the bird that he should fly, than superior strength of body and a firmer texture of mind given to man, that he might preside in the deep and daring scenes of action and of council; in government, in arms, in science, in commerce, and in those professions which demand a higher reach, and a wider range of powers. The true value of woman is not diminished by the imputation of inferiority in *these* respects; she has other requisites better adapted to answer the end and purposes of her being...

Let her not then view with envy the keen satirist, hunting vice through all the doublings and windings of the heart; the sagacious politician leading senates, and directing the fate of empires; the acute lawyer detecting the obliquities of fraud; and the skilful dramatist exposing the pretensions of folly: but let her ambition be consoled by reflecting, that those who thus excel; to all that Nature bestows and books can teach, must add besides that consummate knowledge of the world to which a delicate woman has no fair avenues, and which could she attain she would never be supposed to have come honestly by.

In almost all that comes under the description of polite letters, in all that captivates by imagery or warms by just and affecting sentiment, women are excellent. They possess in a high degree that delicacy and quickness of perception, and that nice discernment between the beautiful and defective, which comes under the denomination of taste. Both in composition and in action they excel in details; but they do not so much generalize their ideas as men, nor do their minds seize a great subject with so large a grasp. They are acute observers, and accurate judges of life and manners, as far as their own sphere of observation extends; but they describe a smaller circle. A woman sees the world, as it were, from a little elevation in her own garden, whence she takes an exact survey of home scenes, but takes not in that wider range of distant prospects, which he who stands on a loftier eminence commands.

In summing up the evidence, if I may so speak, of the different powers of the sexes, one may venture, perhaps, to assert, that women have equal *parts*, but are inferior in *wholeness* of mind, in the integral understanding: that though a superior woman may possess single faculties in equal perfection, yet there is commonly a juster proportion in the mind of a superior man: that if women have in an equal degree the faculty of fancy which creates images, and the faculty of memory which collects and stores ideas, they seem not to possess in equal measure the faculty of comparing, combining, analysing, and separating these ideas; that deep and patient thinking which goes to the bottom of a subject; nor that power of arrangement which knows how to link a thousand consecutive ideas in one dependent train, without losing sight of the original idea out of which the rest grow, and on which they all hang. The female too in her intellectual pursuits is turned aside by her characteristic tastes and feelings. Woman in the career of genius, is the Atalanta, who will risk losing the race by running out of her road to pick up the golden apple; while her male competitor, without, perhaps, possessing greater natural strength or swiftness, will more certainly attain his object, by being less exposed to the seductions of extraneous beauty, and will win the race by despising the bait.*

Here it may be justly enough retorted, that, as it is allowed the education of women is so defective, the alleged inferiority of their minds may be accounted for on that ground more justly than by ascribing it to their natural make. And, indeed, there is so much truth in the remark, that till women shall be more reasonably educated, and till the native growth of their mind shall cease to be stinted and cramped, we have no juster ground for pronouncing that their understanding has already reached its

* What indisposes even reasonable women to concede in these points is, that the weakest man instantly lays hold on the concession; and on the mere ground of sex, plumes himself on his own individual superiority; inferring that the silliest man is superior to the first-rate woman.

highest attainable perfection, than the Chinese would have for affirming that their women have attained to the greatest possible perfection in walking, while the first care is, during their infancy, to cripple their feet: or rather, till the female sex are more carefully instructed, this question will always remain as undecided as to the *degree* of difference between the understandings of men and women, as the question between the understandings of blacks and whites; for until Africans and Europeans are put more nearly on a par in the cultivation of their minds, the shades of distinction between their native powers, can never be fairly ascertained...

And when we see (and who will deny that we see it frequently?) so many women nobly rising from under all the pressure of a disadvantageous education and a defective system of society, and exhibiting the most unambiguous marks of a vigorous understanding, a correct judgment, and a sterling piety, it reminds us of those shining lights which have now and then burst out through all the "darkness visible" of the Romish church, have disencumbered themselves from the gloom of ignorance and the fetters of prejudice, and risen superior to all the errors of a corrupt theology.

But whatever characteristical distinctions may exist; whatever inferiority may be attached to woman from the slighter frame of her body, the more circumscribed powers of her mind, from a less systematic education, and from the subordinate station she is called to fill in life; there is one great and leading circumstance which raises her importance, and even establishes her equality. *Christianity* has exalted women to true and undisputed dignity; in Christ Jesus, as there is neither "rich nor poor," "bond nor free," so there is neither "male nor female." In the view of that immortality, which is brought to light by the Gospel, she has no superior. Women...make up one half of the human race; equally with men redeemed by the blood of Christ. In this their true dignity consists; here their best pretensions rest, here their highest claims are allowed...

Women also bring to the study of Christianity fewer of those prejudices which persons of the other sex too often contract early. Men, from their classical education, acquire a strong partiality for the manners of Pagan antiquity, and the documents of Pagan philosophy; this, together with the impure taint caught from the loose descriptions of their poets, and the licentious language even of their historians, (in whom we reasonably look for more gravity,) often weakens the good impressions of young men, and at least confuses their ideas of piety, by mixing them with so much heterogeneous matter... While women, though struggling with the same natural corruptions, have commonly less knowledge to unknow, and no schemes to unlearn...

And as women are naturally more affectionate than fastidious, they are likely both to read and to hear with a less critical spirit than men: they will not be on the watch to detect errors, so much as to gather improvement; they have seldom that hardness which is acquired by dealing deeply in books of controversy, but are more inclined to the perusal of works which quicken the devotional feelings, than to such as awaken a spirit of doubt and scepticism...Women are also, from their domestic habits, in possession of more leisure and tranquillity for religious pursuits, as well as secured from those difficulties and temptations to which men are exposed in the tumult of a bustling world. Their lives are more uniform, less agitated by the passions, the businesses, the contentions, the shock of opinions and interests which convulse the world.

If we have denied them the talents which might lead them to excel as lawyers, they are preserved from the peril of having their principles warped by that too indiscriminate defence of right and wrong, to which the professors of the law are exposed. If we should question their title to eminence as mathematicians, they are happily exempt from the danger to which men devoted to that science are said to be liable; namely, that of looking for demonstration on subjects, which, by their very nature, are incapable of affording it. If they are less conversant in the powers of nature, the structure of the human frame, and the knowledge of the heavenly bodies, than philosophers, physicians, and astronomers; they are, however, delivered from the error into which many of each of these have sometimes fallen, from the fatal habit of resting in second causes, instead of referring all to the first...And let the weaker sex take comfort, that in their very exemption from privileges, which they are sometimes disposed to envy, consists their security and their happiness. If they enjoy not the distinctions of public life and dignified offices, do they not escape the sin of mis-employing, and the mortification of being dismissed from them? If they have no voice in deliberative assemblies, do they not avoid the responsibilities attached to such privileges? Preposterous pains have been taken to excite in women an uneasy jealousy, that their talents are neither rewarded with public honours nor emoluments in life; nor with inscriptions, statues, and mausoleums after death. It has been absurdly represented to them as a hardship; that, while they are expected to perform duties, they must yet be contented to relinquish honours, and must unjustly be compelled to renounce fame while they must labour to deserve it...

If women should lament the disadvantage attached to their sex, that their character is of so delicate a texture, as to be sullied by the slightest breath of calumny, and that the stain once received is indelible; yet are they not led by that very circumstance more instinctively to shrink from all those irregularities to which the loss of character is so inseparably attached; and, to shun with keener circumspection the most distant approach towards the confines of danger? Let them not lament it as a hardship, but enjoy it as a privilege, that the delicacy of their sex impels them more scrupulously to avoid the very appearance of evil, since that very necessity serves to defend their purity, by placing them at a greater distance and in a more deep intrenchment, from the evil itself...

CHAP. XIV.

CONVERSATION. – *Hints suggested on the subject.* – *On the tempers and dispositions to be introduced in it.* – *Errors to be avoided.* – *Vanity under various shapes the cause of those errors.*

The sexes will naturally desire to appear to each other, such as each believes the other will best like; their conversation will act reciprocally; and each sex will wish to appear more or less rational as they perceive it will more or less recommend them to the other. It is therefore to be regretted, that many men, even of distinguished sense and learning, are too apt to consider the society of ladies, as a scene in which they are rather to rest their understandings, than to exercise them; while ladies, in return, are too much addicted to make their court by lending themselves to this spirit of trifling; they often avoid to make use of what abilities they have; and affect to talk below their natural and acquired powers of mind; considering it as a tacit and welcome flattery to the understanding of men, to renounce the exercise of their own.

But since taste and principles thus mutually operate; men, by keeping up conversation to its proper standard, would not only call into exercise the power of mind which women actually possess; but would even awaken energies which they do not know they possess; and men of sense would find their account in doing this, for their own talents would be more highly rated by companions who were better able to appreciate them. And, on the other hand, if young women found it did not often recommend them in the eyes of those whom they most wish to please, to be frivolous and superficial, they would become more sedulous in correcting their own habits; and, whenever fashionable women indicate a relish for instructive conversation, men will not be apt to hazard what is vain or unprofitable; much less will they ever presume to bring forward what is loose or corrupt, where some signal has not been previously given, that it will be acceptable, or at least that it will be pardoned.

Ladies commonly bring into company minds already too much relaxed by petty pursuits, rather than overstrained by too intense application; the littleness of the employments in which they are usually engaged, does not so strain their minds or exhaust their spirits as to make them stand in need of that relaxation from company which severe application or over-whelming business makes requisite for studious or public men. The due consideration of this circumstance might serve to bring the sexes more nearly on a level in society; and each might meet the other half way; for that degree of lively and easy conversa-tion which is a necessary refreshment to the learned and the busy, would not decrease in pleasantness by being made of so rational a cast as would yet somewhat raise the minds of women, who commonly seek society as a scene of pleasure, not as a refuge from overwhelming thought or labour.

It is a disadvantage even to those women who keep the best company, that it is unhappily almost established into a system, by the other sex, to postpone every thing like instructive discourse till the ladies are withdrawn; their retreat serving as a kind of signal for the exercise of intellect. And in the few cases in which it happens that any important discussion takes place in their presence, they are for the most part considered as having little interest in serious subjects. Strong truths, whenever such happen to be addressed to them, are either diluted with flattery, or kept back in part, or softened to their taste; or if the ladies express a wish for information on any point, they are put off with a compliment, instead of a reason; and are considered as beings who are not expected to see and to judge of things as they really exist.

Do we then wish to see the ladies, whose opportunities leave them so incompetent, and the modesty of whose sex ought never to allow them even to be as shining as they are able; – do we wish to see them take the lead in metaphysical disquisitions? Do we wish them to plunge into the depths of theological polemics,

And find no end in wand'ring mazes lost?[239]

Do we wish them to revive the animosities of the Bangorian controversy,[240] or to decide the process between the Jesuits and the five propositions of Jansenius?[241] Do we wish to enthrone them in the professor's chair, to deliver oracles, harangues, and dissertations? to weigh the merits of every new production in the scales of Quintilian,[242] or to regulate the unities of dramatic composition *by Aristotle's clock*?[243] Or, renouncing those foreign aids, do we desire to behold them, inflated with their original powers, labouring to strike out sparks of wit, with a restless anxiety to shine, which generally fails, and with an anxious affectation to please, which never pleases?...

All this be far from them! – But we *do* wish to see the conversation of well bred women rescued from vapid common places, from uninteresting tattle, from trite and hackneyed communications, from frivolous earnestness, from false sensibility, from a warm interest about things of no moment, and an indifference to topics the most important; from a cold vanity, from the overflowings of self-love, exhibiting itself under the smiling mask of an engaging flattery, and from all the factitious manners of artificial intercourse. We *do* wish to see the time passed in polished and intelligent society, considered among the beneficial, as well as the pleasant portions of our existence, and not too frequently consigned over to premeditated trifling or systematic unprofitableness. Let us not, however, be misunderstood; it is not meant to prescribe that they should affect to talk on lofty subjects, so much as to suggest that they should bring good sense, simplicity, and precision into those common subjects, of which, after all, both the business and the conversation of mankind is in a great measure made up.

It is too well known how much the dread of imputed pedantry keeps off any thing that verges towards *learned*, and the terror of imputed enthusiasm, staves off any thing that approaches to *serious* conversation, so that the two topics which peculiarly distinguish us, as rational and immortal beings, are by general consent in a good degree banished from the society of rational and immortal creatures. But we might almost as consistently give up the comforts of fire because a few persons have been burnt, and the benefit of water because some others have been drowned, as relinquish the enjoyments of reasonable and the blessings of religious intercourse, because the learned world has sometimes been infested with pedants, and the religious world with fanatics.

As in the momentous times in which we live, it is next to impossible to pass an evening in company, but the talk will so inevitably revert to politics, that, without any premeditated design, every one present shall infallibly get to know to which side the other inclines; why, in the far higher concern of eternal things, should we so carefully shun every offered opportunity of bearing even a casual testimony to the part we espouse in religion? Why, while we make it a sort of point of conscience to leave no doubt on the mind of a stranger, whether we adopt the party of Pitt or Fox,[244] shall we choose to leave it very problematical whether we belong to God or Baal?[245] Why, in religion, as well as in politics, should we not act like people who, having their all at stake, cannot forbear now and then adverting for a moment to the object of their grand concern, and dropping, at least, an incidental intimation of the side to which they belong?

Even the news of the day, in such an eventful period as the present, may lend frequent occasions to a woman of principle, to declare, without parade, her faith in a moral Governor of the world; her trust in a particular Providence; her belief in the Divine Omnipotence; her confidence in the power of God, in educing good from evil, in his employing wicked nations, not as favourites but instruments;[246] her persuasion that present success is no proof of the divine favour; in short, some intimation that she is not ashamed to declare that her mind is under the influence of Christian faith and principle. A general concurrence in exhibiting this spirit of decided faith and holy trust, would inconceivably discourage that pert infidelity which is ever on the watch to produce itself: and, as we have already observed, if women, who derive authority from their rank or talents, did but reflect how their sentiments are repeated and their authority quoted, they would be so on their guard, that general society might become a scene of general improvement, and the young, who are looking for models on which to fashion themselves, would be ashamed of exhibiting any thing like levity or scepticism.

Let it be understood, that it is not meant to intimate that serious subjects should make up the bulk of conversation; this, as it is impossible, would also often be improper. It is not intended to suggest that they should be studiously introduced or affectedly prolonged; but only that they should not be systematically shunned, nor the brand of fanaticism be fixed on the person who, with whatever propriety, hazards the introduction of them. It is evident, however, that this general dread of serious topics arises a good deal from an ignorance of the true nature of religion; people avoid it on the principle expressed by the vulgar phrase of the danger of playing with edge tools. They conceive of it as something which involves controversy, and dispute, and mischief; something of an inflammatory nature, which is to stir up ill humours; as of a sort of party business which sets friends at variance. So much is this notion adopted, that I have seen two works announced of considerable merit, in which it was stipulated as an attraction, that religion, as being likely to excite anger and party distinctions, should be excluded. Such is the worldly idea of the spirit of that religion, whose precise object it was to bring "peace and good-will to men!"[247]

Women too little live or converse up to their understandings; and however we have deprecated affectation or pedantry, let it be remembered, that both in reading and conversing the understanding gains more by stretching, than stooping. If by exerting itself it may not attain to all it desires, yet it will be sure to gain something. The mind, by always applying itself to objects below its level, contracts and shrinks itself to the size, and lowers itself to the level, of the object about which it is conversant; while the mind which is active expands and raises itself, grows larger by exercise, abler by diffusion, and richer by communication.

But the taste of general society is not favourable to improvement. The seriousness with which the most frivolous subjects are agitated, and the levity with which the most serious are despatched, bear a pretty exact proportion to each other. Society too is a sort of magic lanthorn; the scene is perpetually shifting. In this incessant change, the evanescent fashion of the existing minute, which, while in many it leads to the cultivation of real knowledge, has also sometimes led even the gay and idle to the affectation of mixing a sprinkling of science with the mass of dissipation. The ambition of appearing to be well informed breaks out even in those triflers who will not spare time from their pleasurable pursuits sufficient for acquiring that knowledge, of which, however, the reputation is so desirable. A little smattering of philosophy often dignifies the pursuits of their day, without rescuing them from the vanities of the night. A course of lectures (that admirable assistant for enlightening the understanding) is not seldom resorted to as a means to substitute the appearance of knowledge for the fatigue of application; but where this valuable help is attended merely like any other public exhibition, and is not furthered by correspondent reading at home, it often serves to set off the reality of ignorance with the affectation of skill. But instead of producing in conversation a few reigning scientific terms...would it not be more modest even for those who are better informed, to avoid the common use of technical terms whenever the idea can be conveyed without them? For it argues no real ability to know the *names* of tools; the ability lies in knowing their *use*: and while it is in the thing, and not in the term, that real knowledge consists, the charge of pedantry is attached to the use of the term, which would not attach to the knowledge of the science.

In the faculty of speaking well, ladies have such a happy promptitude, of turning their slender advantages to account, that there are many who, though they have never been taught a rule of syntax, yet, by a quick facility in profiting from the best books and the best company, hardly ever violate one; and who often possess an elegant and perspicuous arrangement of style, without having studied any of the laws of composition. Every kind of knowledge which appears to be the result of observation, reflection, and natural taste, sits gracefully on women. Yet on the other hand it sometimes happens, that ladies of no contemptible natural parts are too ready to produce, not only pedantic expressions, but crude notions; and still oftener to bring forward obvious and hackneyed remarks, which float on the very surface of a subject, with the imposing air of recent invention, and all the vanity of conscious discovery. This is because their acquirements have not been woven into their minds by early instruction; what knowledge they have gotten stands out as it were above the very surface of their minds, like the *appliquée* of the embroiderer, instead of having been interwoven with the growth of the piece, so as to have become a part of the stuff. They did not, like men, acquire what they know while the texture was forming. Perhaps no better preventive could be devised for this literary vanity, than early instruction: that woman would be less likely to be vain of her knowledge who did not remember the time when she was ignorant. Knowledge that is *burnt in*, if I may so speak, is seldom obtrusive.

Their reading also has probably consisted much in abridgements from larger works, as was observed in a former chapter;[248] this makes a readier talker, but a shallower thinker, than books of more bulk. By these scanty sketches their critical spirit has been excited, while their critical powers have not been formed. For in those crippled mutilations they have seen nothing of that just proportion of parts, that skilful arrangement of the plan, and that artful distribution of the subject, which, while they prove the master hand of the writer, serve also to form the taste of the reader, far more than a dis-jointed skeleton, or a beautiful feature or two, can do. The instruction of women is also too much drawn from the scanty and penurious sources of short writings of the essay kind: this, when it comprises the best part of a person's reading, makes smatterers and spoils scholars; for though it supplies ready talk, yet it does not make a full mind; it does not furnish a store house of materials to stock the understanding, neither does it accustom the mind to any trains of reflection; for the subjects, besides being each succinctly, and, on account of this brevity, superficially treated, are distinct and disconnected; they form no concatenation of ideas, nor any dependent series of deduction. Yet on this pleasant but desultory reading, the mind which has not been trained to severer exercise, loves to repose itself in a sort of creditable indolence, instead of stretching its powers in the wholesome labour of consecutive investigation.*

I am not discouraging study at a late period of life, or even slender knowledge; information is good at whatever period and in whatever degree it be acquired. But in such cases it should be attended with peculiar humility; and the new possessor should bear in mind, that what is fresh to her has been long known to others; and she should be aware of advancing as novel that which is common, and obtruding as rare that which every body possesses. Some ladies are eager to exhibit proofs of their reading, though at the expence of their judgment, and will introduce in conversation quotations quite irrelevant to the matter in hand, because they happen to recur to their recollection, or were, perhaps, found in the book they have just been reading. Inappropriate quotations or strained analogy may shew reading, but they do not shew taste. That just and happy allusion which knows by a word how to awaken a corresponding image, or to excite in the mind of the hearer the idea which fills the mind of the speaker, shews less pedantry and more taste than bare citations; and a mind imbued with elegant knowledge will inevitably betray the opulence of its resources, even on topics which do not relate to science or literature. Well informed persons will easily be discovered to have read the best books, though they are not always detailing catalogues of authors. True taste will detect the infusion which true modesty will not display; and even common subjects passing through a cultivated understanding, borrow a flavour of its richness. A power of apt selection is more valuable than any power of

---

* The writer cannot be supposed desirous of depreciating the value of those many beautiful periodical essays which adorn our language. But, perhaps, it might be better to regale the mind with them singly, at different times, than to read at the same sitting, a multitude of short pieces on dissimilar and contradictory topics, *by way of getting through the book.*

general retention; and an apposite remark, which shoots straight
to the point, demands higher powers of mind than an hundred
simple acts of mere memory: for the business of the memory is
only to store up materials which the understanding is to mix
and work up with its native faculties, and which the judgment is
to bring out and apply. But young women, who have more
vivacity than sense, and more vanity than vivacity, often risk the
charge of absurdity to escape that of ignorance, and will even
compare two authors who are totally unlike rather than miss the
occasion to shew that they have read both.

Among the arts to spoil conversation, some ladies possess that
of suddenly diverting it from the channel in which it was
beneficially flowing, because some *word* used by the person who
was speaking has accidentally struck out a new train of thinking
in their own minds, and not because the *idea* expressed has struck
out a fresh idea, which sort of collision is indeed the way of
eliciting the true fire. Young ladies, whose sprightliness has not
been disciplined by a correct education, are sometimes willing to
purchase the praise of being lively at the risk of being thought rash
or vain. They now and then consider how things may be prettily
said, rather than how they may be prudently or seasonably
spoken; and hazard being thought wrong for the chance of being
reckoned pleasant. The flowers of rhetoric captivate them more
than the justest deductions of reason; and to repel an argument
they arm themselves with a metaphor. Those also who do not aim
so high as eloquence, are often surprised that you refuse to accept
of a prejudice instead of a reason; they are apt to take up with a
probability instead of a demonstration, and cheaply put you off
with an assertion, when you are requiring a proof. The same
mode of education renders them also impatient of opposition;
and if they happen to possess beauty, and to be vain of it, they may
be tempted to consider that as an additional proof of their being
in the right. In this case, they will not ask the conviction of your
judgment to the force of their argument, so much as to the
authority of their charms; for they prefer a sacrifice to a convert,
and submission to their will flatters them more than proselytism
to their "pleaded reason."

The same turn of mind, strengthened by the same cause, (a neglected education,) leads lively women often to pronounce on a question without examining it: on any given point they seldomer *doubt* than men; not because they are more clear-sighted, but because they have not been accustomed to look into a subject long enough to discover its depths and its intricacies; and, not discerning its difficulties, they conclude that it has none. Is it a contradiction to say, that they seem at once to be quick-sighted and short-sighted? What they see at all, they commonly see at once; a little difficulty discourages them; and, having caught a hasty glimpse of a subject, they rush to this conclusion, that either there is no more to be seen, or that what is behind will not pay them for the trouble of searching. They pursue their object eagerly, but not regularly; rapidly, but not pertinaciously; for they want that obstinate patience of investigation which grows stouter by repulse. What they have not attained, they do not believe exists; what they cannot seize at once, they persuade themselves is not worth having.

Is a subject of moment started in company? While the more sagacious are deliberating on its difficulties, and viewing it under all its aspects, in order to form a competent judgment what to say, you will often find the most superficial woman present determine the matter without hesitation. Not seeing the perplexities in which the question is involved, she wonders at the want of penetration in him whose very penetration keeps him silent. She secretly despises the dull perception and slow decision of him who is patiently *untying* the knot which she fancies she exhibits more dexterity by *cutting*. By this shallow sprightliness, the person whose opinion was best worth having is discouraged from delivering it, and an important subject is dismissed without discussion, inconsequent flippancy[249] and voluble rashness. It is this abundance of florid talk, from superficial matter, which has brought on so many of the sex the charge of *inverting* the Apostle's precept, and being *swift* to *speak*, *slow* to *hear*.[250]

...But the silence of listless ignorance, and the silence of sparking intelligence, are two things almost as obviously distinct, as the wisdom and the folly of the tongue. And an inviolable and marked attention may shew that a woman is pleased with a subject, and an illuminated countenance may prove that she understands it, almost as unequivocally as language itself could do; and this, with a modest question, is in many cases as large a share of the conversation as it is decorous for feminine delicacy to take. It is also as flattering an encouragement as men of sense require, for pursuing such topics in their presence, which they would do, did they oftener gain by it the attention which it is natural to wish to excite.

Yet do we not sometimes see an impatience to be heard (nor is it a *feminine* failing only) which good breeding can scarcely subdue? And even when these incorrigible talkers are compelled to be silent, is it not evident that they are not listening to what is said, but are only thinking of what they themselves shall say when they can seize the first lucky interval for which they are so narrowly watching?...

But society, as was observed before, is not a stage on which to throw down our gauntlet, and prove our own prowess by the number of falls we give to our adversary; so far from it, that good breeding as well as Christianity, considers as an indispensable requisite for conversation, the disposition to bring forward to notice any talent in others, which their own modesty, or conscious inferiority, would lead them to keep back. To do this with effect requires a penetration exercised to discern merit, and a generous candour which delights in drawing it out. There are few who cannot converse tolerably on some one topic; what that is, we should try to find out, and introduce that topic, though to the suppression of any one on which we ourselves are supposed to excel: and however superior we may be in other respects to the persons in question, we may, perhaps, in that particular point, improve by them; and if we do not gain information, we shall at least gain a wholesome exercise to our humility and self-denial; we shall be restraining our own impetuosity; we shall be giving confidence to a doubting, or cheerfulness to a depressed spirit. And to place a just remark, hazarded by the diffident in the most advantageous point of view; to call the attention of the inattentive to the observation of one, who, though of much worth, is perhaps of little note; these are requisites for conversation, less brilliant, but far more valuable, than the power of exciting bursts of laughter by the brightest wit, or of extorting admiration by the most poignant sallies.

For wit is of all the qualities of the female mind that which requires the severest castigation; yet the temperate exercise of this fascinating quality throws an additional lustre round the character of an amiable woman; for to manage with discreet modesty a dangerous talent, confers a higher praise than can be claimed by those whom the absence of the talent takes away the temptation to misemploy it. But to women, wit is a peculiarly perilous possession, which nothing short of the soberminded-ness of Christianity can keep in order. Intemperate wit craves admiration as its natural aliment; it lives on flattery as its daily bread. The professed wit is a hungry beggar that subsists on the extorted aims of perpetual panegyric; and, like the vulture in the Grecian fable,[251] the appetite increases by indulgence. Simple truth and sober approbation become tasteless and insipid to the palate, daily vitiated by the delicious poignancies of exaggerated commendation.

But if it be true that some women are too apt to affect brilliancy and display in their own discourse, and to undervalue the more humble pretensions of less showy characters; it must be confessed also, that some of more ordinary abilities are now and then guilty of the opposite error, and foolishly affect to value themselves on not making use of the understanding they really possess. They exhibit no small satisfaction in ridiculing women of high intellectual endowments, while they exclaim with much affected humility, and much real envy, that "they are thankful *they* are not geniuses." Now, though one is glad to hear gratitude expressed on any occasion, yet the want of sense is really no such great mercy to be thankful for; and it would indicate a better spirit, were they to pray to be enabled to make a right use of the moderate understanding they possess, than to expose with a too visible pleasure the imaginary or real defects of their more shining acquaintance. Women of the brightest faculties should not only "bear those faculties meekly," but should consider it as no derogation, cheerfully to fulfil those humbler duties which make up the business of common life, always taking into account the higher responsibility attached to higher gifts. While women of lower attainments should exert to the utmost such abilities as Providence has assigned them; and while they should not deride excellences which are above their reach, they should not despond at an inferiority which did not depend on themselves...

Vanity, however, is not the monopoly of talents; let not a young lady, therefore, fancy that she is humble, merely because she is not ingenious. Humility is not the exclusive privilege of dullness. Folly is as conceited as wit, and ignorance many a time outstrips knowledge in the race of vanity. Equally earnest competitions in conversation spring from causes less worthy to excite them than wit and genius. Vanity insinuates itself into the female heart under a variety of unsuspected forms, and seizes on many a little pass which was not thought worth guarding.

Who has not seen a restless emotion agitate the features of an anxious matron, while peace and fame hung trembling in doubtful suspense on the success of a soup or a sauce, on which sentence was about to be pronounced by some consummate critic, as could have been excited by any competition for literary renown, or any struggle for contested wit?

There is another species of vanity in some women which disguises itself under the thin veil of an affected humility; they will accuse themselves of some fault from which they are remarkably exempt, and lament the want of some talent which they are rather notorious for possessing. This is not only a clumsy trap for praise, but there is a disingenuous intention, by renouncing a quality they eminently possess, to gain credit for others in which they are really deficient. All affectation involves a species of deceit ...Some are also attacked with such proud fits of humility, that while they are ready to accuse themselves of almost every sin in the lump, they yet take fire at the imputation of the slightest *individual* fault; and instantly enter upon their own vindication as warmly as if you, and not themselves, had brought forward the charge. The truth is, they ventured to condemn themselves, in the full confidence that you would contradict them; the last thing they intended was that you should believe them, and they are never so much piqued, and disappointed as when they are taken at their word.

Of the various shapes and undefined forms into which vanity branches out in conversation there is no end. Out of a restless desire to please, grows the vain desire to astonish: from vanity as much as from credulity, arises that strong love of the marvellous, with which the conversation of the ill-educated abounds. Hence that fondness for dealing in narratives hardly within the compass of possibility. Here vanity has many shades of gratification; those shades will be stronger or weaker, whether the relater have been an eye witness of the wonder she recounts; or whether she claim only the second hand renown of its having happened to her friend, or the still remoter celebrity of its having been witnessed only by her friend's friend: but even though that friend only knew the man, who remembered the woman, who actually beheld the thing which is now causing admiration in the company, still *self*, though in a fainter degree, is brought into notice, and the relater contrives in some circuitous way to be connected with the wonder.

To correct this propensity "to elevate and surprise,"* it would be well in mixed society to abstain altogether from hazarding stories, which though they may not be absolutely false, yet lying without the verge of probability, are apt to impeach the credit of the narrator; in whom the very conscious-ness that she is not believed, excites an increased eagerness to depart still farther from the soberness of truth, and induces a habit of vehement asseveration, which is too often called in to help out a questionable point.†

* The Rehearsal.[252]
† This is also a good rule in composition. An event, though it may actually have happened, yet if it be out of the reach of probability, or contrary to the common course of nature, will seldom be chosen as a subject by a writer of good taste; for he knows that a probable fiction will interest the feelings more than an unlikely truth. Verisimilitude is, indeed, the poet's truth, but the truth of the moralist is of a more sturdy growth.

There is another shape, and a very deformed shape it is, in which loquacious vanity shews itself; I mean, the betraying of confidence. Though the act be treacherous, yet the fault, in the first instance, is not treachery, but vanity. It does not so often spring from the mischievous desire of divulging a secret, as from the pride of having been trusted with it. It is the secret inclination of mixing *self* with whatever is important. The secret would be of little value, if the revealing it did not serve to intimate our connection with it: the pleasure of its having been deposited with us would be nothing, if others may not know that it has been so deposited. – When we continue to see the variety of serious evils it involves, shall we persist in asserting that vanity is a slender mischief?...

Again, it is surprising to mark the common deviations from strict veracity which spring, not from enmity to truth, not from intentional deceit, not from malevolence or envy, or the least design to injure, but from mere levity, habitual inattention, and a current notion that it is not worth while to be correct in small things. But here the doctrine of habits comes in with great force, and in that view no error is small. The cure of this disease in its more inveterate stages being next to impossible, its prevention ought to be one of the earliest objects of education...

Good natured young people often speak favourably of un-worthy, or extravagantly of common characters, from one of these motives; either their own views of excellence are low, or they speak respectfully of the undeserving, to purchase for themselves the reputation of tenderness and generosity; or they lavish unsparing praise on almost all alike, in the usurious hope of buying back universal commendation in return; or in these captivating characters in which the simple and masculine lan-guage of truth is sacrificed to the jargon of affected softness; and in which smooth and pliant manners are substituted for intrinsic worth, the inexperienced are too apt to *suppose* virtues, and to *forgive* vices. But they should carefully guard against the error of making *manner* the criterion of merit, and of giving unlimited credit to strangers for possessing every perfection, only because they bring into company the engaging exterior of alluring gentleness. They should also remember that it is an easy, but not an honest way of obtaining the praise of candour to get into the soft and popular habit of saying of all their acquaintance, when speaking of them, that *they are so good!* ...

True good nature, that which alone deserves the name, is not a holiday ornament, but an every-day habit. It does not consist in servile complaisance, or dishonest flattery, or affected sympathy, or unqualified assent, or unwarrantable compliance, or eternal smiles. Before it can he allowed to rank with the virtues, it must be wrought up from a disposition into a principle, from a humour into a habit. It must be the result of an equal and well-governed mind, not the start of casual gaiety, the trick of designing vanity, or the whim of capricious fondness. It is compounded of kindness, forbearance, forgiveness, and self-denial; "it seeketh not its own,"[253] but is capable of making continual sacrifices of its own tastes, humours, and self-love; but among the sacrifices it makes, it must never include its integrity. Politeness on the one hand, and insensibility on the other, assume its name and wear its honours; but they assume the honours of a triumph, without the merit of a victory; for politeness subdues nothing, and insensibility has nothing to subdue. Good nature of the true cast, and under the foregoing regulations, is above all price in the common intercourse of domestic society; for an ordinary quality which is constantly brought into action, by the perpetually recurring though minute events of daily life, is of higher value than more brilliant qualities which are more seldom called into use...

CHAP. XV.
On the danger of an ill-directed Sensibility.

In considering the human character with a view to improve it, it is prudent to endeavour to discover the natural bent of the mind, and having found it, to apply your force to that side on which the warp lies, that you may lessen by counteraction the defect which you might be otherwise promoting, by applying your aid in a contrary direction. But the misfortune is, people who mean better than they judge, are apt to possess themselves of a set of general rules, good in themselves, perhaps, and originally gleaned from experience and observation on the nature of human things, but not applicable in all cases. These rules they keep by them as nostrums of universal efficacy, which they therefore often use in cases to which they do not apply. For to make any remedy effectual it is not enough to know the medicine, you must study the constitution also; for if there be not a congruity between the two, you may be injuring one patient by the means which are requisite to raise and restore another whose temperament is of a contrary description.

It is of importance in forming the female character that those on whom the task devolves, should possess so much penetration as accurately to discern its degree of sensibility, and so much judgment as to accommodate the treatment to the individual character. By constantly stimulating and extolling feelings naturally quick, those feelings will be rendered too acute and irritable. On the other hand a calm and equable temper will become obtuse by the total want of excitement; the former treatment converts the feelings into a source of error, agitation, and calamity, the latter starves their native energy, deadens the affections, and produces a cold, dull, selfish spirit; for the human mind is an instrument which will lose its sweetness if strained too high, and will be deprived of its tone and strength if not sufficiently raised.

It is cruel to chill the precious sensibility of an ingenuous soul, by treating with supercilious coldness, and unfeeling ridicule, every indication of a warm, tender, disinterested, and enthusiastic spirit, as if it exhibited symptoms of a deficiency in understanding or prudence. How many are apt to intimate, with a smile of mingled pity and contempt, that when she knows the world, that is, in other words, when she shall be grown cunning, selfish, and suspicious, she will be ashamed of her present glow of honest warmth, and of her lovely susceptibility of heart. May she never know the world, if the knowledge of it must be acquired at such an expence!...

For young women of naturally warm affections, in whom those affections have not been carefully disciplined, are in danger of incurring an unnatural irritability; and while their happiness falls a victim to the excess of uncontrolled feelings, they are liable at the same time to indulge a vanity of all others the most preposterous, that of being vain of their defects. They have heard sensibility highly commended, without having heard any thing of those bounds and fences which were intended to confine its excesses, or without having been imbued with that principle which would have given it a beneficial direction; and, conscious that they possess the quality itself in the extreme, and not conscious that they want all that makes that quality safe and delightful, they plunge headlong into those miseries from which they conceitedly imagine, that not principle, but coldness, has preserved the more sober-minded and well instructed of their sex.

But as it would be foreign to the present design to expatiate on those sad effects of ungoverned passion which terminate in criminal excesses, it is only intended here to hazard a few remarks on those lighter consequences of the same defect, which injure the comfort without injuring the character, and impair the happiness of life without incurring any very censurable degree of guilt or discredit. Let it, however, be incidentally remarked, and let it be carefully remembered, that if no women have risen so high in the scale of moral excellence as those whose natural warmth has been conscientiously governed by its true guide, and directed to its true end; so none have furnished such deplorable instances of extreme depravity as those who, through the ignorance or the dereliction of principle, have been abandoned by the excess of this very temper to the violence of ungoverned passions and uncontrolled inclinations. And, perhaps, if we were to enquire into the remote cause of some of the blackest crimes which stain the annals of mankind, profligacy, murder, and especially suicide,[254] we might trace them back to this original principle, an ungoverned Sensibility.

Notwithstanding all the fine theories in prose and verse to which this topic has given birth, it will be found that very exquisite sensibility contributes so little to *happiness*, and may yet be made to contribute so much to *usefulness*, that it may, perhaps, be considered as bestowed for an exercise to the possessor's own virtue, and as a keen instrument with which he may better work for the good of others.

Women of this cast of mind are less careful to avoid the charge of unbounded extremes, than to escape at all events the imputation of insensibility. They are little alarmed at the danger of *exceeding*, though terrified at the suspicion of *coming short* of what they take to be the extreme point of feeling. They will even resolve to prove the warmth of their sensibility, though at the expence of their judgment, and sometimes also of their justice. Even when they earnestly desire to *be* and to *do* good, they are apt to employ the wrong instrument to accomplish the right end. They employ the passions to do the work of the judgment; forgetting, or not knowing, that the passions were not given us to be used in the search and discovery of truth, which is the office of a cooler and more discriminating faculty; but that they were given to animate us to warmer zeal in the pursuit and practice of truth, when the judgment shall have pointed out what *is* truth.

Through this natural warmth, which they have been justly told is so pleasing, but which, perhaps, they have not been told will be continually exposing them to peril and to suffering, their joys and sorrows are excessive. Of this extreme irritability, as was before remarked, the ill-educated learn to boast as if it were an indication of superiority of soul, instead of labouring to restrain it as the excess of a temper which ceases to be interesting when it is no longer under the control of the governing faculty. It is misfortune enough to be born more liable to suffer and to sin, from this conformation of mind; it is too much to allow its unrestrained indulgence; it is still worse to be proud of so misleading a quality.

Flippancy, impetuosity, resentment, and violence of spirit, grow out of this disposition, which will be rather promoted than corrected, by the system of education on which we have been animadverting; in which system, emotions are too early and too much excited, and tastes and feelings are considered as too exclusively making up the whole of the female character; in which the judgment is little exercised, the reasoning powers are seldom brought into action, and self-knowledge and self-denial scarcely included.

The propensity of mind which we are considering, if unchecked, lays its possessors open to unjust prepossessions, and exposes them to all the danger of unfounded attachments. In early youth, not only love, but also friendship, at first sight, grows out of an ill-directed sensibility; and in after-life, women under the powerful influence of this temper, conscious that they have much to be borne with, are too readily inclined to select for their confidential connections, flexible and flattering companions, who will indulge and perhaps admire their faults, rather than firm and honest friends, who will reprove and would assist in curing them. We may adopt it as a general maxim, that an obliging, weak, yielding, complaisant friend, full of small attentions, with little religion, little judgment, and much natural acquiescence and civility, is a most dangerous, though generally a too much desired confidant: she soothes the indolence, and gratifies the vanity of her friend, by reconciling her to her own faults, while she neither keeps the understanding nor the virtues of that friend in exercise. These obsequious qualities are the "soft green"*[255] on which the soul loves to repose itself. But it is not a refreshing or a wholesome repose: we should not select, for the sake of present ease, a soothing flatterer, who will lull us into a pleasing oblivion of our feelings, but a friend, who, valuing our soul's health above our immediate comfort, will rouse us from torpid indulgence to animation, vigilance, and virtue.

An ill-directed sensibility leads a woman to be injudicious and eccentric in her *charities* also; she will be in danger of proportioning her bounty to the immediate effect which the

* Burke's *Sublime & Beautiful*.

distressed object produces on her senses: and she will be more liberal to a small distress which presents itself to her own eyes, than to the more pressing wants and better claims of those miseries of which she only hears the relation. There is a sort of stage effect which some people require for their charities; and she will be apt too to desire, that the object of her compassion shall have something interesting and amiable in it, such as shall furnish pleasing images and lively pictures to her imagination, and engaging subjects for description...nay, the more uninviting and repulsive cases may be better tests of the principle on which we relieve, than those which abound more in pathos and interest, as we can have less suspicion of our motive in the one case than in the other: but, while we ought to neglect neither of these supposed cases, yet the less our feelings are caught by pleasing circumstances, the less danger we shall be in of indulging self-complacency...

But through the want of that governing principle which should direct her sensibility, a tender-hearted woman, whose hand, if she be actually surrounded with scenes and circumstances to call it into action, is

Open as day to melting charity,[256]

yet her feelings being acted upon solely by local circumstances and present events, only remove her into another scene, distant from the wants she has been relieving; place her in the lap of indulgence, so surrounded with ease and pleasure, so immersed in the softnesses of life, that distress no longer finds any access to her presence, but through the faint and unaffecting medium of a distant representation: thus removed from the sight and sound of that misery which, when present, so tenderly affected her, she is apt to forget that misery exists; and as she hears but little, and sees nothing of want and sorrow, she is ready to fancy that the world is grown happier than it was: in the meantime, with a quiet conscience and a thoughtless vanity, she has been lavishing on superfluities that money which she would cheerfully have given to a charitable case, had she not forgotten that any such were in existence, because *Pleasure* had blocked up the avenues through which misery used to find its way to her heart; and now, when again such a case forces itself into her presence, she laments with real sincerity that the money is gone which should have relieved it.

In the meantime, perhaps, other women of less natural sympathy, but whose sympathies are under better regulation, or who act from a principle which requires little stimulus, have, by a constant course of self-denial, by a constant attention in refusing themselves unnecessary indulgences, and by guarding against that dissolving PLEASURE which melts down the firmest virtue that allows itself to bask in its beams, have been quietly furnishing a regular provision for miseries, which their know-ledge of the state of the world tells them are every where to be found, and which their obedience to the will of God tells them it is their duty to find out and to relieve; and for the general expectation to be called upon to relieve which, the conscien-tiously charitable will always be prepared.

On such a mind as we have been describing, *Novelty* also will operate with peculiar force, and in nothing more than in this article of charity. Old established institutions, whose continued existence must depend on the continued bounty of that afflu-ence to which they owed their origin, will be sometimes neglected, as presenting no variety to the imagination, as having by their uniformity ceased to be interesting; and having of course ceased to excite those springs of mere sensitive feeling which set the charity agoing, and which are no longer capable of awakening those sudden emotions of tenderness and gusts of pity, which newer forms of distress are necessary to excite afresh. As age comes on, that charity which has been the effect of mere feeling, having been often disappointed in its high expectations of the gratitude and subsequent merit of those it has relieved, grows cold and rigid; and by withdrawing its bounty, because some of its objects have been undeserving, it gives clear proof that what it bestowed was for its own gratifica-tion; and now finding that self-complacency at an end, it bestows no longer. Probably too the cause of so much disappointment may have been the ill choice of the objects which feeling has led them to make. The summer showers of mere sensibility soon dry up, while the living spring of Christian charity flows alike in all seasons.

The impatience, levity, and fickleness, of which women have been somewhat too generally accused, are perhaps not a little strengthened by the littleness and frivolousness of female pursuits. The sort of education they commonly receive, teaches girls to set a great price on small things. Besides this, they do not always learn to keep a very correct scale of degrees for the value of the objects of their admiration and attachment; but by a kind of unconscious idolatry, they rather make a merit of loving *supremely* things and persons which ought to be loved with moderation and in a subordinate degree the one to the other. Unluckily, they consider moderation as so necessarily indicating a cold heart and narrow soul, and they look upon a state of indifference with so much horror, that either to love or hate with energy is supposed by them to proceed from a higher state of mind than is possessed by more steady and equable characters. Whereas it is in fact the criterion of a warm but well directed sensibility, that while it is capable of loving with energy, it must be enabled by the judgment which governs it, to suit and adjust its degree of interest to the nature and excellence of the object about which it is interested; for unreasonable prepossession, disproportionate attachment, and capricious or precarious fondness, is not sensibility.

Excessive but unintentional *flattery* is another fault into which a strong sensibility is in danger of leading its possessor. A tender heart and a warm imagination conspire to throw a sort of radiance round the object of their love, till they are dazzled by a brightness of their own creating. The worldly and fashionable borrow the warm language of sensibility without having the same warm feeling; and young ladies get a habit of saying, and especially of writing, such over obliging and flattering things to each other, that this mutual politeness, aided by the self-love so natural to us all, and by an unwillingness to search into our own hearts, keeps up the illusion, and we get a habit of taking our character from the good we *hear* of ourselves, which others do not very well know, rather than from the evil we *feel* in ourselves, and which we therefore ought to be too thoroughly acquainted with.

Ungoverned sensibility is apt to give a wrong direction to its anxieties; and its affection often falls short of the true end of friendship. If the object of its regard happens to be sick, what enquiries! what prescriptions! what an accumulation is made of cases in which the remedy its fondness suggests has been successful! What an unaffected tenderness for the perishing body! Yet is this sensibility equally alive to the immortal interests of the sufferer? Is it not silent and at ease when it contemplates the dearest friend persisting in opinions essentially dangerous; in practices unquestionably wrong? Does it not view all this, not only without a generous ardour to point out the peril and rescue the friend; but if that friend be supposed to be dying, does it not even make it the *criterion* of kindness to let her die undeceived? What a want of real sensibility, to feel for the pain, but not for the danger, of those we love!...

Those young women in whom feeling is indulged to the exclusion of reason and examination, are peculiarly liable to be the dupes of prejudice, rash decisions, and false judgment. The understanding having but little power over the will, their affections are not well poized, and their minds are kept in a state ready to be acted upon by the fluctuations of alternate impulses; by sudden and varying impressions; by casual and contradictory circumstances; and by emotions excited by every accident. Instead of being guided by the broad views of general truth, and having one fixed principle, they are driven on by the impetuosity of the moment. And this impetuosity blinds the judgment as much as it misleads the conduct; so that, for want of a habit of cool investigation and inquiry, they meet every event without any previously formed opinion or rule of action: and as they do not accustom themselves to appreciate the real value of things, their attention is as likely to be led away by the under parts of a subject, as to seize on the leading feature. The same eagerness of mind which hinders the operation of the discriminating faculties, leads also to the error of determining on the rectitude of an action by its success, and to that of making the event of an undertaking decide on its justice or propriety: it also leads to that superficial and erroneous way of judging which fastens on exceptions, if they make in one's own favour, as grounds of reasoning, while they lead us to overlook received and general rules which tend to establish a doctrine contrary to their wishes.

Open hearted, indiscreet girls, often pick up a few strong notions which are as false in themselves as they are popular among the class in question: such as "that warm friends must make warm enemies;" – that "the generous love and hate with all their hearts;" – that "a reformed rake makes the best husband;" – that "there is no medium in marriage, but that it is a state of exquisite happiness, or exquisite misery;" with many other doctrines of equal currency and equal fondness. These they consider as axioms, and adopt as rules of life. From the two first of these oracular sayings girls are in no small danger of becoming unjust through the very warmth of their hearts: for they will get a habit of making their estimate of the good or ill qualities of others, merely in proportion to the greater or less degree of kindness which they themselves have received from them. Their estimation of general character is thus formed on insulated and partial grounds; on the accidental circumstance of personal predilection or personal pique. Kindness to themselves or their friends involves all possible excellence; neglect includes all imaginable defects. Friendship and gratitude can and should go a great way; but as they cannot convert vice into virtue, so they ought never to convert truth into falsehood. And it may be the more necessary to be upon our guard in this instance, because the very idea of gratitude may mislead us, by converting injustice into the semblance of a virtue. Warm expressions therefore should be limited to the conveying a sense of our own individual obligations which are real, rather than employed to give an impression of general excellence in the person who has obliged us, which may be imaginary. A good man is still good though it may not have fallen in his way to oblige or serve us; nay, though he may have neglected or even unintentionally hurt us; and sin is still sin though committed by the person in the world we best love, and to whom we are most obliged.

We come next to that fatal and most indelicate, nay gross maxim, that a reformed rake makes the best husband; an aphorism to which the principles and the happiness of so many young women have been sacrificed. It goes upon the preposterous supposition, not only that effects do not follow causes, but that they oppose them; on the supposition, that habitual vice creates rectitude of character, and that sin produces happiness: thus flatly contradicting what the moral government of God uniformly exhibits in the course of human events, and what revelation so evidently and universally teaches.

For it should be observed, that the reformation is generally, if not always, supposed to be brought about by the all-conquering force of female charms. Let but a profligate young man have a point to carry by winning the affections of a vain and thoughtless girl; he will begin his attack upon her heart by undermining her religious principles, and artfully removing every impediment which might have obstructed her receiving the addresses of a man without character. And while he will lead her, not to hear named without ridicule that change of heart which Scripture teaches and experience proves the power of Divine grace can work on a vicious character; while he will teach her to sneer at a change which he would treat with contempt, as a really miraculous conversion; yet he will not scruple to swear that the power of her beauty has worked an instantaneous equally complete revolution in his own loose practice.[257]

But supposing it possible that his reformation were genuine, it would even then by no means involve the truth of her proposition, that past libertinism insures future felicity; yet many a weak girl, confirmed in this palatable doctrine, by examples she has frequently admired of these surprising reformations, so conveniently effected in the last scene of most of our comedies, has not scrupled to risk her earthly and eternal happiness with a man, who is not ashamed to ascribe to the influence of her beauty that power of changing the heart which he impiously denies to Omnipotence itself.

As to the last of these practical aphorisms, "that there is no medium in marriage, but that it is a state of exquisite happiness or exquisite misery;" this, though not equally sinful, is equally delusive; for marriage is only one certain modification of human life, and human life is not commonly in itself a state of exquisite extremes, but is usually that mixed and moderate state, so naturally dreaded by those who set out with fancying this world a state of rapture, and so naturally expected by those who know it to be a state of probation and discipline. Marriage, therefore, is only one condition, and often the best condition, of that imperfect state of being which, though seldom very exquisite, is often very tolerable;[258] and which may yield much comfort to those who do not look for constant transport. But unfortunately, those who find themselves disappointed of the unceasing raptures they had anticipated in marriage, disdaining to sit down with so poor a provision as comfort, and scorning the acceptance of that moderate lot which Providence commonly bestows, with a view to check despondency and to repress presumption; give themselves up to the other alternative; and, by abandoning their hearts to discontent, make to themselves that misery with which their fervid imaginations had filled the opposite scale.

The truth is, these young ladies are very apt to pick up their opinions, less from the divines than the poets; and the poets, though it must be confessed they are some of the best embellishers of life, are not *quite* the safest conductors through it: as in travelling through a wilderness, though we avail ourselves of the harmony of singing birds, to render the grove delightful, yet we never think of following them as guides, to conduct us through its labyrinths.

Those women, in whom the natural defects of temper have been strengthened by an education which fosters their faults, are very dexterous in availing themselves of a hint, when it favours a ruling inclination, soothes vanity, indulges indolence, or gratifies their love of power. They have heard so often from their favourite sentimental authors, and their more flattering male friends, "that when nature denied them strength, she gave them fascinating graces in compensation; that their strength consists in their weakness;" and that "they are endowed with arts of persuasion which supply the absence of force, and the place of reason;" that they learn, in time, to pride themselves on that very weakness, and to become vain of their imperfections; till at length they begin to claim for their defects, not only pardon, but admiration. Hence they get to cherish a species of feeling which, if not checked, terminates in excessive selfishness; they learn to produce their inability to bear contradiction as a proof of their tenderness; and to indulge in that sort of irritability, in all that relates to themselves, which inevitably leads to the utter exclusion of all interest in the sufferings of others. Instead of exercising their sensibility in the wholesome duty of relieving distress and visiting scenes of sorrow, that sensibility itself is pleaded as a reason for their not being able to endure sights of woe, and for shunning the distress it should be exerted in removing. That exquisite sense of feeling which God implanted in the heart as a stimulus to quicken us in relieving the miseries of others, is thus introverted, and learns to consider *self* not as the agent, but the object of compassion. Tenderness is made an excuse for being hard-hearted; and instead of drying the weeping eyes of others, this false delicacy reserves its own selfish and ready tears for the more elegant and less expensive sorrows of the melting novel or the pathetic tragedy.

When feeling stimulates only to self-indulgence; when the more exquisite affections of sympathy and pity evaporate in sentiment, instead of flowing out in active charity, exerting itself in all the various shapes of assistance, protection, or consolation for every species of distress; it is an evidence that the feeling is of a spurious kind; and instead of being nourished as an amiable tenderness, it should be subdued as a fond and base self-love.

That idleness, to whose cruel inroads many women of fortune are unhappily exposed, from not having been trained to consider wholesome occupation, vigorous exertion, and systematic employment as making part of the indispensable duties of life, lays them open to a thousand evils of this kind, from which the useful and the busy are exempted: and, perhaps, it would not be easy to find a more pitiable object than a woman with a great deal of time and a great deal of money on her hands, who, never having been taught the conscientious use of either, squanders both at random, or rather moulders both away, without plan, without principle, and without pleasure; all whose projects begin and terminate in self; who considers the rest of the world only as they may be subservient to her gratification; and to whom it never occurred, that both her time and money were given for the gratification and good of others.

It is not much to the credit of the other sex, that they now and then lend themselves to the indulgence of this selfish spirit in their wives, and cherish by a kind of false fondness those faults which should be combated by good sense and a reasonable counteraction; slothfully preferring a little false peace, the purchase of precarious quiet, and the popular reputation of good nature, to the higher duty of forming the mind, fixing the principles, and strengthening the character of her with whom they are connected. Perhaps too, a little vanity in the husband helps out his good nature; he secretly rewards himself by the consciousness of his superiority; he feels a self-complacency in his patient condescension to her weakness, which tacitly flatters his own strength: and he is, as it were, paid for stooping by the increased sense of his own tallness. Seeing also, perhaps, but little of other women, he gets to believe that they are all pretty much alike, and that, as a man of sense, he must content himself with what he takes to be the common lot. Whereas, in truth, by his misplaced indulgence, he has rather *made* his own lot than *drawn* it; and thus, through an indolent despair in the husband of being able to improve by opposing them, it happens that helpless, fretful, and dawdling wives often acquire a more powerful ascendancy than the most discreet and amiable woman; and that the most absolute female tyranny is established by these sickly and capricious humours.

The poets again, who, to do them justice, are always ready to lend a helping hand when any mischief is to be done, have contributed their full share towards confirming these feminine follies: they have strengthened by adulatory maxims, sung in seducing strains, those faults which their talents and their

influence should have been employed in correcting. When fair
and youthful females are complimented with being

Fine by defect and delicately weak![259]

Is not a standard of feebleness held out to them, to which vanity
will gladly resort, and to which softness and indolence can easily
act up, or rather *act down*, if I may be allowed the expression?

When ladies are told by the same misleading, but to them
high, authority, that "smiles and tears are the irresistible arms
with which Nature has furnished them for conquering the
strong," will they not eagerly fly to this cheap and ready
artillery, instead of labouring to furnish themselves with a
reasonable mind, an equable temper, and a meek and quiet
spirit?

Every animal is endowed by Providence with the peculiar
powers adapted to its nature and its wants; while none, except
the human, by grafting art on natural sagacity, injures or mars
the gift. Spoilt women, who fancy there is something more
picquant and alluring in the mutable graces of caprice, than in the
monotonous smoothness of an even temper, and who also
having heard much, as was observed before, about their
"amiable weakness," learn to look about them for the best
succedaneum to strength, the supposed absence of which they
sometimes endeavour to supply by artifice. By this engine the
weakest woman frequently furnishes the converse to the famous
reply of the French Minister, who, when he was accused of
governing the mind of that feeble Queen Mary de Medicis by
sorcery, replied, "that the only sorcery he had used was that
influence which strong minds naturally have over weak ones."[260]

But though it be fair so to study the tempers, defects, and
weaknesses of others as to convert our knowledge of them to
the promotion of their benefit and our own; and though it be
making a lawful use of our penetration to avail ourselves of the
faults of others for "their good to edification;" yet all deviations
from the straight line of truth and simplicity; every plot insi-
diously to turn influence to unfair account; all contrivances to

extort from a bribed complaisance what reason and justice would refuse to our wishes; these are some of the operations of that lowest and most despicable engine, selfish cunning, by which *little minds sometimes govern great ones*.

And unluckily, women, from their natural desire to please, and from their sometimes doubting by what means this grand end may be best effected, are in more danger of being led into dissimulation than men; for dissimulation is the result of weakness, it is the refuge of doubt and distrust, rather than of conscious strength, the dangers of which lie another way. Frankness, truth, and simplicity, therefore, as they are inexpressibly charming, so are they peculiarly commendable in women, and nobly evince that while they wish to please, (and why should they not wish it?) they disdain to have recourse to any thing but what is fair, and just, and honourable to effect it; that they scorn to attain the most desired end by any but the most lawful means. The beauty of simplicity is indeed so intimately felt and generally acknowledged by all who have a true taste for personal, moral, or intellectual beauty, that women of the deepest artifice often find their account in assuming an exterior the most foreign to their character, and by affecting the most studied *naïveté*. It is curious to see the quantity of *art* some people put in practice in order to appear *natural*; and the deep *design* which is set at work to exhibit *simplicity*. And indeed this feigned simplicity is the most mischievous, because the most engaging of all the Proteus forms which dissimulation can put on. For the most free and bold sentiments have been sometimes hazarded with fatal success under this unsuspected mask. And an innocent, quiet, indolent, artless manner has been adopted as the most refined and successful accompaniment of sentiments, ideas, and designs, neither innocent, quiet, nor artless.

CHAP. XVI.
On dissipation and the modern habits of fashionable life.

Perhaps the interests of true friendship, elegant conversation, mental improvement, social pleasure, maternal duty, and conjugal comfort, never received such a blow as when Fashion issued out that arbitrary and universal decree, that *every body must be acquainted with every body*; together with that consequent, authoritative, but rather inconvenient clause that *everybody must go every where every night*. The devout obedience paid to this law is incompatible with the very being of friendship; for as the circle of acquaintance expands, and it will be continually expanding, the affections will be beaten out into such thin lamina as to leave little solidity remaining. The heart which is continually exhausting itself in professions grows cold and hard. The feelings of kindness diminish in proportion as the expression of kindness becomes more diffuse and indiscriminate. The very traces of "simplicity and godly sincerity," in a delicate female, wear away imperceptibly by constant collision with the world at large. And perhaps no woman takes so little interest in the happiness of her real friends, as she whose affections are incessantly evaporating in universal civilities; as she who is saying fond and flattering things at random to a circle of five hundred people every night.

The decline and fall of animated and instructive conversation has been in a good measure effected by this barbarous project of assembling *en masse*. An excellent prelate,* with whose friendship the author was long honoured, and who himself excelled in the art of conversation, used to remark, that a few years had brought about a great revolution in the manners of society; that it used to be the custom, previously to going into company, to think that something was to be communicated or received,

* The late Bishop Horne.[261]

taught or learnt; that the powers of the understanding were expected to be brought into exercise, and that it was therefore necessary to quicken the mind, by reading and thinking, for the share the individual might be expected to take in the general discourse; but that knowledge, and taste, and wit, and erudition, seemed now to be scarcely considered as necessary materials to be brought into the pleasurable commerce of the world; in which there was little chance of turning them to much account; and, therefore, he who possessed them, and he who possessed them not, were nearly on a footing.

It is obvious also that multitudinous assemblies are so little favourable to that *cheerfulness* which it should seem to be their very end to promote, that if there were any chemical process by which the quantum of spirits animal or intellectual could be ascertained the diminution would be found to have been inconceivably great, since the transformation of man and woman from a social to a gregarious animal.

But if it be true as to the injury which friendship, society, and cheerfulness, have sustained by this change of manners, how much more pointedly does the remark apply to family happiness!

Notwithstanding the known fluctuation of manners and the mutability of language, could it be foreseen, when the Apostle Paul exhorted "married women to be keepers *at home*,"[262] that the time would arrive when that very phrase would be selected to designate one of the most decided acts of dissipation? Could it be foreseen that when a fine lady should send out a notification that on such a night she shall be AT HOME, these two words (besides intimating the rarity of the thing) would present to the mind an image the most *undomestic* which language can convey? My country readers, who may require to have it explained that these two magnetic words now possess the powerful influence of drawing together every thing *fine* within the sphere of their attraction, may need also to be apprized that the guests afterwards are not asked what was *said* by the company, but whether the *crowd* was prodigious. The rule for deciding on the merit of a fashionable society not being by the taste or the spirit, but by the *score* and the *hundred*. The question of pleasure, like a Parliamentary question, is now carried by numbers. And when two parties modish, like two parties political, are run one against another on the same night, the same kind of mortification attends the leader of a defeated minority, the same triumph attends the exulting carrier of superior numbers, in the one case as in the other.

...Ladies...while they are devoted to the enjoyments of the world, yet retain considerable solicitude for the instruction of their daughters. But if they are really in earnest to give them a Christian education, they must themselves renounce a dissipated life. Or if they resolve to pursue the chace of pleasure they must renounce this prime duty. Contraries cannot unite. The moral nurture of a tall daughter can no more be administered by a mother whose time is absorbed by crowds abroad, than the physical nurture of her infant offspring can be supplied by her in a perpetual absence from home. And is not that a preposterous affection which leads a mother to devote a few months to the inferior duty of furnishing aliment to the mere animal life, and then to desert her post when the more important moral and intellectual cravings require sustenance? This great object is not to be effected with the shreds and parings rounded off from the circle of a dissipated life; but in order to its adequate execution the mother should carry it on with the same spirit and perseverance at home, which the father thinks it necessary to be exerting abroad in his public duty or professional engagements.

The usual vindication, and in theory it has a plausible sound, which has been offered for the large portion of time spent by women in acquiring ornamental talents is, that they are calculated to make the possessor love home, and that they innocently fill up the hours of leisure. The plea has indeed so promising an appearance that it is worth inquiring whether it be in fact true. Do we then, on fairly pursuing the inquiry, discover that those who have spent most time in such light acquisitions, are really remarkable for loving home or staying quietly there? or that when there, they are sedulous in turning time to the best account? I speak not of that rational and respectable class of

women, who, applying (as many of them do) these elegant
talents to their true purpose, employ them to fill up the
vacancies of better occupations, and to embellish the leisure of a
life actively good. But do we *generally* see that even the most
valuable and sober part of the reigning female acquisitions leads
their possessor to scenes most favourable to the enjoyment of
them? to scenes which we should naturally suppose she would
seek, in order to the more effectual cultivation of such rational
pleasures?

Would not those delightful pursuits, botany and drawing, for
instance, seem likely to court the fields, the woods, and gardens
of the paternal seat, as more congenial to their nature, and more
appropriate to their exercise, than barren watering places,
destitute of a tree, or an herb, or a flower, or an hour's interval
from successive pleasures, to profit by them even if they
abounded with the whole vegetable world from the "Cedar of
Lebanon to the Hyssop on the wall."[263]

From the mention of watering places, may the author be
allowed to suggest a few remarks on the evils which have arisen
from the general conspiracy of the gay to usurp the regions of
the sick; and converting the health-restoring fountains, meant as
a refuge for disease, into the resorts of vanity for those who have
no disease but idleness?

This inability of staying at home, as it is one of the most
infallible, so it is one of the most dangerous, symptoms of the
reigning mania. It would be more tolerable, did this epidemic
malady only break out as formerly, during the winter, or some
one season. Heretofore, the tenantry and the poor, the natural
dependents on the rural mansions of the opulent, had some
definite period to which they might joyfully look forward for
the approach of those patrons, part of whose business in life it
is, to influence by their presence, to instruct by their example,
to sooth by their kindness, and to assist by their liberality, those,
whom Providence in the distribution of human lots, has placed
under their more immediate protection. Though it would be far
from truth to assert, that dissipated people are never charitable,
yet I will venture to say, that dissipation is inconsistent with the

spirit of charity. That affecting precept followed by so gracious a promise, "Never turn away thy face from any poor man, and then the face of the Lord shall never be turned away from thee,"[264] cannot literally mean that we should *give* to all, as then we should soon have nothing left to give: but it seems to intimate the habitual attention, the duty of inquiring out all cases of distress, in order to judge which are fit to be relieved; now for this inquiry, for this attention, for this sympathy, the dissipated have little taste and less leisure.

Let a reasonable conjecture (for calculation would fail!) be made of how large a diminution of the general good has been effected in this single respect, by causes, which, though they do not seem important in themselves, yet make no inconsiderable part of the mischief arising from modern manners: and I speak now to persons who *intend* to be charitable. What a deduction will be made from the aggregate of charity, by a circumstance apparently trifling, when we consider what would be the beneficial effects of that regular bounty which must almost unavoidably result from the evening walks of a great and benevolent family among the cottages of their own domain: the thousand little acts of, comparatively, unexpensive kindness which the *sight* of petty wants and difficulties would excite; wants, which will scarcely be felt in the relation; and which will probably be neither seen, nor felt, nor fairly represented, in their long absences, by an agent. And what is even almost more than the good done, is the habit of mind kept up in those who do it: would not this habit exercised on the Christian principle, that "even a cup of cold water," given upon *right motives*, shall not lose its reward;[265] while the giving "all their goods to feed the poor,"[266] without the true *principle* of charity shall profit them nothing; would not this habit, I say, be almost the best part of the education of daughters?*

---

* It would be a pleasant summer amusement for our young ladies of fortune, if they were to preside at such spinning feasts as are instituted at Nuneham for the promotion of virtue and industry in their own sex. Pleasurable anniversaries of this kind would serve to combine in the mind of the poor two ideas, which ought never to be separated, but which *they* are

But transplant this wealthy and bountiful family periodically amidst the frivolous and uninteresting bustle of the watering place; where it is not denied that frequent public and fashionable acts of charity may make a part, and it is well they do make part, of the business and of the amusement of the day; with this latter, indeed, they are sometimes good-naturedly mixed up. But how shall we compare the regular systematical good these persons would be doing at their own home, with the light, and amusing, and bustling bounties of these public places? The illegal raffle[267] at the toy-shop, for some distress, which though it may be real, and which if real it ought to be relieved, is yet less easily ascertained than the wants of their own poor, or the debts of their distressed tenants. How shall we compare the broad stream of bounty which should be flowing through, and refreshing whole districts, with the penurious current of the subscription breakfast for the needy musician, in which the price of the gift is taken out in the diversion, and in which pleasure dignifies itself with the name of bounty? How shall we compare the attention, and time, and zeal which would otherwise, perhaps, be devoted to the village school, spent in hawking about benefit tickets for a broken player, while the kindness of the benefactress, perhaps, is rewarded by scenes in which her charity is not always repaid by the purity of the exhibition?

Far be it from the author to wish to check the full tide of charity wherever it is disposed to flow! Would she could multiply the already abundant streams, and behold every source purified! But in the public resorts there are many who are able and willing to give. In the sequestered, though populous village, there is, perhaps, only one affluent family: the distress which they do not *behold*, will probably not be attended to: the distress

---

not very forward to unite, – that the great wish is to make them *happy* as well as good. Occasional approximations of the rich and poor, for the purpose of relief and instruction, and annual meetings for the purpose of innocent pleasure, would do much towards wearing away discontent, and contribute to reconcile the lower class to that state in which it has pleased God to place them.

which *they* do not relieve will probably not be relieved at all: the wrongs which *they* do not redress will go unredressed: the oppressed whom *they* do not rescue will sink under the tyranny of the oppressor. Through their own rural domains too, charity runs in a clearer current, and is less polluted with any suspicion of that muddy tincture which it is sometimes apt to contract in passing through the impure soil of the world.

But to return from this too long digression: the old standing objection formerly brought forward by the prejudices of the other sex, and too eagerly laid hold on as a shelter for indolence and ignorance by ours, was, that intellectual accomplishments too much absorbed the thoughts and affections, took women off from the necessary attention to domestic duties, and superinduced a contempt or neglect of whatever was useful. – But it is peculiarly the character of the present day to detect absurd opinions, and to expose plausible theories by the simple and decisive answer of experiment; and it is presumed that this popular error, as well as others, is daily receiving the refutation of actual experience. For it cannot surely be maintained on ground that is any longer tenable, that acquirements truly rational are calculated to draw off the mind from real duties. Whatever removes prejudices, whatever stimulates industry, whatever rectifies the judgment, whatever corrects self-conceit, whatever purifies the taste, and raises the understanding, will be likely to contribute to moral excellence: to woman, moral excellence is the grand object of education; and of moral excellence, domestic life is to woman the appropriate sphere.

Count over the list of females who have made shipwreck of their fame and virtue, and have furnished the most lamentable examples of the dereliction of family duties; and the number will not be found considerable who have been led astray by the pursuit of knowledge. And if a few deplorable instances of this kind be produced, it will commonly be found that there was little infusion in the minds of such women of that correcting principle without which all other knowledge only "puffeth up."[268]

The time nightly expended in late female vigils is expended

by the light of far other lamps than those which are fed by the student's oil; and if families *are* to be found who are neglected through too much study in the mistress, it will probably be proved to be Hoyle,[269] and not Homer, who has robbed her children of her time and affections. For one family which has been neglected by the mother's passion for books, an hundred have been deserted through her passion for play. The husband of a fashionable woman will not often find that the library is the apartment the expences of which involve him in debt or disgrace. And for one literary slattern, who now manifests her indifference to her husband by the neglect of her person, there are scores of elegant spendthrifts who ruin theirs by excess of decoration.

May I digress a little while I remark, that I am far from asserting that literature has never filled women with vanity and self-conceit; but I will assert, that in general those whom books are supposed to have spoiled, would have been spoiled in another way without them. She who is a vain pedant because she has read much, has probably that defect in her mind which would have made her a vain fool if she had read nothing. It is not her having more knowledge but less sense, which makes her insufferable; and illiteracy would have added little to her value, for it is not what she has, but what she wants, which makes her unpleasant. These instances too only furnish a fresh argument for the general cultivation of the female mind. The wider diffusion of sound knowledge would remove that temptation to be vain which may be excited by its rarity.

But while we would assert that a woman of a cultivated intellect is not driven by the same necessity into the giddy whirl of public resort; who but regrets that real cultivation does not *inevitably* preserve her from it? No wonder that inanity of character, that vacuity of mind, that torpid ignorance, should plunge into dissipation as their natural refuge; should seek to bury their insignificance in the crowd of pressing multitudes, and hope to escape analysis and detection in the undistinguished masses of mixed assemblies! *There* attrition rubs all bodies smooth, and makes all surfaces alike; thither superficial and external accomplishments naturally fly as to their proper scene of action; as to a field where competition is in perpetual exercise; where the laurels of admiration are to be won, and the trophies of vanity triumphantly carried off!

It would indeed be matter of little comparative regret, if this corrupt air were only breathed by those of the above description whose natural element it seems to be; but who can forbear regretting that the power of fashion attracts also into this impure and unwholesome atmosphere minds of a better make, of higher aims and ends, of more ethereal temper? Minds who, renouncing enjoyments for which they have a genuine taste, and which would make them really happy, neglect society they love and pursuits they admire, in order that they may *seem* happy and *be* fashionable in the chace of pleasures they despise, and in company they disapprove!...

This contagion is so deep, so wide, and fatal, that if I were called upon to assign the predominant cause of the greater portion of the misfortunes and corruptions of the great and gay in our days, I should not look for it principally in any seemingly great or striking cause; not in the practice of notorious vices, not originally in the dereliction of Christian principle; but I should not hesitate to ascribe it to a growing, regular, systematic series of amusements; to an incessant, boundless, and not very disreputable DISSIPATION. Other corruptions, though more formidable in appearance, are yet less fatal in some respects, because they leave us intervals to reflect on their turpitude, and spirit to lament their excesses: but dissipation is the more hopeless, as by engrossing almost the whole of life, and enervating the whole moral and intellectual system, it leaves neither time for reflection, nor space for self-examination, nor temper for the cherishing of right affections, nor leisure for the operation of sound principles, nor interval for regret, nor vigour to resist temptation, nor energy to struggle for amendment.

The great master of the science of pleasure among the ancients,[270] who reduced it into a system, which he called *the chief good of man*, directed that there should be interval enough between the succession of delights to sharpen inclination; and accordingly instituted periodical days of abstinence: well-knowing that gratification was best promoted by previous self-denial. But so little do our votaries of fashion understand the true nature of pleasure, that one amusement is allowed to overtake another without any interval, either for recollection of the past, or preparation for the future. Even on their own selfish principle, therefore, nothing can be worse understood than this unremitted degree of enjoyment: for to such a degree of labour is the pursuit carried, that the pleasures exhaust instead of exhilarating; and their recreations require to be rested from.

And, not to argue the question on the ground of religion, but merely on that of present enjoyment; look abroad and see who are the people that complain of weariness, listlessness, and dejection. You will not find them among such as are overdone with work, but with pleasure. The natural and healthful fatigues of business are recruited with natural and cheap gratifications; but a spirit worn down with the toils of amusement, requires pleasures of poignancy; varied, multiplied, stimulating!

It has been observed by medical writers, that that sober excess in which many indulge, by constantly eating and drinking a little too much at every day's dinner and every night's supper, more effectually undermines the health, than those accidental excesses with which others now and then break in upon a life of general sobriety. This illustration is not introduced with a design to recommend occasional deviations into gross vice, by way of a pious receipt for mending the morals; but merely to suggest that there is more probability that those who are sometimes driven by unresisted passion into irregularities which shock their cooler reason, are more liable to be roused to a sense of their danger, than persons whose perceptions of evil are blunted by a round of systematical, excessive, and yet not scandalous dissipation. And when I affirm that this system of regular indulgence relaxes the soul, enslaves the heart, bewitches the senses, and thus disqualifies for pious thought or useful action, without having any thing in it so gross as to shock the conscience; and when I hazard an opinion that this state is more formidable because less alarming than that which bears upon it a more determined character of evil, I no more mean to speak of the latter in slight and palliating terms, than I would intimate that because the sick sometimes recover from a fever, but seldom from a palsy, that a fever is therefore a safe or a healthy state.

But there seems to be an error in the first concoction, out of which the subsequent errors successively grow. First then, as has been observed before, the showy education of women tends chiefly to qualify them for the glare of public assemblies: secondly, they seem in many instances to be so educated, with a view to the greater probability of their being splendidly married: thirdly, it is alleged in vindication of those dissipated practices, that daughters can only be seen, and admirers procured at balls, operas, and assemblies; and that therefore, by a natural consequence, balls, operas, and assemblies must be followed up without intermission till the object be effected. For the accomplishment of this object it is that all this complicated machinery had been previously set a going, and kept in motion with an activity not at all slackened by the disordered state of the system; for some machines, instead of being stopped, go faster because the true spring is out of order; the only difference being that they go wrong, and so the increased rapidity only adds to the quantity of error.

It is also, as we have already remarked, an error to fancy that the love of pleasure exhausts itself by indulgence, and that the very young are chiefly addicted to it. The contrary appears to be true. The desire grows with the pursuit upon the same principle as motion is quickened by the continuance of the impetus.

First then, it cannot be thought unfair to trace back the excessive fondness for amusement to that mode of education we have elsewhere reprobated. Few of the accomplishments, falsely so called, assist the development of the faculties: they do not exercise the judgment, nor bring into action those powers which fit the heart and mind for the occupations of life: they do not prepare women to love home, to understand its occupations, to enliven its uniformity, to fulfil its duties, to multiply its comforts: they do not lead to that sort of experimental logic, if I may so speak, compounded of observation and reflection, which makes up the moral science of life and manners. Talents which have *display* for their object despise the narrow stage of home: they demand mankind for their spectators, and the world for their theatre.

While one cannot help shrinking a little from the idea of a delicate young creature, lovely in person, and engaging in mind and manners, sacrificing nightly at the public shrine of Fashion, at once the votary and the victim; one cannot help figuring to oneself how much more interesting she would appear in the eyes of a man of feeling, did he behold her in the more endearing situations of domestic life. And who can forbear wishing, that the good sense, good taste, and delicacy of the men had rather led them to prefer seeking companions for life in the almost sacred quiet of a virtuous home? *There* they might have had the means of seeing and admiring those amiable beings in the best point of view: *there* they might have been enabled to form a juster estimate of female worth, than is likely to be obtained in scenes where such qualities and talents as might be expected to add to the stock of domestic comfort must necessarily be kept in the back ground, and where such only *can* be brought into view as are not particularly calculated to insure the certainty of home delights.

> O! did they keep their persons fresh and new,
> How would they pluck allegiance from men's hearts,
> And win by rareness![271]

But by what unaccountable infatuation is it that men too, even men of sense, join in the confederacy against their own happiness by looking for their home companions in the resorts of vanity? Why do not such men rise superior to the illusions of fashions? why do they not uniformly seek her who is to preside in *their* families in the bosom of her own? in the practice of every domestic duty, in the exercise of every amiable virtue, in the exertion of every elegant accomplishment? those accomplishments of which we have been reprobating, not the possession, but the application? *there* they would find her exerting them to their true end, to enliven business, to animate retirement, to embellish the charming scene of family delights, to heighten the interesting pleasures of social intercourse, and, rising to their noblest object, to adorn the doctrine of God her Saviour.

If, indeed, woman were mere outside form and face only, and if *mind* made up no part of her composition, it would follow that a ball-room was quite as appropriate a place for choosing a wife, as an exhibition room for choosing a picture. But, inasmuch as women are not mere portraits, their value not being determinable by a glance of the eye, it follows that a different mode of appreciating their value, and a different place for viewing them antecedent to their being individually selected, is desirable. The two cases differ also in this, that if a man select a picture for himself from among all its exhibited competitors, and bring it to his own house, the picture being passive, he is able to *fix* it there: while the wife, picked up at a public place, and accustomed to incessant display, will not, it is probable, when brought home stick so quietly to the spot where he fixes her; but will escape to the exhibition room again, and continue to be displayed at every subsequent exhibition, just as if she were not become private property, and had never been definitively disposed of.

It is the novelty of a thing which astonishes us, and not its absurdity: objects may be so long kept before the eye that it begins no longer to observe them; or may be brought into such close contact with it, that it does not discern them. Long habit so reconciles us to almost any thing, that the grossest improprieties cease to strike us when they are once melted into the common course of action. This, by the way, is a strong reason for carefully sifting every opinion and every practice before we let them incorporate into the mass of our habits, for which they will be no more examined. – Would it not be accounted preposterous for a young man to say that he had fancied such a lady would dance a better minuet, because he had seen her behave devoutly at Church, and *therefore* had chosen her for his partner? and yet he is not thought at all absurd when he intimates that he chose a partner for life because he was pleased with her at a ball. Surely the place of choosing and the motive of choice, would be just as appropriate in one case as in the other, and the mistake, if the judgment failed, not *quite* so serious.

There is, among the more elevated classes of society, a certain set of persons who are pleased exclusively to call themselves, and whom others by a sort of compelled courtesy are pleased to call, *the fine world.* This small detachment consider their situation with respect to the rest of mankind, just as the ancient Grecians did theirs; that is, as the Grecians thought there were but two sorts of beings, and that all who were not Grecians were barbarians; so this *certain set* considers society as resolving itself into two distinct classes, the *fine world* and the *people*; to which last class they turn over all who do not belong to their little *coterie*, however high their rank or fortune. Celebrity, in their estimation, is not bestowed by birth or talents, but by being connected with *them.* They have laws, immunities, privileges, and almost a language of their own; they form a kind of distinct *cast,*[272] and with a sort of *esprit du corps* detach themselves from others, even in general society, by an affectation of distance and coldness; and only whisper and smile in their own little groupes of the initiated; their confines are jealously guarded, and their privileges are incommunicable.

In this society a young man loses his natural character, which, whatever it might originally have been, is melted down and cast into the one prevailing mould of Fashion; all the strong, native, discriminating qualities of his mind being made to take one shape, one stamp, one superscription! However varied and distinct might have been the materials which nature threw into the crucible, plastic Fashion takes care that they shall all be the same, or at least appear the same, when they come out of the mould. A young man in such an artificial state of society, accustomed to the voluptuous ease, refined luxuries, soft accommodations, obsequious attendance, and all the unrestrained indulgences of a fashionable club, is not likely after marriage to take very cordially to a home, unless very extraordinary exertions are made to amuse, to attach, and to interest him: and he is not likely to lend a very helping hand to the happiness of the union, whose most laborious exertions have hitherto been little more than a selfish stratagem to reconcile health with pleasure. Excess of gratification has only served to make him irritable and exacting; it will of course be no part of his project to make sacrifices, but to receive them: and what would appear incredible to the *Paladins* of gallant times, and the *Chevaliers Preux* of more heroic days, even in the necessary business of establishing himself for life, he sometimes is more disposed to expect attentions than to make advances.

Thus the indolent son of fashion, with a thousand fine, but dormant qualities, which a bad tone of manners forbids him to bring into exercise; with real energies which that tone does not allow him to discover, and an unreal apathy which it commands him to feign; with the heart of a hero, perhaps, if called into the field, he affects the manners of a Sybarite;[273] and he, who with a Roman, or what is more, with a British valour, would leap into the gulph at the call of public duty,

Yet in the soft and piping time of peace,[274]

when fashion has resumed her rights, he would murmur if a rose-leaf lay double under him.

The clubs above alluded to, as has been said, generate and cherish luxurious habits, from their perfect ease, undress, liberty, and equality of distinction in rank: they promote a spirit for play, and in short, every temper and spirit which tends to undomesticate; and what adds to the mischief is, all this is attained at a cheap rate compared with what may be procured at home in the same style.

These indulgencies, and that habit of mind, gratify so many passions, that it can never be counteracted successfully by anything of *its own kind*; or which gratifies the *same* habits. Now, a passion for gratifying vanity, and a spirit of dissipation, *is* a passion of the same kind; and therefore, though for a few weeks, a man who has chosen his wife in the haunts of dissipation, and this wife, a woman made up of accomplishments, may, from the novelty of the connexion and of the scene, continue domestic; yet in a little time she will find that those passions, to which she has trusted for making his married life pleasant, will long for the more comfortable pleasures of the club; and *she* will, while they are pursued, be consigned over to solitary evenings at home, or driven back to the old dissipations.

To conquer the passion for club gratifications, a woman must not strive to feed it with sufficient aliment of the same kind in her society, either at home or abroad; for this she cannot do: but she must supplant and overcome it by a passion of a different nature, which Providence has kindly planted within us, the love of fire-side enjoyments. But to qualify herself for administering these, she must cultivate her understanding and her heart; acquiring at the same time that modicum of accomplishments suited to his taste, which may qualify her for possessing, both for him and for herself, greater varieties of safe recreation.

One great cause of the want of attachment in these modish couples is, that by living in the world at large, they are not driven to depend on each other as the chief source of comfort. Now it is pretty clear, in spite of modern theories, that the very frame and being of societies, whether great or small, public or private, is jointed and glued together by dependence. Those attachments, which arise from, and are compacted by, a sense of mutual wants, mutual affection, mutual benefit, and mutual obligation, are the cement which secure the union of the family as well as of the state.

Unfortunately, when two young persons of the above description marry, the union is sometimes considered rather as the end than the beginning of an engagement: the attachment of each to the other is rather viewed as an object already completed, than as one which marriage is to confirm more closely. But the companion for life is not always chosen from the purest motive; she is selected, perhaps, because she is admired by other men, rather than because she possesses in an eminent degree those peculiar qualities which are likely to constitute the individual happiness of the man who chooses her. Vanity usurps the place of affection; and indolence swallows up the judgment. Not happiness, but some easy substitute for happiness is pursued; and a choice which may excite envy, rather than produce satisfaction, is adopted as the means of effecting it.

The pair, not *matched, but joined*, set out separately with their independent and individual pursuits; whether it made a part of their original plan or not, that they should be indispensably necessary to each other's comfort, the sense of this necessity, probably not very strong at first, rather diminishes than increases by time; they live so much in the world, and so little together, that to stand well with their *own set* continues the favourite project of each; while to stand well with each other is considered as an under part of the plot in the drama of life: whereas, did they start in the conjugal race with the fixed idea that they were to look to each other for the principal happiness of life, not only principle, but prudence, and even selfishness would convince them of the necessity of sedulously cultivating each other's esteem and affection as the grand spring of promoting that happiness. But vanity, and the desire of flattery and applause, still continue to operate. Even after the husband is brought to feel a perfect indifference for his wife, he still likes to see her decorated in a style which may serve to justify his choice. He encourages her to set off her person, not so much for his own gratification, as that his self-love may be flattered, by her continuing to attract the admiration of those whose opinion is the standard by which he measures his fame, and which fame is to stand him in the stead of happiness. Thus is she necessarily exposed to the two-fold temptation of being at once neglected by her husband, and exhibited as an object of attraction to other men. If she escape this complicated danger, she will be indebted for her preservation not to his prudence, but to her own principles.

In some of these modish marriages, instead of the decorous neatness, the pleasant intercourse, and the mutual warmth of communication of the once social dinner; the late and uninteresting meal is commonly hurried over by the languid and slovenly pair, that the one may have time to dress for his club, and the other for her party. And in these cold abstracted *têtes-à-*

têtes, they often take as little pains to entertain each other, as if the one was precisely the only human being in the world in whose eyes the other did not feel it necessary to appear agreeable.

But if these young and perhaps really amiable persons could struggle against the imperious tyranny of fashion, and contrive to pass a little time together, so as to get acquainted with each other; and if each would live in the lively and conscientious exercise of those talents and attractions which they sometimes know how to produce on occasions not *quite* so justifiable; they would, I am persuaded, often find out each other to be very agreeable people. And both of them, delighted and delighting, would no longer be driven to the anxious necessity of perpetually flying from home as from the only scene which offers no possible materials for pleasure.

It may seem a contradiction to have asserted that beings of all ages, tempers, and talents, should with such unremitting industry follow up any way of life if they did not find some enjoyment in it; yet I appeal to the bosoms of these incessant hunters in the chace of pleasure, whether they are really happy. No. – In the full tide and torrent of diversion, in the full blaze of gaiety,

> The heart distrusting asks if this be joy?[275]

But there is an anxious restlessness which, if not interesting, is bustling. There is the dread and partly the discredit of being suspected of having one hour unmortgaged, not only to successive, but contending engagements; this it is, and not the pleasure of the engagement itself, which is the object. There is an agitation in the arrangements which imposes itself on the vacant heart for happiness. There is a tumult kept up in the spirits which is a busy though treacherous substitute for comfort. The multiplicity of solicitations soothes vanity. The very regret that they cannot be all accepted has its charms; for dignity is flattered because refusal implies importance. Then there is the joy of being invited when others are neglected; the triumph of showing one's less modish friend that one is going where she cannot come; and the feigned regret at being *obliged* to go, assumed before her who is half wild at being obliged to stay away. These are some of the supplemental shifts for happiness with which vanity contrives to feed her hungry followers.

In the succession of open houses in which Pleasure is to be started and pursued on any given night, the existing place is never taken into the account of enjoyment: the scene of which is always supposed to lie in any place where her votaries happen not to be. Pleasure has no present tense: but in the house which her pursuers have just quitted, and in the house to which they are just hastening, a stranger might conclude the slippery goddess had really fixed her throne, and that her worshippers considered the existing scene, which they seem compelled to suffer, but from which they are eager to escape, as really detaining them from some positive joy to which they are flying in the next crowd; till, if he meets them there, he will find the component parts of each precisely the same. He would hear the same stated phrases interrupted, not answered, by the same stated replies, the unfinished sentence "driven adverse to the winds" by pressing multitudes; the same warm regret mutually exchanged by two friends (who had been expressly denied to each other all the winter) that they had not met before; the same soft and smiling sorrow at being torn away from each other now; the same anxiety to renew the meeting, with perhaps the same secret resolution to avoid it. He would hear described with the same pathetic earnestness the difficulties of getting into this house, and the dangers of getting out of the last! the perilous retreat of former nights, effected amidst the shock of chariots and the clang of contending coachmen! a retreat indeed effected with a skill and peril little inferior to that of the *ten thousand*,[276] and detailed with far juster triumph; for that which happened only once in a life to the Grecian Hero occurs to these British heroines every night.

With "mysterious reverence"[277] I forbear to descant on those serious and interesting rites, for the more august and solemn celebration of which Fashion nightly convenes these splendid myriads to her more sumptuous temples. Rites! which, when engaged in with due devotion, absorb the whole soul, and call every passion into exercise, except indeed those of love, and peace, and kindness, and gentleness. Inspiring rites! which stimulate fear, rouse hope, kindle zeal, quicken dulness, sharpen discernment, exercise memory, inflame curiosity! Rites! in short, in the due performance of which all the energies and attentions, all the powers and abilities, all the abstraction and exertion, all the diligence and devotedness, all the sacrifice of time, all the contempt of ease, all the neglect of sleep, all the oblivion of care, all the risks of fortune (half of which if directed to their true objects would change the very face of the world): all these are concentrated to one point; a point in which the wise and the weak, the learned and the ignorant, the fair and the frightful, the sprightly and the dull, the rich and the poor, the Patrician and the Plebeian, meet in one common and uniform equality; an equality as religiously respected in these solemnities, in which all distinctions are levelled at a blow, and of which the very spirit is therefore democratical, as it is combated in all other instances.

NOTES

[1] Mrs Ann Gwatkin, a wealthy citizen of Bristol, sent her daughter to the Mores' school; her son was to marry the favourite niece of Sir Joshua Reynolds, to whom she introduced More.

[2] *The Rivals* was first performed at Covent Garden on 17 January 1775. The revised version was performed on 28 January 1775. When R. Brimley Johnson included extracts from this letter in his selection, *The Letters of Hannah More*, Bodley Head, 1925, he excluded the section referring to Sheridan's *The Rivals*, and suggested the letter dated from 1773.

[3] *The Maid of the Oaks*, presented by Garrick at Drury Lane, was written in 1774 by General John Burgoyne (1722–92). In September 1774 he went to America and played a major part, commanding British troops, in the American War of Independence.

[4] The Pantheon (1772–92) designed by James Wyatt, stood in Oxford Street, London. It was used for the staging of masquerades and concerts as well as for assemblies.

[5] David Garrick (1717–79), actor and theatre manager, and his wife Eva Marie Garrick (1724–1822) had a town residence at 5, Adelphi Terrace, and a small house in the country, near Hampton Court.

[6] Sir Joshua Reynolds (1723–92), portrait painter, lived with his youngest sister Frances Reynolds at 47, Leicester Fields, now Leicester Square. Frances Reynolds painted More's portrait, now in the Georgian House, Bristol.

[7] Samuel Johnson (1709–84) published his *Journey to the Western Isles of Scotland* in 1775. It was printed by Thomas Cadell, bookseller and publisher, who came from the same parish in Bristol as the Mores.

[8] Elizabeth Montagu (1720–1800), Elizabeth Carter (1726–1806) and Frances Boscawen (1722?-1805) were three of the circle of 'Blue Stockings' of whom More wrote in her 'Bas Bleu', see notes 14, 70 and 75. See also Introduction, above p. xi. Gaius Lælius (f. 140 BC) and Titus Atticus (110–32 BC) were Roman intellectuals and patrons, now known chiefly through the writings of Cicero.

[9] *Braganza* by Robert Jephson (1736–1803) was produced with great success at the Theatre Royal, Drury Lane in February 1775. It was particularly admired by Horace Walpole, who wrote an epilogue for it.

[10] Hester Chapone (1727–1801), writer and another of the *Bas Bleu* set, was widowed in 1761.

[11] More's extreme Sabbatarianism, so much in evidence in her later writings, can be seen here in embryo.

[12] Martha More (1747–1819), known as Patty, was the youngest of More's sisters.

[13] Job, the Old Testament patriarch.

[14] Elizabeth Montagu is here compared to Gaius Mæcenas (died 8 BC), the patron of a literary circle which included Virgil and Horace.

[15] Anna Laetitia Barbauld (1743–1825) had published her first volume of poems in 1773. This included *Corsica*, a poem Elizabeth Montagu much admired.

[16] More published her ballad 'Sir Eldred of the Bower' in 1776.

[17] Sheridan raised the money to become a proprietor, and, with Garrick's active support, became his successor in the management of Drury Lane. Garrick made his final appearance on 10 June 1776.

[18] More published her poem 'The Bleeding Rock' in 1776. It was printed together with 'Sir Eldred' in a single volume.

[19] See Joseph Addison, *The Spectator* No. 271, Thursday, 10 January 1712.

[20] More had just taken an apartment in the centre house in the Adelphi, close to the Garricks.

[21] Richard Berenger (died 1782), Master of the King's Horse, published *The History and Art of Horsemanship* in 1771.

[22] James Boswell (1740–95) published *An Account of Corsica... and memoirs of Pascal Paoli* in 1768. He had known Johnson since 1763.

[23] David Hume (1711–76), philosopher, died on 25 August 1776.

[24] Richard Price (1723–91) published his *Observations on the Nature of Civil Liberty, the Principles of Government and the Policy of the War with America* in 1776. Josiah Tucker (1712–99) responded, in *Four Tracts on Political and Commercial Questions* (1776), *A Humble Address and Earnest Appeal* (1777) and *The Respective Pleas and Arguments of the Mother Country and the Colonies* (1775), in a way which may have disappointed More.

[25] Soame Jenyns (1704–87) published *A View of the Internal Evidence of the Christian Religion* in 1776. Richard Owen Cambridge (1717–1802) had published his mock-heroic poem *The Scribleriad* in 1751; More refers to him in the 'Bas Bleu', see below p. 27.

[26] Mrs Walsingham, daughter of Sir John Hanbury-Williams, a well-educated and strong-minded patron and hostess, became an unlikely friend and critic of More. Elizabeth Newton was the second wife of Thomas Newton (1704–82), Bishop of Bristol and Dean of St Paul's.

[27] Richard Cumberland (1732–1811) published a 27-page volume of *Odes*, London, 1776. He was better known as a dramatist; his comedies *The Wheel of Fortune* and *The Fashionable Lover* were produced at the Theatre Royal, Drury Lane.

[28] Sir James Stonhouse (1716–95), physician and clergyman, was the Mores' neighbour and patron in Bristol. Charles Middleton (1726–1813), later First Lord of the Admiralty and first Baron Barham (1805), his wife Margaret and their friend Mrs Bouverie, were later to inspire More with their passionate commitment to the Anti-Slave Trade movement. Jacques Saurin was a Huguenot preacher whose sermons were published in a translation by the Baptist minister Robert Robinson, 5 vols, Cambridge, 1775–84.

[29] Elizabeth Chudleigh (1720–88) had bigamously married Evelyn Pierrepont, second Duke of Kingston (1711–73) in 1769. A charge of bigamy was instigated by the duke's nephew and her trial before the House of Lords took place in April 1776.

[30] Henry Fiennes Clinton, 2nd Duke of Newcastle (1720–94).

[31] A sacque was originally a loose kind of gown, but by the eighteenth century the word was also being used to mean a silk train attached to the shoulders of such a gown. (*OED*)

[32] John Dunning (1731–83), lawyer and MP for Calne 1768–82. See note 94 below.

[33] Margaret Caroline Rudd was tried at the Old Bailey on 8 December 1775 charged with the forgery of a bond for £10,600 to defraud Sir Thomas Frankland and William Adair. Witnesses contradicted each other and, because of the conflicting evidence, Rudd was found not guilty. Many considered her fortunate in the verdict. See John Bailey, *The Trial at large of Mrs. Margaret Caroline Rudd...*, London, 1775.

[34] Samuel Foote (1720–77), actor and dramatist, planned to portray the duchess as Lady Crocodile in his play *A Trip to Calais*, but she prevented him.

[35] Hannah Pritchard (1711–68), actress, was best known as Garrick's Lady Macbeth. She died about eight years before More moved to London. Her daughter was a friend of More.

[36] Henry Herbert, 10th Earl of Pembroke (1734–94) and Elizabeth, Countess of Pembroke.

[37] Roscius was, of course, a nickname for Garrick, after Quintus Roscius Gallus (died 62 BC) the Roman actor. His fame was enhanced by Shakespeare's reference to 'when Roscius was an actor in Rome', *Hamlet*, II, 2, 386–87. See also 'The Bas Bleu', below p. 31.

[38] Sir John Fielding (died 1780) was a magistrate at Bow Street.

[39] The Duke of Newcastle, whose hospitality More enjoyed at the trial.

[40] David Garrick made a series of farewell appearances in his most famous roles before his retirement in June 1776.

[41] Charles Pratt (1714–94), 1st Earl of Camden, was a lawyer, judge and Lord Chancellor 1766–70.

[42] More's tragedy *Percy* was written in the spring and summer of 1777 and presented at Covent Garden in December 1777 and January 1778.

[43] In the American War of Independence, the British Army commanded by General Burgoyne, had surrendered at Saratoga on 17 October 1777. More was a bitter opponent of the American rebels and her relations with Burke cooled for a while over this issue. See note 85 below.

[44] Thomas Harris (died 1820), was one of the proprietors and manager of Covent Garden Theatre.

[45] Thomas Percy (1729–1811), antiquarian and clergyman, published his *Reliques of Ancient English Poetry* in 1765. His much vaunted hereditary connection with the Percys of Northumberland was, in fact, remote.

[46] Hugh Percy (1715–86), 1st Duke of Northumberland of the third creation, was born Henry Smithson. His only connection with the Percys was his marriage to Elizabeth Percy, who, on her father's death, brought the family estates to him. Their son, Hugh Percy (1742–1817) had commanded British forces in the American War of Independence, rising to the rank of lieutenant general, but returned home in 1777 after a dispute with William Howe. Earl Percy was a courtesy title; he did not become the Earl of Northumberland until his father's death in 1786, when he inherited that title along with the dukedom.

[47] I am a little proud.

[48] Thomas Lyttleton (1744–79), whose licentious behaviour on the Grand Tour shocked London, MP 1768–9, 2nd Baron 1773.

[49] Anne, Lady North (died 1797) was wife to Frederick, Lord North (1732–92), Prime Minister 1770–82.

[50] Lord North was the Prime Minister responsible for the War of American Independence. Any anti-war sentiments she expressed in her play certainly did not express her opinions about the conduct of that war.

[51] Tryphena, Countess Bathurst (died 1807) was the second wife of Henry, Earl Bathurst, Lord Chancellor 1771–8.

[52] William Cadogan (1711–97), physician, lived in George Street, Hanover Square. He was to treat Garrick in his fatal illness, see below p. 21.

[53] Ann Spranger Barry (1734–1801), actress, played the heroine Elwina. Sarah Siddons played the part in the 1787 revival, but More never saw a performance of this production. Her reasons are made clear in the 'Preface to the Tragedies', *Works*, 1801, III, pp. 1–51.

[54] John Gay (1685–1732) satirised the law courts in *The Beggar's Opera*, first produced in 1728.

[55] William 'Gentleman' Lewis (1748?-1811), actor, became deputy-manager at Covent Garden in 1782.

[56] William Ashurst (1725–1807), judge, was to become best known for his attacks from the bench on English radicals in the 1790s, attacks of which More strongly approved.

[57] John Home (1722–1808), Scottish author of the highly successful play *Douglas* (1756), was less successful in 1777 with *Alfred* which closed after four performances.

[58] Mary Delany (1700–88), was a friend of Margaret, Duchess of Portland and, later, of Fanny Burney.

[59] A group of learned men who met weekly, ate sour crout, and frequently invited More to their discussions.

[60] Kitty Clive (1711–85), actress, one of the liveliest of Garrick's company, had retired from the stage in 1769.

[61] David Garrick died on 20 January 1779. More had been in Bristol on 11 January 1779; see Letter to Cadell, MS Oxford, Bodleian Library, Montagu d. 19, ff. 118–200.

[62] David Garrick was buried on 1 February 1779.

[63] John Thomas (1712–93), Bishop of Rochester 1774–93, was also a Prebendary of Westminster Abbey from 1754.

[64] Elizabeth Thomas, the widow of Sir Joseph Yates, judge of King's Bench, had become Bishop Thomas's second wife in 1776.

[65] Elizabeth Vesey, (1723–1791), daughter of an Irish bishop, wife of MP Agmondesham Vesey (died 1785), was eminent as a hostess from 1770–84.

[66] Aspasia of Miletus was the mistress of the Athenian statesman Pericles (c. 495–429 BC). She was reputed to be a woman of intellect who conversed with Socrates.

[67] Lucullus (c.114–57 BC) was a great hedonist, devoted to good food and a lover of literature and the arts.

[68] A phenicopter was a kind of bird, described by Martial (AD c. 40 – c. 104);

their tongues in particular were considered a delicacy. Samuel Johnson, *Dictionary*, (1775).

[69] Seneca the Younger (c.4 BC – AD 65), tutor and later political adviser to the Emperor Nero, was out of sympathy with imperial decadence and ultimately forced to commit suicide.

[70] Frances Boscawen (1722?-1805), highly intelligent but perhaps the least *scholarly* of the circle, was the widow of Admiral Boscawen (1711–61) and mother of the Duchess of Beaufort. See note 8 above.

[71] See note 8 above and note 75 below.

[72] William Pulteney (1729–1805), MP for Shrewsbury 1775–1805, was born William Johnstone and took the name of Pulteney in 1767 when his wife, Frances Pulteney, succeeded to the estates of Lord Bath.

[73] From Molière's 1659 comedy, *Les Précieuses Ridicules*, satirising women aiming at or affecting a ridiculous over-refinement or over-fastidiousness of language and taste. See *Strictures*, below p. 173.

[74] Horace Walpole (1717–97) was a close friend and correspondent of More.

[75] Elizabeth Carter (1717–1806), author of *All the Works of Epictetus which are now extant...translated from the Greek with introduction and notes*, London, 1758 and *Poems on several occasions*, London, 1776. Elizabeth Montagu (1720–1800) published *An Essay on the Writings and Genius of Shakespear, compared with the Greek and French Dramatic Poets*, London, 1769, reprinted by Cass in 1970 in the series *Eighteenth Century Shakespeare* (No. 12). This defended Shakespeare from Voltaire's criticisms in *Lettres Philosophiques*, Paris, 1734.

[76] The Hôtel de Rambouillet, Paris, on the site of the present Palais-Royal, was an intellectual centre of the best Parisian society in the first half of the seventeenth century. It was the town house of Catherine de Vivonne, Marquise de Rambouillet (1588–1665), who, with her daughter Julie d'Angennes, later Duchesse de Montausier, presided over a literary salon. Vincent Voiture (1598–1648) was a poet and letter writer, but was best known for his wit and conversation. Gilles Ménage (1613–92) was a scholar, a man of letters and a philologist.

[77] Marie de Rabutin-Chantal, Marquise de Sévigné (1626–96) was a highly educated woman, best known as a letter writer. She frequented the Hôtel de Rambouillet in the days of its decline.

[78] See note 25 above.

[79] Philip Stanhope (1694–1773), 4th Earl of Chesterfield, told his son he considered 'Vivacity and wit make a man shine in company; but trite jokes and loud laughter reduce him to buffoon', *The Letters of Philip Dormer Stanhope 4th Earl of Chesterfield*, ed. Bonamy Dobrée, 6 vols, London, 1932, Letter No. 1689, To his son, 5 February 1750 (OS), IV, p. 1503; and, 'Loud laughter is...the illiberal and noisy testimony of the joy of the mob at some very silly thing. A gentleman is often seen, but very seldom heard, to laugh', Letter No. 1782, To his son, 13 June 1751 (OS), IV, p. 1753.

[80] The fashion, the vogue, the mode; from 1769 (*OED*).

[81] Elizabeth Vesey broke the formal circle at her gatherings and placed her guests in smaller informal groups.

[82] Rev. William Mason (1724–97), poet and author of a poem *The English Garden*, also published the *Life and Letters of Thomas Gray* in 1774.

[83] Lancelot 'Capability' Brown (1715–83), landscape gardener and architect, was a friend of More.

[84] Samuel Johnson (1709–84) was still living when this was first written, but died before its publication in 1786.

[85] Edmund Burke (1729–97) had been a close friend of More, but the pro-American stance in his *Speech on Conciliation with America* (22 March 1775) alienated her. His *Reflections*, was, of course, to restore him to favour.

[86] Sir William Weller Pepys (died 1825), lawyer, and his wife Elizabeth Dowdeswell lived in Wimpole Street and were good friends of More.

[87] A syrup or cooling drink made from barley, almonds and orange flower water; from 1754 (*OED*).

[88] Soul is a misprint for soil. In the first edition in Bristol Central Library it is so corrected in what (from the evidence of the manuscript letters) is possibly More's own hand.

[89] More's lack of hostility to Freemasonry at this date is surprising. By the 1790s it was clearly linked with the Enlightenment, the *illuminées*, the French Revolution, Jacobinism and the assault on Christianity, and hence anathema to her. See J. M. Roberts, "The Origins of a Mythology: Freemasons, Protestants and the French Revolution", *BIHR* 44 (1971), 78–97, and *The Mythology of the Secret Societies*, London, 1972. See also *Strictures*, below, p. 139 and note 192.

[90] These were, of course, two of the main grounds on which the anti-slave trade movement attacked black slavery.

[91] The term posture-master was in use from the late seventeenth century. Addison in 1712 in the *Spectator* described one as an artist 'to teach them how to nod judiciously, to shrug up their Shoulders in a dubious Case, to connive with either Eye, and in a Word, the whole Practice of *Political Grimace*.' *Spectator*, No. 305, 19 February 1712.

[92] This is, to an extent, wishful thinking on More's part. The playing of cards or dice was not forbidden by common law, though living off the profits of a gaming house was. Any master could license his servant to play cards &c. with himself or with any other gentlemen in his house. The law was clearly concerned to control gambling amongst the lower orders without making it illegal for the wealthy. See Richard Burn, *The Justices of the Peace and Parish Officer*, 13th edition, 4 vols, London, 1776, II, pp. 308–23.

[93] The use of the term 'come out' to mean 'make a formal entry into Society on reaching womanhood', dates from the 1780s; Fanny Burney used the term in *Cecilia* (1782) where she equated it with presentation at court (VI, 4; World Classics edition, OUP, 1988, p.468). See note 220 below.

[94] John Dunning's motion that 'the influence of the crown has increased, is increasing, and ought to be diminished' was approved by the House of Commons on 6 April 1780. See note 32 above.

[95] St Lucia was one of the Windward islands between Martinique and St Vincent. It passed hands between the French and the English many times in the 18th century, and its economy depended upon slave labour.

[96] According to the *OED*, the first usage of 'cat' as short for cat-o'-nine-tails comes in A. Falconbridge, *African Slave Trade*, also published in 1788: 'A cat (an instrument of correction, which consists of a handle or stem, made of a

rope three inches and a half in circumference, and about eighteen inches in length, at one end of which are fastened nine branches, or tails, composed of log line, with three or more knots upon each branch)' p. 40.

[97] The lines 'Rule, Britannia, rule the waves; / Britons never will be slaves' first appeared in James Thomson, *Alfred: a Masque*, II, 5, 42–3, in 1740.

[98] Possibly a reference to the SPCK, founded in 1696, but more likely to the London Foundling Hospital, founded in 1739 and active in this period. See, Ruth K. McClure, *Coram's Children: The London Foundling Hospital in the Eighteenth Century*, Yale University Press, 1981, esp. pp. 152–3. In either case, the foundation preceded by many years the 'Justices of the new Police', see note 102 below, and the use of Botany Bay, see note 104 below. More was obviously not worried by anachronisms in a 'tale for the common people'.

[99] Celebrations traditional on May-day included dancing around a May-pole garlanded with flowers, and, in London, following the May-day sweep, a chimney-sweeper decorated with ribbons and flowers at the London sweeps' May-day festival.

[100] The Seven Dials is an area of London along Monmouth Street, where seven roads meet. It is close to Covent Garden and to Holborn, both mentioned later in the tale.

[101] The term 'cheat' had a much stronger meaning than today's loose usage. It was a legal term covering deceitful practices, fraud and counterfeit. See Burn, *Justice of the Peace*, I, pp. 312–32. See also below, 'Tawney Rachel', pp. 61, 69.

[102] The Middlesex Justices Act of 1792 allowed the appointment of stipendiary magistrates in London. These first paid professionals acted in the police courts from 1792 and the system was reviewed in Patrick Colquhoun, *Treatise on the Police of the Metropolis*, London, 1796, a work which almost certainly influenced More in writing this tale.

[103] Seven pounds and ten shillings; to give present day equivalents is very problematic, but this is perhaps around the figure of £500.

[104] Botany Bay was a convict settlement in New South Wales, Australia. Transportation to America ended in 1776 and, after a period of incarcerating prisoners in the hulks (prison ships, no longer sea-worthy, moored on the Thames), a convict settlement was established near Botany Bay (actually at Port Jackson) in 1788. Tyburn, situated at the junction of the present Oxford Street, Bayswater Road, and Edgware Road, had been the place of public execution for Middlesex until 1783. The word was later used simply to denote a place of execution.

[105] The closing of the quotation marks here and at the end of the next paragraph were omitted probably by the printer, an error corrected by More in later editions.

[106] More never wrote the second part of this story, but did write a ballad on 'The Hackney Coachman, or, the Way to get a good fare'.

[107] This story followed two others in the *Cheap Repository* about Black Giles the Poacher who lived in Somerset.

[108] A cabbage net was used to boil cabbage in.

[109] A cunning woman was one practiced in the occult arts.

[110] Two printer's errors have been corrected in the text to preserve the sense

of the dialogue. This sentence was placed in quotation marks, which have been removed, and the closing quotation marks three sentences above ("O it was this morning, just before I awoke.") were omitted and have been added.

[111] Dream-books contained the interpretation of dreams. A popular example was Thomas Hill, *The Most Pleasaunte Art of the Interpretacion of Dreames*, 1576; see Keith Thomas, *Religion and the Decline of Magic*, Weidenfeld & Nicolson, 1971, Penguin edition, 1978, p. 153.

[112] A popular name for the plant *Sedum Telephium*.

[113] In the Old Testament, Jacob served Laban for seven years to win his daughter Rachel. See Genesis 30: 18–30.

[114] Quotation marks erroneously placed around this last clause, by the printer, have been removed to preserve the sense of the dialogue.

[115] A sideboard or side-table, often ornamental for the disposition of china, plate &c.; from 1718 (*OED*).

[116] The quotation marks around the second half of this sentence, after 'said Rachel', were omitted in error by the printer and have been restored to preserve the sense of the dialogue.

[117] Spelt thus here, and 'southernwood' a few lines below.

[118] Lammas day, the first of August, was celebrated as an harvest festival.

[119] Another printer's error, for 'Robert Price'.

[120] Twenty pounds.

[121] The law against vagrants included not only the idle and disorderly, but also, 'all persons pretending to be gypsies... or pretending to have skill in physiognomy, palmistry, or like crafty science. Or using any subtil craft to deceive and impose on any of his majesty's subjects.' The law against witchcraft had been abolished sixty years earlier, but it was still illegal for any person to 'pretend to exercise or use any kind of witchcraft, sorcery, inchantment, or conjuration; or undertake to tell fortunes; or pretend from his skill or knowledge in any occult or crafty science, to discover where... any goods and chattels, supposed to have been lost, may be found...' Burns, *Justice of the Peace*, IV, pp. 307–13, 374.

[122] Mr Wilson was clearly one of the increasing number of clergymen at this time who served also as a justice of the peace. On the rise and fall of clerical magistrates in this period see Antony Russell, *The Clerical Profession*, London, 1980, pp. 32–42, 146–8, 149–67.

[123] Those guilty of Grand or Petty Larceny, felonious stealing, or the taking of money or goods, and liable to burning in the hand or whipping, could be transported for seven years. This provision was intended to be merciful. See Burns, *Justice of the Peace*, IV, pp. 291–4.

[124] See note 101 above.

[125] The witch of Endor; see 1 Samuel 28: 7, ff.

[126] Kersey was a kind of coarse narrow cloth, woven from long wool and usually ribbed.

[127] Isaiah 1: 18: 'though your sins be as scarlet, they shall be as white as snow; though they be red like crimson, they shall be as wool'.

[128] The village of Weyhill is five miles west of Andover.

[129] The phrase 'cut a dash' dated from 1771 (*OED*); More disliked this new usage.

[130] More, or her printer, failed to close the quotation marks here, an error she corrected in later editions.

[131] The quotation marks are never closed in the original.

[132] Not, as in later usage, a large box for the transportation of tea, but rather, in this period, a tea caddy.

[133] Tiff was the manner of dressing or arranging the hair; in use from 1703 (*OED*).

[134] A gimcrack was a showy, insubstantial thing – a useless ornament, a trumpery article, a knick-knack; a powder-puff may have been a soft pad, usually of down, for applying powder to the skin, but was more likely an instrument like a small bellows used for powdering the hair; a wash-ball was a small ball of soap for washing the hands and face; cards without pips were cards on which to draw or write messages, as opposed to playing cards.

[135] The Fencibles were men of an area who were ready to act as soldiers to defend the land in the case of invasion.

[136] A variant of escritoire, or writing desk.

[137] *The History of Thomas Hickathrift. Printed from the earliest extant copies*, edited by G. L. Gomme, Villon Society, Chap-Books and Folk-Lore Tracts...First Series, No. 1, 1885; Jack the Giant Killer appears in a chap-book of 1711, but note also Shakespeare, *King Lear*, III. iv. 187–8.

[138] See *Strictures*, below pp. 133–40.

[139] See *Strictures*, below p. 171.

[140] Technically, the soldier who carries the standard, but in practice, commissioned officers of the lowest grade in the infantry.

[141] Illustrations and designs cut or engraved on wood &c. Illustrated Bibles were becoming common in the later eighteenth century.

[142] A puzzle in which the syllables of a word are represented by figures, pictures or arrangements of letters; in use from 1605 (*OED*).

[143] 'Bit of a hop' in 1796 was changed to 'little dance' when More reprinted the story in her *Works*, 1801, vol. 4, p. 147.

[144] A funambulist, or rope walker, who performed on the slack-rope, rather than the tight-rope.

[145] The term country bumpkin was used not only of a person, but also of a dance.

[146] 'Beasts' in 1796 was changed to 'cattle' when More reprinted the story in her *Works*, 1818, IV, p. 164; it remained 'beasts' in the 1801 *Works*.

[147] Servants were hired on the four Quarter Days – Lady Day (March 25), Midsummer Day (June 24), Michaelmas (Sept. 29), and Christmas (Dec. 25). Most were hired at Michaelmas for the year and to change servants each quarter was unusual.

[148] 'Station' in 1796 was changed to 'class' when More reprinted the story in her *Works*, 1801, IV, p. 210.

[149] 'Plowmen' in 1796 was changed to 'ploughmen' when More reprinted the story in her *Works*, 1801, IV, p. 210.

[150] 'Turned' in 1796 was changed to 'subdued' when More reprinted the story in her *Works*, 1801, IV, p. 210.

[151] Psalms 111: 10: 'The fear of the Lord is the beginning of wisdom'.

[152] Strolling players were still bracketed with rogues and vagabonds. See Burns, *Justice of the Peace*, IV, pp. 306–38.

[153] By 'the new philosophy' More usually means the French Enlightenment. Thomas Paine, *The Age of Reason*, Paris, 1794, reflected the deist strand of Enlightenment thought.

[154] Proverbs 28: 20: '...he that maketh haste to be rich shall not be innocent.'

[155] From a prayer in The Order for the Burial of the Dead in the 1662 *Book of Common Prayer*.

[156] Luke 15: 18; from the parable of the prodigal son.

[157] Philip Doddridge, *The Rise and Progress of Religion in the Soul, illustrated in a course of serious and practical addresses... With a devout meditation, or prayer, added to each chapter*, London, 1745.

[158] 'Past' in 1797 was changed to 'passed' when More reprinted the story in her *Works*, 1801, IV, p. 266.

[159] Eli the priest was the too indulgent father of Hophni and Phinehas; see 1 Samuel 1: 3–4, 18.

[160] Genesis 49: 4: 'Unstable as water, thou shalt not excel.'

[161] See note 108 above.

[162] 'Past' in 1797 was changed to 'passed' when More reprinted the story in her *Works*, 1801, IV, p. 273.

[163] The Caribbean was one of the main theatres of war for the Anglo-French conflict of the 1790s. Large numbers of soldiers died of disease, especially of yellow fever, in which horrific vomiting of black, digested blood, preceded death. See David Gessus, *Slavery, War and Revolution: the British Occupation of Saint Domingue, 1793–98*, Oxford, 1982.

[164] Again from the parable of the prodigal son; Luke 15: 17. More's memory transforms 'of my father's' in the original to 'of my father'.

[165] Matthew 10: 42: 'And whosoever shall give to drink unto one of these little ones a cup of cold water only in the name of a disciple, verily I say unto you, he shall in no wise lose his reward.'

[166] 'Sunk' in 1797 was changed to 'sank' when More reprinted the story in her *Works*, 1801, IV, p. 282.

[167] A paraphrase of part of the general confession from The Communion service in the 1662 *Book of Common Prayer*.

[168] Job 17: 14.

[169] More changed *unparalled* to *unparalleled* in the second (1799) and subsequent editions. The *OED* recognises the former as an obscure variant, but does not note an example of its use after 1640.

[170] More's reference to the exclusion from light here probably refers, not to the lack of Christianity, but to the Ottoman harem. This was both the part of a Muslim dwelling-house appropriated to the women constructed so as to secure the utmost seclusion and privacy, and a collection of wives and concubines. There is nothing in Koranic law to justify her comment. More's view of Islam and of the prophet Muhammad here, is very different from that of Gibbon in *The History of the Decline and Fall of the Roman Empire*, (1776–88); her lack of toleration for non-Christian faiths contrasts with that of Burke.

[171] In 1799, the threat to England from the French Revolutionary wars had not yet passed. In some ways the crisis was not as acute as it had been. The

Revolution was moving from Directory to Napoleonic rule, and the darkest days of the war had been 1796–7. But there was still a sense of crisis, as Grenville worked to establish a coalition against France.

[172] More's memory was faulty here; it was a Greek, Demosthenes, who first made this much repeated remark. See Plutarch, *The Lives of the Noble Grecians and Romans...*, trans. Sir Thomas North, London, 1657, pp. 701–2.

[173] John Milton, *Paradise Lost, a poem in twelve books*, 1667, VIII, 601–2, in *The Poetical Works of John Milton*, ed. Helen Darbishire, Oxford University Press, 1958, p. 180: 'Those thousand decencies that daily flow /From all her words and actions, ...'

[174] Niccolò Machiavelli (1469–1527), author of *The Prince* (1513); Thalestris was a mythical Amazon Queen who reputedly hastened to Alexander the Great to become a mother by the conqueror of Asia, see Plutarch, *Lives*, p.578.

[175] Anthony Ashley Cooper (1621–83), 1st Earl of Shaftesbury, *Characteristicks of Men, Manners, Opinions, Times*, (1711), 2nd ed., 3 vols, London, 1714, I, p. 61: 'Truth, 'tis supposed, may bear all lights, and one of the principal lights, or natural mediums, by which things are to be viewed, in order to a thorough recognition, is ridicule itself, or that manner of proof by which we discern whatever is liable to just raillery in any subject.' Not only More disagreed with him. Chesterfield repeats his assertion and adds, 'I deny it.' Letter No. 1810, To his son, 6 February 1752 (OS), *Letters*, ed. Dobrée, V, p. 1826. More's friend, Samuel Johnson commented of Akenside, 'He adopted Shaftesbury's foolish assertion of the efficacy of ridicule for the discovery of truth...If ridicule be applied to any position as the test of truth, it will then become a question whether such ridicule be just, and this can only be decided by the application of truth as the test of ridicule.' *Lives of the English Poets*, (1779–81), ed., G. Birkbeck Hill, 3 vols, Oxford University Press, 1905, III, p. 413.

[176] By the 'new philosophy', More meant the ideas of the Enlightenment in general, and of Voltaire in particular.

[177] Persiflage – light banter or raillery; bantering, frivolous talk; a frivolous manner of treating any subject – was first used in English by Chesterfield in a letter of 1774 (*OED*).

[178] The earliest example of this meaning of the word 'bore' applied to a person quoted by the *OED* is dated 1812; an example of 1778 shows it applied to a thing.

[179] The following few paragraphs reflect More's dislike of the French Revolution and the ideas it engendered in 'English Jacobins'. The attitudes she condemns were those of a radical minority, that in the 1790s grew more and more unacceptable to the conservative majority and were, in 1799, less common than she implies. More's arguments reflect closely those of Burke in *Reflections*.

[180] More's imagery here alludes both to the Ghost of Hamlet's father, and Pallas Athena springing fully armed from the head of Zeus. See Shakespeare, *Hamlet* I. ii. 200; Hesiod, *Theogony*, 886–900.

[181] The image of the phoenix was one Voltaire used frequently, but More does not seem to have had a particular reference in mind here.

[182] Jonathan Swift, *Tale of a Tub*, (1704), ed. Herbert Davis, Blackwell, 1939, pp. 83–9. Section Six tells how Jack and Martin had to remove a series of fashion accessories from coats given to them by Lord Peter. Martin removed them gradually and carefully and left his coat intact; Jack ripped them away destroying his coat in the process. The story is similar to those used by More in 'Village Politics' (1792) to show the advantage of slow and organic, political and constitutional change as opposed to revolutionary reform.

[183] Miguel de Cervantes Saavedra (1547–1616), *Don Quixote de la Mancha*, Part One (1605), Part Two (1615); Molière (1622–73), *Tartuffe*, 1664/9.

[184] The law considered that death in a duel was homicide only if the dual was fought in cold blood: 'If two fall out upon a sudden occasion, and agree to fight in such a field, and each of them go and fetch their weapon, and go into the field, and therein fight, and the one killeth the other, this is no malice prepensed; but for the fetching of the weapon, and going into the field, is but a continuance of the sudden falling out, and the blood was never cooled. But if there were deliberation, as that they meet the next day, if there were such a competent distance of time, that in common presumption, they had time of deliberation, then it is murder.' In such cases not only the principal was guilty of murder but his seconds too; the seconds of the dead man were guilty as accessories. Burns, *Justice of the Peace*, II, pp. 475–6.

[185] The French Enlightenment mounted its critique of Christianity and the abuses of contemporary society and government in a wide variety of forms, including: Montesquieu, *Persian Letters*, 1721, Voltaire, *Philosophical Letters*, (from England) 1734, and Diderot's *Encyclopédie*, 1751–65, though his *Supplément au Voyage de Bougainville*, 1772, was still unpublished in 1799.

[186] Rousseau's *La Nouvelle Héloïse* was published in 1761, and first appeared in an English translation by William Kendrick in the same year under the title *Eloisa: or, a series of original letters collected and published by J. J. Rousseau*. More was a French reader, but there is no definitive evidence whether she read it in English or French.

[187] On the English novel in this period see *inter alia* Gary Kelly, *The English Jacobin Novel 1780–1805*, Oxford University Press, 1976, and Terry Castle, *Masquerade and Civilization: The Carnivalesque in Eighteenth-Century English Culture and Fiction*, Methuen, 1986.

[188] Exodus 20: 14: 'Thou shalt not commit adultery'.

[189] Friedrich Schiller (1759–1805) wrote *Die Räuber* in 1781. It is a late example of the *Sturm und Drang* school and is written in passionate and violent prose. It also includes the suicide of the villain, Franz. A translation by Alexander Tytler, Lord Woodhouselee, (1747–1813), Professor of Universal History at the University of Edinburgh, was published in 1792. Other translations by William Render and Elizabeth Craven appeared in 1799.

Bagshot was a respectable, suburban, English town, situated between Windsor and Basingstoke.

[190] Milton, *Paradise Lost*, II, 628, *Works*, p. 42. More added the exclamation point.

[191] To a significant extent, it was the experience of the French Revolution and the Revolutionary War which turned many English people against the writers of the French Enlightenment.

[192] The English translation of the Abbé Barruel's *Memoirs of... Jacobinism* (1797) and John Robison's *Proofs of a Conspiracy against All the Religions and Governments of Europe* (1797) alleged two connected conspiracies; one that of the French *philosophes*, the other of freemasons and *illuminées*. Robison concentrated on the latter, outlining the role of Dr Adam Weishart in founding the Order of Illuminati in 1775, and chronicling the order's later history in Germany. See above note 89.

[193] August von Kotzebue (1761–1819), *Menschenhaß und Reue*, 1789, appeared in translation as, *The Stranger: a comedy. Freely translated from Kotzebue's German comedy of Misanthropy and repentance*, London, 1798. Sheridan wrote an air for inclusion in the fourth act.

[194] Mary Wollstonecraft was so described in W. Godwin, *Memoirs of the Author of a Vindication of the Rights of Woman*, London, 1798, p. 112. However, the phrase does not come in the context of her suicide attempts of May and October, 1795, which he describes pp. 132–6. Rather, it appears before the birth of Imlay's child when Mary was still in Paris, in the context of a discussion of extreme sensibility and the pains it can cause a person: 'This character is finely pourtrayed by the author of the Sorrows of Werter. Mary was in this respect a female Werter.' Johan Wolfgang von Goethe (1749–1832) wrote *Die Leiden des jungen Werthers* in 1774. It was alleged to have inspired a number of imitative suicides, notably that of Christel von Laßberg in 1777, who died with a copy of the novel in her pocket.

[195] In the second and subsequent editions, this final phrase becomes the *Wrongs of Woman*. William Godwin published Mary Wollstonecraft's *Maria or The Wrongs of Women* in 1798, a few months after her death. This novel, defending women's right to sexual freedom, evidently disturbed More profoundly. In the second edition of *Strictures* and thereafter, she inserted a long and passionate passage at this point which shows clearly her fear of the power of female sexuality: 'And this leads me to dwell a little longer on this most destructive class in the whole wide range of modern corruptors, who effect the most desperate work of the passions, without so much as pretending to urge the *violence* of the passions as a plea to extenuate their corruptions. They solicit the indulgence of the grossest appetites with a sort of cold-blooded speculation, and abandon themselves, and debauch the reader, to the most unbounded gratification of the senses, with all the saturnine coolness of a geometrical calculation...

This cool, calculating, intellectual wickedness eats out the very heart and core of virtue, and like a deadly mildew blights and shrivels the blooming promise of the human spring. Its benumbing touch communicates a torpid sluggishness, which paralyzes the soul. It descants on depravity, and details its grossest acts as frigidly as if its object were to *allay* the tumult of the passions, while it is letting them loose on mankind, by "plucking off the muzzle" of the present restraint and future accountableness. The system is a dire infusion compounded of bold impiety, brutish sensuality, and exquisite folly, which creeping fatally around the heart checks the moral circulation, and totally stops the pulse of goodness by the extinction of the vital principle. Thus not only choaking up the stream of actual virtue, but drying up the very fountain of future remorse and remote repentance.

The ravages which some of the old offenders against purity made in the youthful heart, by the exercise of a fervid but licentious imagination on the passions, was like the mischief effected by floods, cataracts, and volcanos. The desolation indeed was terrible, and the ruin tremendous: yet it was a ruin which did not *infallibly* preclude the possibility of recovery...

But the heart once infected with this newly medicated venom, subtil though sluggish in its operation, resembles what travellers relate of that blasted spot the dead-sea, where those devoted cities once stood which for their pollutions were burnt with fire from heaven. It continues a stagnant lake of putrifying waters. No wholesome blade evermore shoots up; the air is so tainted that no living thing subsists within its influence. Near the sulphureous pool the very principle of life is annihilated. – All is death...' See Introduction, above, p. xxxii.

[196] See 'Mr Bragwell and his two daughters' (1795–7), above.

[197] *Minauderie*, meaning to put on coquettish airs and affected expressions, dates in English from 1763 (*OED*).

[198] A paraphrase of Hamlet's passionate condemnation of women at the end of the nunnery scene: 'you jig, you amble, and you lisp, and nick-name God's creatures, and make your wantonness your ignorance.' Shakespeare, *Hamlet* III. i. 146–8.

[199] The *OED* notes, '*Contemporary* is the original form, and that approved by Latin analogies... But the variant *co-temporary* was used by some in the 17th c., and... it became so prevalent after c. 1725, as almost to expel *contemporary* from use. Towards the end of the 18th c., the latter rapidly recovered its ground...' 'Cotemporary', is still unchanged in the eleventh edition of *Strictures* in 1811, but when More revised the work for inclusion in her 1818 *Works*, she changed it to 'contemporary', VII, p. 77.

[200] A vehicle with four horses driven by one person.

[201] Circassians, from the northern Caucasus were, in fact Greek Orthodox Christians; More's allusion is to the belief that some of them were kept in Ottoman harems as slaves or wives.

[202] *The Spectator*, No. 334, 24 March 1712.

[203] Gaius Sallustius Crispus (86–35 BC) was a Roman historian whose *Bellum Catilinae* dealt with the Catiline conspiracy of 63 BC.

[204] Worse was to come. More was alerted to the dangers of the Waltz by Charles Burney in a letter of 1799 congratulating her on *Strictures*: '... perhaps you have not seen a party of French or German *Waltz* dancers.' Roberts, *Memoirs*, III, p. 71. In 1818, when she included *Strictures* in the new edition of her *Works,* she added the footnote, 'When this little work was written, the indecent and offensive Waltz had not been added to the amusements of our virtuous young ladies.' The earliest *OED* reference to the Waltz, as a German dance, is in 1781; Helen M. Williams records it in her *Tour of Switzerland* in 1798 and W. Hamilton defined it in 1825 as 'the name of a riotous and indecent German dance', (*OED*).

[205] More added the following footnote to the second, and subsequent, editions: 'Since the first edition of this Work appeared, the author has received from a person of great eminence the following statement, ascertaining the *time* employed in the acquisition of music in one instance. As a *general*

calculation, it will perhaps be found to be so far from exaggerated. The statement concludes with remarking, that the individual who is the subject of it is now married to a man who *dislikes music*!

Suppose your pupil to begin at six years of age and to continue at the average of four hours a-day *only*, Sunday excepted, and thirteen days allowed for travelling annually, till she is eighteen, the statement stands thus; 300 days multiplied by four, the number of hours amount to 1200; that number multiplied by twelve, which is the number of years, amounts to 14,400 hours!'

[206] Nobles families in Athens and Sparta, members of whom feature in the *Lives* of Plutarch (c. AD 46–c.120).

[207] Hetaerae, or prostitutes and courtesans: Phryne from Thespiae in Boeotia, Aspasia, the mistress of Pericles, Lais the lover of Diogenes the Cynic.

[208] Horace, *Satires*, I, ii. For once, More is not exaggerating when she complains of its gross indelicacies.

[209] More added the following footnote to the second, and subsequent, editions: 'Let me not be suspected of bringing into any sort of comparison the gentleness of British government with the rapacity of Roman conquests, or the principles of Roman dominion. To spoil, to butcher, and to commit every kind of violence, they call, says one of the ablest of their historians, by the lying name of *government*, and when they have spread a general desolation they call it *peace*. (Tacitus's Life of Agricola, speech of Galgacus to his soldiers.)

With such *dictatorial*, or, as we might now read, *directorial* inquisitors, *we* can have no point of contact; and if I have applied the servile flattery of a delightful poet to the purpose of English happiness, it was only to show wherein true national grandeur consists, and that every country pays too dear a price for those arts and embellishments of society, which endanger the loss of its morals and manners.'

[210] Ecclesiastes 3: 1. More evidently quoted from memory, transforming 'a time to' into 'a time for'. This remained unchanged in the second and third editions. In a letter of 1800, More claimed that 'the chapters in the 'Strictures' on Human Corruption and Baby Balls, are the two which give most offence.' Roberts, *Memoirs*, III, pp. 107–8.

[211] Milton, *Paradise Lost*, VIII, 280–2, *Works*, p.172:

> 'Tell me, how I may know him, how adore,
> From whom I have that thus I move and live,
> And feel that I am happier then I know.'

[212] Scythia was an ancient region extending over a large part of European and Asiatic Russia, inhabited by a nomadic people.

[213] Many French aristocrats and clergy escaped to England during the Revolution. More helped organise support for the émigré clergy in particular.

[214] Sempronia was the wife of Decimus Junius Brutus, a woman of literary accomplishments and allegedly profligate character. Unknown to her husband, she took part in the Catiline conspiracy of 63 BC. Sallust, *Bellum Catilinae* XXV, 40. See note 203 above.

[215] Luke 10: 42.

[216] Thomas Paine, *Rights of Man*, Part One (1791) and Part Two (1792), was a response to Burke, *Reflections*, which had given rise to a large number of works similar to Paine's.

[217] Mary Wollstonecraft published *A Vindication of the Rights of Men* in 1790 and *A Vindication of the Rights of Woman* in 1792.

[218] Kowaleski-Wallace, *Their fathers' daughters*, considers this from a feminist perspective in chapter 2, 'Milton's Bogey Reconsidered', pp. 27–55.

[219] Isaiah 36: 8: '...the wayfaring men, though fools, shall not err therein.' More's slight error remained unchanged in the second and third editions.

[220] See note 93 above.

[221] Isaiah 65: 5: 'Stand by thyself, come not near to me; for I am holier than thou.'

[222] More was probably referring here to Louis René de Caradeuc de la Chalotais, *Essai d'éducation nationale, ou Plan d'études pour la jeunesse*, 1763.

[223] More, who saw an early performance of Sheridan's *The Rivals* (see above p. l), may have agreed with Sir Anthony Absolute that, 'a circulating library in a town is as an evergreen tree of diabolical knowledge!' *Rivals*, I, 2.

[224] Isaac Watts (1674–1748), *Logick: or the right use of reason in the enquiry after truth...*, London, 1725; William Duncan (1717–60) was Professor of Philosophy at the University of Aberdeen and author of *The Elements of Logick*, London, 1748; John Locke (1632–1704), *An Essay Concerning Human Understanding*, 1690; Joseph Butler (1692–1752), *The Analogy of Religion, Natural and Revealed, to the Constitution and Course of Nature*, 1736.

[225] In April 1799, Charles Burney (1726–1814), musician and father of Fanny Burney, commented in his letter of congratulation to More, 'I was a little mortified by the stigma you put upon Italian poetry, in putting it on a level with English sentiment, French philosophy, and German magic wonders. Was it not Italy that taught the rest of Europe all the fine arts; and, indeed, first instructed its inhabitants in the divine principles of Christianity? And in later times, did not Dante, Petrarch, Tasso, Trissino, Tansillo, and Giraldi, furnish models to the poets of other countries?... And is Metastasio, the most chaste, moral, and pious of all modern poets of a high class, to be thrown into such company? If females are allowed to read or sing poetry of any kind, but particularly dramatic, where are to be found better models of heroism and virtue, more refined sentiments, and more elegance of language and versification, than in his secular dramas, or more piety than in his oratorios, or sacred dramas?... If you wish to dissuade young ladies from the study of Italian poetry in general, I could almost take the liberty to intreat you in your next edition, to make a few exceptions in favour of some of those I have mentioned...' Roberts, *Memoirs*, III, pp. 71–2. More's early play *The Inflexible Captive* was a translation of Mestastasio's *Attilio Regolo*. The phrase 'Italian Poetry' remained in the second edition, but was replaced in the third edition (1799) with 'Italian Love-Songs'.

[226] Swift, "A Letter to a Young Lady on her Marriage" (1723), in *Irish Tracts 1720–1723 And Sermons*, ed. Herbert Davis, Blackwell, pp. 85–94. Swift's comment needs to be seen in context: 'I know very well, that those that are commonly called learned Women, have lost all Manner of Credit by their

impertinent Talkativeness, and Conceit of themselves: But there is an easy Remedy for this; if you once consider, that after all the Pains you may be at, you never can arrive, in Point of Learning, to the Perfection of a School-Boy. But the Reading I would advise you to, is only for Improvement of your own good Sense, which will never fail if being mended by Discretion. It is a wrong Method, and ill Choice of Books, that make those learned Ladies just so much worse for what they had read.' p. 92.

227 Correggio (c.1489–1534) is reputed to have exclaimed '*Anch' io sono pittore!*' on seeing Raphael's *St Cecilia* at Bologna in c. 1525.

228 This is clearly a reference to the 'show of eight kings' in Shakespeare, *Macbeth* IV. i. 112–24, but the phrase More quotes, presumably from memory again, does not in fact appear; 'Another yet? – A seventh? – I'll see no more: – ' does (IV. i. 118), as does, later in the play, 'To-morrow, and to-morrow, and to-morrrow,' (V. v. 19). For another example of her imperfect memory of Shakespeare, see below, note 271.

229 See 'Mr. Bragwell and his two daughters', above p. 87. A mantua-maker was a dressmaker.

230 When More republished this as part of her *Works* in 1801, she added a note at this point: 'May I be allowed to strengthen my own opinion with the authority of Dr. Johnson, that *a woman cannot have too much arithmetic?* It is a solid, practical acquirement, in which there is much use and little display; it is a quiet sober kind of knowledge, which she acquires for herself and her family, and not for the world.' VIII, p. 3.

231 See note 73 above.

232 Milton, *A Mask presented at Ludlow Castle, 1634,* [Comus], 1637, lines 5–6: '...of this dim spot / Which men call Earth', *Works*, p. 458.

233 More uses the term 'economy' in its original sense of the management of a house and a household, particularly concerning expenditures.

234 Alexander Pope, 'Epistles to Several Persons', Epistle II, To a Lady (1735), lines 217–18: 'Men, some to Quiet, some to Public Strife; / But ev'ry Lady would be Queen for life.' Pope, *Poetical Works*, ed. Herbert Davis, Oxford University Press, 1965, p. 297.

235 The Salic law was the alleged fundamental law of the French monarchy, by which females were excluded from succession to the crown. In her first published work, *A Search after Happiness*, More wrote, 'I scorn'd the salique laws of pedant schools, / Which chain our genius down by tasteless rules. / I long'd to burst these female bonds which held/My sex in awe, by vanity impell'd:' *Works*, 1801, II, p. 296.

236 Psalms 9: 6. More's three examples of flatterers are Pierre de Bourdeilles, ségneur de Brantôme (c.1540–1614), *Recueil d'aucuns discours*, which flattered great captains, and *Recueil des dames*, which flattered princesses, both were published posthumously in 1665–6; Pierre, le Père Le Moyne (1602–72), *Saint Louis ou le héros chrétien*, 1653, 1658; Antoine-Léonard Thomas (1732–85), *Éloges,* 1763–65, academic discourses in praise of men like Sully (1559–1641), Duguay-Trouin (1673–1736), and Descartes (1596–1650).

237 When she revised *Strictures* for inclusion in the new edition of her *Works* in 1818, More added a footnote here acknowledging that this was a reference to Wollstonecraft's *Rights of Woman*.

[238] 1 Peter 3: 4. This comes in the passage in which St Peter says 'wives, be in subjection to your own husbands', see above, Introduction, p. xxxiii.

[239] Milton, *Paradise Lost*, II, 561: 'And found no end, in wandering mazes lost.' *Works*, p. 40.

[240] The Bangorian controversy arose from the sermon, 'The Nature of the Kingdom or Church of Christ', preached by Benjamin Hoadley (1676–1761), Bishop of Bangor, before King George I, in 1717. Hoadley argued that there was no authority in the Gospels for any visible church authority.

[241] The dispute between the Jesuits and the Jansenists concerning the five propositions on divine grace, set out in Cornelius Otto Jansen, *Augustinus*, 1640, and condemned as heretical by Pope Innocent X.

[242] Quintilian (AD 35–post 95) was a teacher of rhetoric and an advocate in the courts, hence the scales of justice.

[243] The dramatic unities of time, place and action were set out in the *Poetics* of Aristotle (384–322 BC) and were observed by the French classical dramatists more rigidly than Aristotle required.

[244] William Pitt the Younger (1759–1806) was the Tory Prime Minister 1783–1801 and 1804–6. Charles James Fox (1749–1806) was one of his leading Whig opponents.

[245] Baal was the chief male deity of the Phœnician and Canaanitish nations whose name has become generally used for any false god. See Judges 2: 13.

[246] This was the common explanation for the success of the 'godless' French in the war.

[247] Luke 2: 14: '...peace, good will toward men.'

[248] See above p. 166.

[249] More clarified her meaning by inserting the words 'by this' before 'inconsequent flippancy' in the second and subsequent editions.

[250] James 1: 19: '...let every man be swift to hear, slow to speak, slow to wrath'.

[251] The vulture fed on Prometheus's liver. See Hesiod, *Theogony*, 534 ff. and Aeschylus, *Prometheus Bound*.

[252] George Villiers, Duke of Buckingham and others, wrote *The Rehearsal* in 1672 and revised it in 1675. It was revived at Covent Garden in 1767. The phrase appears in I, 1:

'Johnson: "...Fellows that scorn to imitate Nature, but are given altogether to elevate and surprize."

Smith: "Elevate and surprize! Prithee make me understand the meaning of that."

Johnson: "...'Tis a Phrase they have got among them, to express their No-meaning by...Let me see; 'tis Fighting, Loving, Sleeping, Rhyming, Dying, Dancing, Singing, Crying, and every Thing but Thinking and Sense."'

The Rehearsal: with a Key, or Critical View of The Authors, and their Writings, exposed in this Play, London, 1768, p. 6.

[253] 1 Corinthians 13: 5: Charity 'seeketh not her own'.

[254] Suicide, or self-murder, was a crime; the goods and chattels, but not the land, of a suicide were forfeited. See Burns, *Justice of the Peace*, II, p. 480.

[255] Once again, More's habit of quoting from memory leads to a slight

inaccuracy. Burke's list of the milder colours which are appropriated to beauty are, 'light greens; soft blues...' *A Philosophical Enquiry into the Origin of Our Ideas of the Sublime and Beautiful*, (1756), ed. James T. Boulton, revised ed., Blackwell, 1987, p. 117, (III, 17).

[256] Shakespeare, *2 Henry IV*, IV. iv. 32: 'Open as day for melting charity'.

[257] There is no evidence to show whether or not More had read Pierre Choderlos de Laclos (1741–1803), *Les Liaisons dangereuses*, 1782, but she was a French reader, and the work appeared in an English translation in 1784 under the title *Dangerous Connections*.

[258] The word 'tolerable' survived in all editions of *Strictures* until More revised it for inclusion in the new edition of her *Works* in 1818, when she replaced it with 'happy'.

[259] Pope, 'Epistle to a Lady', line 44, in Pope, *Poetical Works*, p. 297. More has omitted the comma after 'defect' and added the exclamation point at the end of the line.

[260] Cardinal Armand-Jean du Plessis, Duc de Richelieu (1585–1640).

[261] George Horne, Bishop of Norwich (1790–2). See introduction pp. xix–xx.

[262] Titus 2: 4–5: 'That they may teach the young women to be sober, to love their husbands, to love their children, to be discreet, chaste, keepers at home, good, obedient to their husbands, that the word of God be not blasphemed.'

[263] 1 Kings 4: 33: 'from the cedar tree that is in Lebanon even unto the hyssop that springeth out of the wall'.

[264] Tobit 4: 7. Tobit was one of the deuterocanonical books which were excluded from the Authorised Version of the Bible. More's translation is that found in the 1662 *Book of Common Prayer*, where it appears as one of the Offertory sentences in The Communion service. Quoting from memory, as usual, she made two slight errors: '...never turn thy face from any poor man, and then the face of the Lord shall not be turned away from thee.'

[265] See note 165 above.

[266] 1 Corinthians 13: 3: 'And though I bestow all my goods to feed the poor...and have not charity, it profiteth me nothing.'

[267] The original meaning of raffle as a game with three dice, was beginning to give way at this time to the sense of a lottery. It was used in this sense in Bath by 1766, and by Fanny Burney, in *Cecilia*, (V, 12; World Classics edition, Oxford University Press, 1988, p.408).

[268] 1 Corinthians 8: 1: '...Knowledge puffeth up, but charity edifieth.'

[269] Edmond Hoyle was the authority on card playing. His many publications included *The Polite Gamester: containing short treatises on the games of Whist, Quadrille, Back-gammon, Piquet and Chess...*, Dublin, 1745.

[270] Epicurus (341–271 BC) was the founder of philosophical hedonism.

[271] A somewhat confused memory of Henry IV's speech to Prince Hal advising him not to be seen too much in public:

> And then I stole all courtesy from heaven,
> And dress'd myself in such humility
> That I did pluck allegiance from men's hearts,
> Loud shouts and salutations from their mouths,

Even in the presence of the crowned King.
Thus did I keep my person fresh and new,
My presence, like a robe pontifical,
Ne'er seen but wonder'd at: and so my state,
Seldom, but sumptuous, show'd like a feast
And won by rareness such solemnity.

Shakespeare, *1 Henry IV*, III. ii. 50–59.

[272] 'Cast' is an alternative spelling of 'caste'. More italicises it for emphasis; it was accepted English usage before the establishment of the link with India.

[273] A native or citizen of Sybaris, an ancient Greek city of southern Italy, traditionally noted for its effeminacy and luxury, and hence, a person devoted to luxury or pleasure; an effeminate voluptuary or sensualist.

[274] Shakespeare, *Richard III*, I. i. 24: '...in this weak piping time of peace,'

[275] Oliver Goldsmith, *The Deserted Village*, line 263.

[276] '...he thought himself dishonoured for ever, that the ten thousand GRECAANS which were returned back from the farthest part of ASIA...' Plutarch, *Lives*, p. 512. North added in his 'Notes and Explications', 'This is the famous story of the ten thousand *Grecians*, who being on *Cyrus* side, and he being killed in fight, made good their retreat through *Asia* into *Europe* in a most notable manner, being led by *Zenophon*.'

[277] Milton, *Paradise Lost*, VIII, 599, *Works*, p. 180.